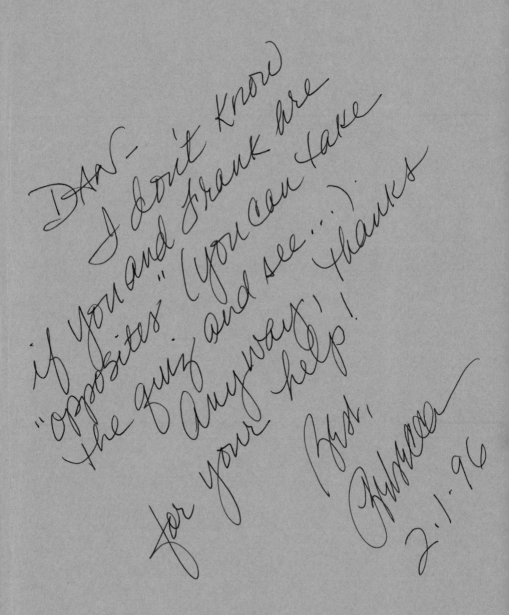

DAN –
I don't know
if you and Frank are
"opposites" (you can take
the quiz and see...).
Anyway, thanks
for your help!

Best,
Rebecca
2·1·96

When
OPPOSITES
Attract

REBECCA CUTTER

When OPPOSITES *Attract*

Right Brain/Left Brain
Relationships and How
to Make Them Work

A DUTTON BOOK

DUTTON

Published by the Penguin Group
Penguin Books USA Inc., 375 Hudson Street, New York, New York 10014, U.S.A.
Penguin Books Ltd, 27 Wrights Lane, London W8 5TZ, England
Penguin Books Australia Ltd, Ringwood, Victoria, Australia
Penguin Books Canada Ltd, 10 Alcorn Avenue, Toronto, Ontario, Canada M4V 3B2
Penguin Books (N.Z.) Ltd, 182–190 Wairau Road, Auckland 10, New Zealand

Penguin Books Ltd, Registered Offices:
Harmondsworth, Middlesex, England

First published by Dutton, an imprint of Dutton Signet,
a division of Penguin Books USA Inc.
Distributed in Canada by McClelland & Stewart Inc.

First Printing, October, 1994
1 3 5 7 9 10 8 6 4 2

Copyright © Rebecca Cutter, 1994
All rights reserved

REGISTERED TRADEMARK—MARCA REGISTRADA

LIBRARY OF CONGRESS CATALOGING IN PUBLICATION DATA:

Cutter, Rebecca.
When opposites attract : right brain/left brain relationships
and how to make them work / by Rebecca Cutter
p.   cm.
Includes bibliographical references.
ISBN 0-525-93731-5
1. Man-woman relationships. 2. Gay couples.
3. Cerebral dominance. 4. Interpersonal communication.
5. Communication in marriage. I. Title.
HQ801.C88   1994
158'.2—dc20   *94–10234*
                                                   CIP

Printed in the United States of America
Set in Garamond Light and Gill Sans Light

Designed by Steven N. Stathakis

To
Rick
*For teaching me the art
of commitment*

To
Sarah Dustin
and
Anna Nicole
*Two of the best decisions
I ever made*

ACKNOWLEDGMENTS

The birth of a book requires many midwives; it is not a solitary act. Those who helped deliver this body of work deserve special mention.

At conception there were only a few, who with very little information from me—other than a rough outline—managed to form a small chorus of encouragement. These include: my agent, Rhoda Weyr, who could "see" what I could only imagine and whose wisdom kept me on track; Miriam Polster, Ph.D., who showed me that midlife could also be a beginning; Susan Challen, the first to enjoy the way I put words together on paper; Nora Clark, whose enthusiasm rang over the long-distance wires; and Ellen Rose Lavin, Ph.D., with her perfectly timed invitations to tea and thoughtful messages left on my machine.

As the project grew, several couples joined in to offer support. They provided good food and terrific company and—most helpful of all—shared their own stories as committed life partners. Thank you: Pat and Mike Goldhamer, M.D.; Doug Braun and Al Killen; Sara Rosenthal, M.D., and Julie Prazich, M.D.; Eve Boyer and Russ Hamm; John Davis and Janet Bowermaster; Mary Ann Petino and John Curtis; coministers Tom and Carolyn Owen-Towle; and Dorothy Johnson, Ph.D., and Donald Johnson, M.D., my mother- and father-in-law with whom I have been absolutely blessed.

The last stage of creating this book brought the greatest challenge—and along with it my editor, Carole DeSanti, who made it all seem effortless, as she expertly coached me through the final editing process, suggesting changes, while remaining sensitive to the fact that this was *my* baby and I thought it was beautiful just the way it was.

It goes without saying that this book could not have happened without the courage of my clients, who were willing to open their relationships to me and who expressed the hope that what was discovered could be used to help others.

Finally, I must say a few words about the "father" of this book, my husband, Rick Johnson. From day one he had faith in me and faith in this project. He believed in it long before I did, and he was dedicated to making it happen. Night or day he was "on call" to help me troubleshoot a variety of difficulties with my computer. Unfailingly he read every word and—serving as the left-brain contingent—provided valuable feedback, as I struggled to present as balanced a perspective as possible. Most of all, through all his effort, he taught me that love is in our actions, as reflected in these words from our wedding ceremony years ago: "You have come to give yourselves in love without giving yourselves away. You have come neither to overpower the other nor to be absorbed by the other, but to live gracefully alongside one another."*

---

*Tom Owen-Towle.

CONTENTS

INTRODUCTION

I have always been curious about relationships. Fascinated by their complexity and humbled by their simplicity, I have wondered: Why is it that some couples seem so well matched and others live in a constant state of turmoil? What makes one relationship easy and the next one a daily effort? Why do some partners frequently feel connected while others share that experience only on rare occasions?

The impetus for writing this book is rooted in both my personal and professional experiences. Within my own marriage I have encountered all the positives and negatives inherent in any relationship created by two people who conceptualize, communicate, and connect in very different ways.

The frustration, at times, has seemed overwhelming. In the first years our mismatched needs and discordant styles propelled us into daily conflict. On many occasions my husband and I could see no solution but dissolution. Yet through it all, our commitment to make it work was a driving force that brought us back again and again to the "editing room," where we would rewind an argument and study our interactions frame by frame. Earlier in our relationship we did this to prove who was right. As the years passed, we began to review things in order to understand not only what went wrong but what it would take to get us back on track and keep us there.

As we got better at processing our disagreements, it became clear that each of us had seen an entirely different movie! I did not know what my husband was talking about, could not imagine how he had come to the conclusions he held, and was confused about his description of my role in the misunderstanding. He voiced a similar reaction to me. We had moved from suspecting that there was one crazy person in our marriage to the possibility that there were two.

The most obvious conclusion was the traditional one: Men and women are very different. This satisfied me for a brief time until I began to notice that couples in psychotherapy had similar complaints and that these complaints frequently failed to fall into place along gender lines. With some couples, the concerns I voiced at home were echoed by the husband, and those of my own husband were similar to those of the wife. An identical pattern emerged in other couples, both partners of which were the same sex. It did not appear that gender was the culprit after all.

Simultaneously I ran across a small book that explored couple dynamics in the high-tech world of Silicon Valley, and although it did not answer all my questions, I was introduced to the concept of "right" and "left" brain, and the seeds for further observation were planted.

Couples come together, separate, and come together again for a variety of reasons. They identify numerous factors that both attract them and contribute to their misunderstandings. They search for a reason for their difficulties. The powerful impact of traditional socialization can easily lead partners to conclude that "That's the way women/men are" and begin to think of the opposite sex as the "enemy."

When Opposites Attract invites you to consider a different perspective, one that is not gender-bound and therefore available for either sex to explore in terms of individual behavior, as well as contributes to relationship building for both heterosexual and same-sex couples.

This perspective is based on the observation that people possess, to varying degrees, dominant characteristics associated with either right (RB) or left (LB) brain activity, and these form certain patterns in their way of relating to self and others, communicating, problem solving, and even making love.

When an RB-dominant person and an LB-dominant person form a couple, it is a joining of "opposites" and the focus of this book. These "opposites" can be male/female, male/male, and female/female. These couples often report high levels of frustration and low levels of satisfaction as they struggle to become compatible.

It is even more distressing when "opposites" discover that they cannot agree on what "compatible" means. To one partner it may mean more closeness, increased intimacy, and being in sync most of the time (*soul* mates). For the other the ideal relationship might offer more individual freedom, greater psychological space, and the ability to problem solve (*team*mates). "Opposites" expend great amounts of time and energy in the effort to become compatible but fail to recognize that their conflict is rooted in the fact that they possess two very different, but *equally valid,* blueprints for change.

With increasing movement toward a holistic perspective on human problems, there is a call to bring more balance to our lives. In this spirit I imagine a model for relationships that does not focus on those differences as barriers to understanding but rather appreciates those differences as merely dissimilar paths to satisfaction of common basic needs.

Currently a number of popular books are available which formulate relationship problems within the single framework of gender. While gender cannot be denied as a factor, it is certainly not the *only* factor. There are millions of men and women who simply do not fit gender stereotype and to whom these books do not speak.

There are men who possess many traits associated with female socialization, as well as women who are not disposed to traditionally "feminine" ways of thinking, problem solving, and communicating. Where can these men and women find guidance in their attempts to create and maintain satisfying relationships? Certainly not in books with titles like *Why Men* . . . or *Why Women* . . . Where does this leave the woman who has faith in logic or the man who seeks knowledge through relationships? What about same-sex partners?

Gender is a social construct; concepts associated with "masculinity" and "femininity" do not exist in nature. Our culture creates artificial distinctions between what we can expect from males and females. The problem is that while growing up, we do not experience these guidelines as arbitrary. We learn them as "givens," which we then take for granted as we make our way about the world. These messages not only set the stage for later misunderstanding between the sexes but color our feelings about our own gender as well. In order to achieve a satisfying relationship, it is imperative that we unlearn these, for no two people of the same gender will necessarily respond the same way to the same situation. To expect them to is the essence of sexism.

As a therapist concerned with equality I regard gender-based expectations as a major contributing factor in stress, chronic personal dissatisfaction, low self-esteem, chemical dependency, eating disorders, depression, and relationship dysfunction in the lives of both men and women.

When we attempt to live out our lives within this rigid framework, we find it oppressive, stunting, and deadening. When men and women step outside those expectations, stretch themselves, and embrace greater possibilities, they report a stronger sense of self, more freedom for expression, and an increased optimism. Going against the grain is a difficult task, a struggle many give up, because they choose to conform to others' expectations of what is "feminine" or "masculine" and, in the process, abandon what feels natural.

In his book *Fire in the Belly* Sam Keen reminds us that:

Manliness and womanliness are both defined by a process of decision and denial. Each gender is assigned half of the possible range of human virtues and vices. . . . We do not know what human beings would be like if encouraged to develop their intimate promise without the systematic crippling effect of the gender game. Every man and every woman is half of a crippled whole [p. 208].

Pasting simplistic labels—"masculine," "feminine"—on the feelings and modes of perception and action is like trying to make people goose-step in orderly ranks. Good men and women alike can be intuitive, reasonable, playful, wise, erotic or loyal [p. 214].

In my work as a marriage and family therapist, I have witnessed countless couples* as they have alternately avoided and confronted the frustration, conflict, pain, and unmet needs that are present in a relationship of "opposites." I will share with you what my journeys with these couples have taught me. In some cases I will describe exactly what transpired in session. At other times what you read will be a composite made from a variety of similar experiences and used to illustrate or emphasize a point. The most tragic couples are those who do not seek professional help, whose relationships needlessly end because lovers believe that they simply have chosen the "wrong" partner.

Partners who seem most satisfied with their relationship are not "opposites" but rather people who are "wired" the same way (RB/RB, LB/LB). They are described as having similar natures and tend to mirror, rather than complement, each other. These couples come in two styles: *Siamese twins* (RB/RB) and *parallel partners* (LB/LB). The first type feels merged, bonded at a deep, almost spiritual level. The second type holds a respect and preference for individual space. Although these two types of couples relate differently, within each partnership the members use similar approaches, regardless of their gender.

Unless opposites reach an understanding of how their differing styles contribute to their issues and learn specific skills for managing their polarized ways of being, they will enter a crisis state. My purpose in bringing this information to others is to prevent couples from having to reach a crisis in their relationship before they begin to explore the problems associated with being opposites and learn ways of relating that are mutually satisfying. If, in your reading this

---

I work with both heterosexual and homosexual couples. In those instances where I use the term "marriage," it is understood that this refers to any significant, committed relationship between lovers.

book, nothing else is gained but the knowledge that this is a common problem—one that *can be solved*—then I will have succeeded.

This book is also for anyone who may not be in a relationship but is seeking a companion. In addition to my private practice, I lecture and teach workshops. Frequently a participant will complain that it is impossible to find a mate. After a brief exchange between us, it is usually revealed that this person has dated several people but is almost always disappointed. A common conclusion is "We're the exact opposite of each other. It would never work."

Well, I am here to say that it *can* work, but it takes a great deal more effort than those relationships in which the partners are similar. Family therapist Israel Charny speaks eloquently about the possibilities and limitations that exist within marital life. Those possibilities and limitations are never more present than in a union of opposites.

In the beginning, as with any challenge, it is more difficult because your skill level is underdeveloped. If you make the commitment to read, discuss, and practice what these pages hold for you, the goal of "meeting in the middle," and the greater satisfaction that accompanies that goal, can be yours. People *do* change. If that weren't true, therapists wouldn't exist. A word of caution, however: The most significant factor is the *commitment* to change. Without that this book will be of little value to you.

I realize that the classification of persons as right brain (RB) or left brain (LB) dominant is an oversimplification. It goes without saying that human beings are far too complex to be captured so easily. To categorize behaviors and attitudes as belonging to certain groups can be dangerous and is the root of such social ills as sexism, racism, and homophobia.

The categorizing of information in this book is done for the purpose of organizing others' research and my own observations so that the data can be presented in a fashion that may be readily understood. To do so does not mean that these categories are absolutes, and they should not be taken as such. They are simply ideas to consider, to accept or toss out as the reader sees fit. They are but one more way of trying to understand the nature of relationships. ·

Because the categories of RB and LB are abstractions, generalizations are made at the expense of individual reality. Human beings are beautiful and mysterious creatures, and many factors contribute to their behavior. The collective observations of one person, presented here, are made with the knowledge that they are just that.

Some men and women will identify with the material presented in these pages. Others may find little value in what they read, as it does not relate to life as they experience it. Each reader will have a unique response, and that is as it should be.

If you are an RB, you may want your LB to read the whole book, but this is a book about relationships, patterns, and connecting, which are all right-brain functions. It is written in terms of professional opinion, but the data are anecdotal rather than "hard" and therefore may have less appeal to an LB. He or she is more likely to read bits and pieces here and there.

This book is the product of hundreds of hours of observing couples in therapy. If you are an LB, you may prefer some kind of shortcut in order to get to the main points without having to wade through descriptions of various couples. If that is the case, then I suggest concentrating on Chapters 1, 2, and 12. Even though these couples were not part of a carefully controlled experiment, I believe that you will be able to recognize some of the dynamics as those occurring in your own life.

Finally, this is not a book about *why* opposites connect, although some thoughts about this are included. It is a book about *how:* how to live, work, and love within such a match. It is a book about the challenge of human relationships: growing beyond one's own ego-defined world, accepting, learning, stretching beyond the familiar, and, above all, bridging and celebrating diversity. Annie Dillard says it well in *Teaching a Stone to Talk:* "What is the difference between a cathedral and a physics lab? Are not they both saying: Hello?"

LEFT BRAIN,
RIGHT BRAIN:
WHAT'S THE DIFFERENCE?

*The test of a first-rate intelligence
is the ability to hold two opposed ideas
in the mind at the same time, and
still retain the ability to function.*
—F. SCOTT FITZGERALD

I am curled up on our rug, organizing notes for writing this chapter. It is a warm October day, and sun floods the room through the open French doors. At various moments each of our three cats marches across my work space and settles down on an island of paper that I will inevitably need. We will spend the afternoon taking turns disturbing one another.

I absentmindedly lift, move, and transplant each curious, furry interloper. They are persistent as only cats can be. Yet throughout this I manage to keep my train of thought. I operate in terms of relationships, and that is what is going on in this moment. I am doing multiple tasks simultaneously without consciously working at it, so these interruptions have little impact.

Periodically I glance up at my husband, who is sitting across the room deeply focused on his reading. I ask him a question. It is a question I already know the answer to, but I like to hear his voice; I like having something transpiring between us, connecting us, even if for a few seconds.

I can see that my interruption has disturbed his concentration, that he is taking time to shift gears mentally from whatever held his attention to what I have now asked of him. This shifting seems to be taking an inordinate amount of time, and I become frustrated and say, "Never mind."

For me it is over. Rearranging my note cards, I am on to other things. I look up to see that he is still thinking about my question. A familiar flicker passes across his face, indicating I have offended him by dismissing him when he did not spontaneously respond.

I apologize and ask him for his answer. He begins a thorough, detailed, fact-loaded reply. I get my answer and lots of extra information that he believes will be valuable to me at some future time, if not immediately.

This, then, is our pattern, a typical pattern for opposites: I want to connect, so I ask a question, interrupting his deeply focused inner world. This derails him, and he has to shift gears before responding. I am impatient and shrug it off, unaware that I am rejecting a chance for him to demonstrate his support for my writing by offering me a rich, well-thought-out answer. Able to jump easily from one thing to another, I am involved elsewhere when I intuitively look up to discover that he is waiting for me to accept his offering.

This time I listen, and even though I thought I had the answer, I am pleased to discover that he has considered another angle, one that eluded me. I thank him. He smiles and says jokingly, "Would you like to know *more?*" Both of us laughing, we return to our separate projects. He has come to understand my low tolerance for waves of facts. I have grown to realize that giving me information is one of the ways he demonstrates his caring and that when I become overly invested in my own style, I become blind to his.

We are very different. To complete this book, I am counting on *my* creativity and *his* keen, critical eye. I am more comfortable writing; he is more comfortable editing. We are opposites, and have learned to bridge the differences. It has been a difficult, often painful, and sometimes lonely journey to get to this place, because we began in polarized positions, not knowing how to "meet in the middle." I now know this is very typical of right-brain/left-brain couples. It is this, my own intimate relationship with a man whom I initially did not understand at all, that has inspired me to help other couples, as a therapist, a lecturer, and now through this book. The journey has been tough but worth every step.

The idea that opposites attract has always held a certain appeal. As a therapist specializing in relationship problems and as someone married to an opposite, I see both sides of the issue: The attraction is compelling, but there are difficulties that arise from such a union. I believe that these differences are related to the partners having different styles, which will be referred to as **RB** and **LB.**

In order to determine whether your style is more RB (right brain), more LB (left brain), or a balance of the two, complete the following exercise. (If you also want your partner to answer the questions, make a copy before marking your own.)

RIGHT-BRAIN/LEFT-BRAIN PREFERENCE

Even though each of us is constantly using both hemispheres of our brain, at certain times and under certain conditions one will be more dominant. Over time patterns develop which reflect a preference for one or the other. This is a simple exercise to assist you in understanding your own style. When unsure of which answer to choose, ask someone who knows you well.

Each of these statements might in some way relate to you, but in order to determine whether you are more right or left brain, it is important to **CHOOSE ONLY ONE STATEMENT IN EACH SET.** We are in a constant state of flux, ever-changing, so it may be difficult to select only one response. Circle the one that describes you better or most of the time (**either** "A" or "B"). There are no right or wrong answers.

1. A. I tend to concentrate on one task at a time.
   B. I often juggle many tasks at the same time without any problem.
2. A. I prefer to do things in logical sequence, beginning at the beginning and working through to the end.

    B. I have no preference; I just jump in at any point and work on something; I figure out the order later.

3. A. When communicating, I prefer the language of facts.
    B. When communicating, I prefer the language of feelings.

4. A. I am often told I am too rational/logical.
    B. I am often told I am too emotional.

5. A. I am uncomfortable with ambiguity and "gray" areas.
    B. I am uncomfortable with things needing to be well defined or definite.

6. A. Before I accept something as true, I want the facts, documentation, proof.
    B. I can accept something as true simply on faith, or using my intuition.

7. A. I am a critical thinker; things must make sense to me before they register as "true."
    B. Something can seem true to me simply because that's the way it feels.

8. A. When problem solving I tend to break things down and analyze the smaller parts to understand.
    B. When problem solving I tend to connect things and look at the relationships between them to understand.

9. A. I am uncomfortable in social situations where I have not had previous experience.
    B. New social situations are exciting to me.

10. A. I am told that I am very predictable.
    B. I am told that I am often unpredictable.

11. A. I prefer to think things through before sharing them with others.
    B. I tend to be spontaneous with my thoughts; the words are out before I know it.

12. A. When it comes to making love, I prefer to be told what I'm supposed to do to please my partner; I don't like taking chances.
    B. When it comes to making love, I think my partner should know what to do to please me; that's the romantic way.

13. A. When making love, I focus on doing what is "technically" right (pushing all the right buttons).

    B. When making love, I focus on the "merging" of our two bodies as we become "one."

14. A. I often have difficulty recognizing people.
    B. I can recognize someone I haven't seen in years.

15. A. I tend to experience an event for what it is and nothing more.
    B. I tend to emphasize the symbolic value of an event as much as the event itself.

16. A. I am often told I seem preoccupied.
    B. I am often told I don't stay on one topic.

17. A. I tend to be shy; more of an introvert, thinker, or loner.
    B. I am more of an extrovert, outgoing.

18. A. I am often accused of being self-centered.
    B. I am often accused of taking things too personally.

19. A. I prefer to spend leisure time alone with a hobby.
    B. I prefer to spend leisure time with people.

20. A. When I am upset I tend to withdraw to think things over.
    B. When I am upset I tend to reach out to talk things over.

21. A. I speak in monitored, carefully thought-out phrases.
    B. I speak spontaneously, not thinking about what I'm saying.

22. A. I am somewhat inhibited and have trouble interacting with others.
    B. I often draw attention to myself.

23. A. I am told I am too serious; that I need to "lighten up."
    B. I am told that I jump to conclusions.

24. A. I want to be precise in my communication.
    B. I want to connect with others in my communication.

25. A. I have difficulty knowing what I am feeling.
    B. I rely on my feelings to guide me in decisions.

26. A. I am good at remembering names.
    B. I have trouble remembering names.

27. A. I prefer using a tool for its intended purpose.
    B. I often use the wrong tool to get a job done.

28. A. I prefer to get the details of what I am learning.
    B. I prefer to get an overall sense of what I am learning.

29. A. I am interested in how something works.
    B. I am interested in how something looks.

30. A. I have stick-to-it-iveness and tend to "hang in there."

     B. If a project takes too long, I get discouraged easily.

31. A. I prefer being called "accurate."

     B. I prefer being called "creative."

32. A. I prefer to play it safe.

     B. I like taking risks.

33. A. I prefer discussing actualities.

     B. I prefer discussing possibilities.

34. A. I like helping someone solve a problem.

     B. I like helping someone explore his or her feelings.

35. A. I like my living space to stay the same way for a long time.

     B. I like to change my living space frequently by rearranging furniture or painting different colors.

SCORING

Count the number of "A" responses you have circled: ____

Count the number of "B" responses you have circled: ____

(Remember that we are all *both* right and left brain. What you may find in your responses is a pattern that indicates you are either right or left-brain **dominant** in certain areas of interaction within your relationships. You may also discover that you are more or less balanced in your style.

A	B	
35–25	0–10	Extremely Left Brain
24–20	11–15	Moderately Left Brain
19–16	16–19	Balanced Left/Right
15–11	20–24	Moderately Right Brain
10–0	25–35	Extremely Right Brain

    The purpose of this book is to help partners alter their perceptions, expectations, and attitudes about each other, in order to coexist in more cooperative, respectful, and compassionate love relationships. To do so, each must be willing to learn more about the reality of the other's world. That learning begins with a basic understanding of how our brain functions and a brief review of the research that has opened new doors.

We have come a long way in our understanding of the human brain since Plato thought it secreted semen and Aristotle declared it worked primarily as a cooling agent. Throughout the ages scientists, fascinated by how the mind functions, have continued to probe its mysteries. Among their many discoveries is one particular finding, which contributes to our discussion of behavior within relationships: the realization that *the right and left hemispheres of the brain have distinctly different functions.*

While I was examining the research in this area, it became clear to me that there are multiple opinions on the application of this knowledge. Scientists, physicians, psychologists, educators, and other related professionals are unable to agree. As in other fields, the results of one study cancel out the results in another. Meanwhile . . .

In 1981 Dr. Roger Sperry was awarded the Nobel Prize in Medicine for his "split-brain" work. What he discovered is as follows:

The *left* hemisphere is responsible for analytical thought and language. Think of it as a computer. It processes information serially, one piece at a time. Data entering are *reduced* to ever-smaller units. This sequential processing is important to language: "Sue wrecked Gordon's car" means something entirely different from "Gordon wrecked Sue's car." The left brain focuses on the parts that make up the whole, on breaking things down to understand them. (taking a clock apart to see why it has stopped working).

The *right* hemisphere is the center of creativity and intuition. It works with images and relationships, expanding on the entering data. It organizes patterns (some real, others imagined) in people's behavior—as well as events—assigning meaning to them. Processing bits of information simultaneously, it works like a kaleidoscope. Emphasis is on integration, "seeing" the missing parts, on wholeness (for instance, visualizing how a room will look after it has been decorated).

The same task can be completed in different ways, depending on which hemisphere is dominant. Take the example of balancing a checkbook: A left-brain person keeps it to the penny, whereas a right-brain person "knows" there's "somewhere around" a hundred dollars in the bank. There are some tasks that require specific hemisphere dominance (math calculations by the left, and brainstorming by the right). Other tasks might require a "cooperative" effort from both hemispheres. (While you drive a car, one part is determining the speed, while the other is picturing the destination.)

Many individuals tend to show a preference for behaviors associated with either the right or left hemisphere of the brain. Because of the way that these color a person's nature, it could be said that they are either right or left brain dominant.

Opposites are couples made up of one individual who is right brain (RB) dominant and another who is left brain (LB) dominant. They become, in the context of this book, an "RB/LB" couple. We will be looking at the common complaints and problems these couples have and discussing solutions. These hemispheric differences related to our discussion of RB/LB couples and their relationships are:

Left Hemisphere (Brain)	*Right Hemisphere (Brain)*
Factual	Experiential
Logical, rational	Intuitive, non-verbal knowing
Mathematical/symbols	Focused on patterns
Sequential	Simultaneous
Language skills	Dreaming
(reading, writing, spelling)	(brainstorming ideas)
Directed	Spontaneous, unordered
Linear	Spatial
Objective	Subjective
Analysis	Synthesis
Explicit	Implicit
Stores practical information	Stores emotions (nostalgia)
Denotative (literal)	Connotative (associative)
(Goal in language is to	(Goal in language is to
be precise)	create rapport)
Remembers names	Remembers faces
Metaphorically: a computer	Metaphorically: a kaleidoscope

The right hemisphere controls the left side of the body, and likewise, the left hemisphere controls the right side of the body. A stroke (hemorrhage) in the right hemisphere can result in paralysis of the left arm and leg. Some stroke victims are no longer able to remember familiar melodies, compute simple mathematical problems, copy geometric figures, or recognize loved ones, depending on where in the brain the damage occurred. However the power of the brain to reprogram itself is tremendous. This has been proved repeatedly in studies of brain-damaged patients, who during rehabilitation relearned skills in one hemisphere that were originally housed in the now-damaged or missing portion of the other hemisphere.

Another way of appreciating the different functions of the right and left brain is to look at the Japanese culture. Japanese writing uses two systems of signs. *Kana* is like an alphabet, but it is not one. It is sixty-nine symbols, each corresponding to a distinct sound. Kana is phonetic (symbols representing sounds). *Kanji,* on the other hand, is not phonetic but ideographic (symbols representing ideas). Each sign has a specific meaning, but the relationship between the sign and its sound is arbitrary. In school kana is taught first, with kanji being taught later. People who develop lesions in the left hemisphere of the brain have difficulty with kana (language); those with right-hemisphere lesions have trouble with kanji (patterns).

Each side of the face is controlled by the opposite side of the brain. If you take a photograph of a face and print one of the negatives backward, you create a mirror image of that face. These two prints (the original print and the "backward" print), when cut in half and then reassembled, form two new faces. The right sides make up one face of that person, and the two left sides make up another face of the same person. Very interesting images result. The photo of the face made up of the right side and its mirror image (which represents a whole face under the control of the left brain) shows expressions that are keen, determined, hard, and somewhat closed. The photo of the face made up on the left side and its mirror image (representing a face under total right-brain control) creates images that are more pleasant, relaxed, and benign. The person's two different natures become more evident through this exaggeration. It is precisely these differences that we all have that will be the focus in the remainder of this book.

9

In your own everyday activities, when you are engaged in two complex tasks simultaneously, they are controlled by *different* hemispheres. Tasks that cannot be done at the same time are functions of the *same* hemisphere that are interfering with each other. (For this reason NASA designed many tasks to be done by astronauts using opposite hands and feet, which ensures that they are from separate, and therefore noninterfering, hemispheres.)

The right and left hemispheres must be able not only to coordinate these different activities, but also to work in unison. They do so by communicating through signals sent back and forth via a bundle of fibers known as the corpus callosum, which acts as a bridge between the two halves. It is because of the corpus callosum that the left hand knows what the right hand is doing. It is this integration of our right and left brain that allows us to express the essence of who we are.

When there are significant problems with *both* hemispheres, this is not possible. For instance, with schizophrenia, there is incoherence, looseness of association, and illogical thinking (suggesting disturbance of language and cognitive activities of the left brain), and there may be a blunting of—as well as inappropriate—affect (suggesting disturbance of emotional aspects of the right brain).

Our right and left hemispheres operate in different modes and in different rhythms, with the exception of situations like deep meditation and intense creativity, when both hemispheres participate in a unified effort known as whole-brain thinking or synchrony. For instance a composer while in his or her left brain might concentrate on the number of beats per measure. A shift to the right brain would mean a loss of real time, but would allow a plunge into artistic expression.

Both halves of the brain can, and do, work in harmony as well as independently. An amazing example is that of the father of the writer Eudora Welty. He was capable of writing with both hands at the same time and could write the letters either right side up or upside down. He could even write *different* words simultaneously!

It would seem that the most obvious sign of hemisphere dominance is handedness, since we've noted that the right hemisphere controls the left side of the body and vice versa, but handedness does not indicate dominance. About 90 percent of us are right-handed and process language in the left hemisphere. Ten percent of us are left-handed, but left-handers are less lateralized (meaning the degree to which specific functions are *exclusively* under the control of one hemisphere). Eight percent of left-handers, like right-handers, process language in the left brain. But two percent of left-handers have language centered in the *right* brain. They are easy to spot, because they write with their hands in backward, hooked positions.

There was a time when teachers did not allow children to express themselves freely and forced them to write "correctly" (right hand, unhooked position). Since hemisphere dominance is deeply ingrained, this insistence can lead to problems with stuttering, confusion in following directions, and reading difficulties. Fortunately, we are taking a more humane approach as we approach the twenty-first century. One has to wonder what would have happened to Leonardo da Vinci, Michelangelo, and Picasso if they had been forced to use their right hands.

Other cultures have appreciated the differences between the right and left hemispheres. For instance, Hopi Indians distinguish one hand for writing and one for making music. For Mojave Indians the left hand (controlled by the right brain) is regarded as the passive, maternal, nurturing side, and the right (controlled by the left brain) is seen as the more active, decision-making father.

There is more than one way of knowing, more than one way to validate experience. Each hemisphere has particular strengths, and each contributes in its own way to thinking and consciousness. Yet we are taught that intuitive thoughts (right brain) do not represent the "truth," that real "truth" can be expressed only mathematically, with hard data.

At the time of the ancient Greeks, Western thought emphasized a dichotomous world; a thing was either true or not true and could not be both at the same time (the essence of today's computers). This viewpoint, the end product of (left brain) logic, has dominated Western civilization throughout history with the exception of the Renaissance, with its emphasis on the arts and humanities. For the past four hundred years, since the Renaissance, a premium has once again been placed on left-brain functions. The left-brain process of analytical thinking has been favored at the expense of the "irrational" right brain in both education and our society at large.

This emphasis on rational thought and analytical reasoning is acknowledged as responsible for the advances in science we benefit from today, yet it is equally important to grant credit to the right brain.

The classic problem-solving process used in scientific experiments actually begins with *right*-brain activity. The work that follows is the cooperative effort of both hemispheres in an alternating sequence. This is eloquently described by Betty Edwards in her book *Drawing on the Artist Within*. The first stage involves an appreciation of the whole problem by the right brain. This is followed by a stage of saturation, during which the left brain gathers, sorts, and categorizes information. At some point bits of data refuse to yield to analysis, and the thinking process loses structure as frustration sets in. The puzzle resists a logical solution.

In exasperation the effort is "set aside" as it enters the unconscious (right brain), while the person moves on to unrelated activity. Here it "incubates" while the right brain attempts to synthesize the material, pulling it into a meaningful pattern by completing the gestalt. When this occurs, the person experiences a spontaneous burst of insight. Suddenly everything makes sense! This stage is so unconscious that the person often thinks, "Where did *that* come from?" Following insight, the process switches again to the left brain for testing and application.

Albert Einstein understood the significance of the right brain when he commented that the really valuable thing in his work was his intuition, which often came to him in visual images. Convinced that beauty and elegance were a guiding principle in theoretical physics, he was also reported to have lost interest in "ugly" equations. Average scientists are motivated by the challenge in their work. "Revolutionary" scientists are equally motivated by enjoyment, the sheer "fun" of doing what they do. This ability to access their "inner child" requires that the left brain pull back and allow the right to participate fully.

This intentional back-and-forth shifting of dominance indicates a person who is open to all paths of understanding, what Oliver

Sacks refers to as a "romantic" scientist. In his book *Flow,* psychologist Mihaly Csikszentmihalyi shares stories of people dedicated to playing with ideas and flirting with methodologies that their colleagues might find suspect. These are obviously scientists who feel equally at home in either hemisphere.

The best researchers in the world appreciate the weakness in using only the computing functions of the left brain. They avoid the pitfalls of getting the right answer to the wrong question. Nature often reveals herself in unpredictable—even paradoxical—ways. At first what seems chaotic and unrelated in a flash of insight is suddenly comprehended. Utilizing both the right and left hemispheres provides the opportunity to be creative *and* productive.

This can be illustrated in everyday life by a couple who wants to build a house. They begin with a dream, an idea, created in their right brain. This stage requires both partners to utilize right-brain thinking, to conjure up that which does not yet exist. If the partners are opposites, these images are not at all alike. The RB partner is more inclined to be working with a gestalt of the finished house. This mental picture may include landscaping, even at this early stage.

RBs are more visionary, but the LB partner will begin to rely on his left-brain skill for calculating linear feet of lumber. The RB partner has an idea: What about a deck off the bedroom? The picture is clear. The LB partner considers whether or not this is logistically possible or structurally feasible. LBs are problem solvers, but *both* partners will need to utilize left-brain thinking when they sit down to discuss the financial reality of such a project, to make the dream manifest.

Later, when it is time to decorate, the relationship will once again shift back to relying on the RB's ability to visualize and his or her skill for spatial problems. An RB/LB couple who has learned the value of appreciating differences as a strength, and to negotiate and integrate them, will end up building a house they both have contributed to. To do so, they must be willing to accept and work with their opposite approaches, rather than criticize and judge each other, personalize their partner's differing responses, and use the differences to justify an end to the relationship. (All this will be discussed later in more detail.)

Although cooperation and teamwork between the hemi-spheres is ideal at times, there are also situations in which one hemisphere's dominance can interfere. To look at a work of art without analyzing it requires discipline, because the left brain in-sists on reasoning, while the right attempts simply to experience the images and appreciate their beauty. Research on drawing indi-cates that individuals who "can't" draw are those people who have difficulty accessing their right brain and are unable to turn off their critical left hemisphere. The left brain perceives in a way that interferes with drawing. By learning to shut off this internal analyzer, those who thought they couldn't draw are able to pro-duce work that challenges their reported inability.

The right brain can also prove disruptive. By creating images and fantasies of failure, a person can convince himself or herself of the "impossibility" of learning math rather than be open to the fact that given time, the concepts can be grasped.

We are in a revolution in our thinking about human capabilities and our assumptions regarding human potential. Research has been done on both coasts (the Institute of Living in Hartford, Connecticut, and the Salk Institute for Biological Sciences in La Jolla, California) which confirms that we constantly shift from our right brain to our left brain and back. When we experience a shock (sudden illness, partner abandonment, loss of business), we search for details and examine earlier behavior in order to make sense out of what's hap-pened, which requires left-brain involvement. Then we shift to our right brain to project into the future and occupy ourselves with what we imagine lies ahead. Through a series of exercises it is even pos-sible to influence which hemisphere is being utilized at any given moment.

When we try to problem solve, insight is aided by suspending left-hemisphere activity and accessing the right. This is assisted by our doing any repetitive, mindless task (such as raking leaves). Any-thing that puts you on "automatic pilot" will shift you to your right brain. Daydreaming is a full-blown right-brain activity.

When you are overcome with an emotion such as anxiety in a doctor's waiting room, the left brain can be called into action as a distracting agent by doing calculations: What is the square footage of the room? How many floor tiles are there?

ACTIVITIES THAT ACCESS YOUR RIGHT BRAIN

Meditation/guided imagery
Picturing a familiar face
Writing with your nondominant hand
Stimulation of your senses
Fantasizing/daydreaming
Free association of thoughts
Appreciating the beauty of something
Boring, repetitive movements
Making love
Imagining how you would decorate a room
Remembering a sad moment in childhood

ACTIVITIES THAT ACCESS YOUR LEFT BRAIN

Crossword puzzles
Calculations
Writing with your dominant hand
Categorizing, organizing
Speaking out loud
Remembering a name
Analyzing a work of art
Debating an issue
Rewiring a house
Making a list of sequential events
Fixing a toaster

(In the section on Exercises, you will find one on hemisphere shifting.)

Throughout this book, when I use the terms "right brain (RB) dominant," "left brain (LB) dominant," and "hemisphere dominance" I do not mean that a person is either one or the other at *all* times. I mean that in such areas as communication, conflict, problem solving, and relating to self and others, the person—more often than not—operates in a way that reflects the functions of either the right or left hemisphere. Over time such individuals habitually prefer one mode over the other and often become fixed and predictable in their behavior.

Even though scientists disagree on whether humans are actually hemisphere "dominant," people *do* perform differently on tests that measure the separate functions of each hemisphere. They also tend to select employment in jobs that are aligned with a particular hemisphere's function. For this reason, and for our purposes, an artist can be said to have selected a more "right brain" profession than a computer programmer, whose work is more "left brain." Some occupations compare as follows:

Left Brain (LB)	Right Brain (RB)
Accountant	Social worker
Doctor	Nurse
Engineer	Teacher
Financial analyst	Volunteer coordinator
Pilot	Homemaker
Attorney	Decorator
Computer programmer	Artist

Each of these professions can also be represented along a right-brain/left-brain continuum. For instance, a doctor's choice of specialty reflects more or less interest in establishing an ongoing relationship with patients:

Left brain ....Right brain

PATHOLOGY ....FAMILY PRACTICE
EMERGENCY ROOM ....PEDIATRICS
ANESTHESIOLOGY ....GERIATRICS

Many people become dissatisfied with their career choice, once they have accumulated enough on-the-job experience, because they discover the work does not match their hemisphere preference. I had a client who was an engineer, but one who thought in colors and spoke in metaphors. He was miserable in his job and never felt that he fitted in. By not losing the knowledge he had gained, he decided to turn to teaching in order to give himself a place where he could "bloom." Fortunately some occupations are inherently more balanced than others, and teaching is one of them.

Although humans seem to be heavily influenced by family and society while developing hemisphere dominance, one occasionally develops the less preferred side later in life. One of the most famous examples is the French postimpressionist artist Paul Gauguin, who was a successful banker until he was over thirty-five, when he abandoned his job (and family) to paint.

Hundreds of books have been written about why adults act as they do. There are as many theories as there are behaviors. As I've said, many thinkers, writers, and theorists would argue that behavior is based on gender. I believe this type of thinking contributes to a sense of alienation between men and women. There *are* differences, but there are also many, many exceptions to the gender-based paradigm. In today's world, where women are fine engineers and men make terrific nurses, we must reconsider our expectations. Imagine the following, if you will:

> A female is raised in a household with both parents employed as research scientists and a home environment that values logic over emotion. Watching her parents over the years, she observes the way they are reluctant to express affection publicly, how they weigh their words before they speak, their tendency to spend large blocks of time in individual activities, and their emphasis on facts over feelings. Consequently, although *most* females are socialized to be right brain dominant, she develops a more left-brain preference in her thought processes and behavior.

> A male is brought up in a home where both parents are social workers, and communication is free-flowing. Relationship and involvement with others are more prized than financial success. Even though the *majority* of males are more left brain, given an environment that encourages characteristics associated with right-brain activity, a male could easily mature into an adult who prefers awareness to analysis, expresses himself artistically and

has a keen sense of what others are feeling at any given moment.

My work with heterosexual, gay, and lesbian couples supports the above perspective. I do not see any of these couples' problems and complaints as gender-specific. It isn't just a matter of being male or female, but rather, the way in which a person has learned to exercise certain brain functions that over time become fixed in particular patterns. Being "wired" differently from their opposite partner creates problems for couples. This is the root of so many issues, and this is what you are about to explore.

2

WHEN
OPPOSITES
ATTRACT

The heart has its reasons
which reason knows nothing of.

—*BLAISE PASCAL*

Each of us wants to be understood by the person we love. Such a task is easy, when that man or woman is "in sync" with us: Communication is effortless and we, in turn, are generous with our compassion. When partners have difficulty relating to each other, too often they give up out of frustration rather than commit themselves to bridging the gap.

The best way to describe the root of these difficulties is to visualize people as being "wired" differently, as having different ways of conceptualizing, processing what they are receiving from the world, communicating their thoughts and feelings to the world, and relating to the "self" and others. Stephen Covey, in his book *The 7 Habits of Highly Effective People,* reminds us that "people tend to stay in the 'comfort zone' of their dominant hemisphere."

Before I explain these differences in detail, let's eavesdrop on several couples as they describe the problems of being in a relationship of opposites. As you read through their comments, see if you identify with one partner more than the other.

DAVE: (LB) Sheila is just too emotional. I can't get her to discuss our problems in a rational manner. We start to talk, and before I know it, she is yelling at me about something, and then she's crying. I can't figure her out at all. I just give up and walk out, 'cause there's no making sense of it.

SHEILA: (RB) Dave is not emotionally available to me. He lives in his own little world. I swear I could get hit by a car and he might not even notice. He seems so cold to me. I don't think he has any feelings. I don't think anything gets to him like it does to normal people.

For Dave there is only one path to understanding: a rational discussion focusing on the facts of the situation. If something does not make sense to him, he has difficulty accepting it as real. Sheila, on the other hand, feels cut off and alienated from Dave, because he is unable to regard her experiences as valid and worthy of discussion. Because she is overly focused on her internal state, she is unable to concentrate on the facts that are so important to him. Each feels unheard and therefore invisible.

BEN: (RB) Leo is married to his work. He spends all his "spare" time working. I would rather do things together. I will often have dinner waiting, only to be called and told that a project is going to take more time than he had expected. I wonder if he really cares.

LEO: (LB) Ben is too dependent on me for companionship. He needs to get a hobby or something. I am the main source of income for us, and I can't just go off and play when he feels like it.

Ben derives a great deal of satisfaction from being in a relationship with Leo. He enjoys doing things with Leo and feels strongly identified as a couple. Leo, however, is mostly occupied with keeping his head above water at work, and when he is deeply engaged in a project, he forgets everything else. Ben boasts that *he* never forgets Leo, and so he personalizes Leo's tardiness, believing that it is an indication of Leo's not caring about him. Ben does not understand that it is not about him; it is about Leo's tendency to get on one "channel" and stay there, because he is left-brain dominant. Ben's thoughts can easily weave back and forth between work and play, but that kind of shift requires a great deal more effort for Leo.

Opposites who do not truly understand that they are wired differently complain, "If I can do it, why can't she?" or "If he really wanted to he would." Ben becomes mired in the belief that the only thing preventing Leo from being different (and more like Ben) is stubbornness, self-interest or the absence of love. The moment Ben questions Leo's motives, a major change occurs and Ben begins to see Leo through a more critical lens.

One of the most frustrating aspects of being with an opposite (and remember that *both* partners are) is also one of the most difficult shifts to incorporate into one's thinking: What appears to be a simple, almost unconscious act for one spouse, may require significant effort by the other, and that which comes as second nature for one lover may never even occur to the other.

In the middle of a misunderstanding, when opposites are in conflict and when tension is high, the easiest move is to attack each other's character. Opposites who are heavily invested in their own ways and fail to consider alternative possibilities and explanations, never reach that point where they can appreciate the innocence behind certain acts that, at first, might seem intentionally thoughtless or neglectful. Ben's "If you really loved me, you wouldn't be late," would then become "I'm disappointed when you're late, but I know you love me and that you don't really want to be late." This shift allows Leo the room to see how he uses his time, and how he unrealistically tries to pack too much into each day.

MARIA: (RB) Ron is insensitive to my needs and selfish. He seems always to be focused on Ron. Sometimes I think we shouldn't have gotten married. I would like him to think about me more.

RON: (LB) Maria takes everything personally; she is too sensitive. If I've had a bad day and I come home thinking about it, she thinks I'm mad at her and gets all upset. Then I tell her to stop crying, and she tells me I don't care about her like I used to. It's crazy now.

Maria requires attention. Like the character in the movie *When Harry Met Sally,* she is "high maintenance" (a common aspect of being right-brain dominant). In contrast, Ron is "low maintenance" (a common aspect of left-brain dominance). Ron spends much of his time and energy focused on himself. Like many LBs, Ron played alone as a child, preferring hobbies to interacting with other kids. Consequently, he has never developed a strong need for companionship and continues to prefer his own world to most others.

Maria is therefore not so much a part of Ron's world as she is orbiting around it. Problems develop when she believes Ron's self-focus is a negation of her. Being an RB, Maria will relate almost everything to herself, and then react to that, without checking it out. Maria must come to understand that although Ron's style may not work well for her, it is not *in reaction to* her.

Ron will need to expand his world to include her, even if it means being "mechanical" about it in the beginning. Maria must not criticize his early efforts and demand that he respond naturally. She must come to understand that his natural state is to exclude others.

Although change is usually slow and often defended against, opposites are capable of making significant alterations in the way they interact. RBs tend to change first and rather quickly, but because that action is rooted in a desire for reciprocity—rather than in a true individual commitment to doing things differently—if the LB does not soon follow suit, the RB will shift back to his or her old behavior. The RB is "giving to get" and when the giving isn't returned in kind, resentment sets in. The RB turns self-righteous, saying, "Well I did everything I could, but it didn't do any good."

Frequently the problem is not so much that LBs have no interest in change, but rather that RBs and LBs operate with different time frames. By the time an LB has gotten used to the idea of doing things differently, and about the time he or she initiates a change, the RB has given up waiting and announces, "It's too late," which places them back at square one.

An LB spends great blocks of time internally debating all the permutations of a new behavior before engaging in it. Once an LB truly invests in it, that change becomes integrated, but all of this takes time. RBs jump right into new behaviors, but an RB has greater difficulty remaining committed to change, because that change may not have been thought through. Opposites need each other for balance in this area, as they do in many others. RBs are good at jump-starting a relationship when the action slows down, and LBs are good at maintaining a constant, if slow, forward momentum.

FRANCINE: (LB) I like a lot of warning. I'm much more comfortable planning ahead. I like to cover all my bases. Then I can really relax. Nick is always throwing things at me suddenly, and then he gets upset when I say, "No." He never thinks ahead.

NICK: (RB) It takes Fran two weeks to plan for a two-day trip. Forget coming home and suggesting we try to make a movie in twenty minutes. That's out of the question. She's never willing to just take her chances. It's like a movie is an incredibly serious decision to make.

Francine's world is one in which only thoroughly calculated risks are taken. As an LB, she will go to great lengths to make sure she does not make a mistake. It may seem unnecessary to Nick, but by taking the time to plan what she is going to take with her on a trip, Francine is not going to be caught off-guard with a mismatched belt or too much time on her hands with not enough reading material.

This attention to detail may serve Francine well, but it has a negative impact on Nick, who is always trying to interject some playfulness and excitement into their lives, which he experiences as overly organized and too predictable. The problems arise when Francine denies that the way she lives affects Nick, and when Nick diminishes what Francine needs in order to feel secure.

My work as a therapist has enabled me to witness the common complaints of many couples like these and to appreciate how frustrating and painful a relationship can become when there is so much misunderstanding. The weekly argument expands into a daily event. The partners sense a growing alienation and withdraw into themselves in order to feel safer. Eventually they may needlessly separate, each believing that he or she has selected the "wrong" partner.

When opposites first get together, they are usually excited by their differences. They view their polarized ways of being in the world as part of the attraction. Later those same differences become the focus of many a heated argument, and the erroneous conclusion is made that the relationship is doomed.

TODD: (RB) When I met Alice, she was very introverted, quiet, and shy. I really liked that about her, especially after dating so many women who always needed to be the center of attention.

THERAPIST: And now?

TODD: I realize what I thought was charming is really a problem. I can't get her to talk to me. We never have very long conversations.

SARA: (RB) I remember how independent Lynn was when I first knew her. I liked the way she didn't need me to entertain her. That left me plenty of time to study.

THERAPIST: How has her independent spirit created problems for you as a couple?

SARA: Well, I'm finding out that it wasn't independence as much as she simply prefers her own company over our doing things as a couple. I feel abandoned.

In order to relate all this to your own relationship, it might be helpful to outline particular characteristics that can be found more often in either a right-brain (RB) or left-brain (LB) partner. As you read through these, decide if you identify with one list more than the other and which one might apply to your mate.

Remember that all of us have *both* right- and left-brain tendencies. Many people seem to be somewhat balanced, and those readers will identify with several items from both lists. Others will find that they lean more one way than the other and tend to connect with the items on one list almost exclusively.

LEFT-BRAIN PARTNERS

- Focus on one thing at a time; resist getting side-tracked
- Prefer to have an order about all things; approach problems sequentially; are systematic, thorough

- Love to learn; seek knowledge; are open to new information
- Prefer a straightforward approach; are blunt; can be accused of being rigid
- Use black and white thinking; are uncomfortable with gray areas; hate ambiguity
- Are very logical, rational, and analytical in their approach to problem solving
- Are critical thinkers; must have things make sense to register as "true"; have a critical eye
- Depend on previous experiences; have difficulty with new social situations
- Are predictable; prefer not to take risks
- Deal in facts; reject intuition as source
- Are more "technical" lovers; emphasize pushing the right buttons ("Just tell me what you want me to do")
- Have difficulty recognizing faces
- Communicate in a reserved, somewhat constricted manner; may have flat, unmodulated speech; use minimal facial expressions, few gestures
- Are more invested in "actual" than "possible"
- Avoid emotional conflict; prefer to debate
- Are comfortable with routine
- Are oriented to the practical value of things (function over form)
- Are dependent on others to initiate activity
- Are good at hanging in there
- Expect others to operate with same rules of logic

RIGHT-BRAIN PARTNERS

- Are jugglers; often do many things at once
- Do not require tasks to be ordered/structured
- Deal in hunches; use intuition
- Focus on feelings
- Will accept or reject information on faith; have no need for documentation
- Emphasize connections; are comfortable in gray areas
- Can tolerate concurrent, diverse emotions; do not have to have things make sense to register as "true"

- Are comfortable with ambiguity, confusion, ambivalence
- Often emphasize the symbolic value of an event more than the event itself
- Are unpredictable, spontaneous, risk takers
- Are more "romantic" lovers; emphasize merging and knowing each other deeply ("If you love me, you'll know what I want")
- Have difficulty separating emotion and fact
- Have difficulty remembering names
- Communicate using expressive speech with varied intonation, using many facial expressions and gestures
- Tend to initiate emotional conflict (in order to engage less emotional partner)
- Avoid routine if possible
- Are oriented to the aesthetic value of things (form over function)
- Stimulate others into action
- Lack stick-to-itiveness; are easily discouraged
- Expect others to be as interested in relationship as they are

It is important to appreciate that we all possess characteristics from *both* lists but that we tend to live our lives emphasizing one more than the other. Even though there are obvious differences, couples need to recognize the *strengths* that are present in a relationship of opposites. Just as society is the collaborative effort of both right- and left-brain activities (the arts and the legal system, music and science), a couple is an exercise in complementarity. Together the partners weave an atmosphere that promotes growth for the individuals as well as the relationship itself.

Adjusting to an opposite is no small task, but a significant one, as beautifully described in Betty Berzon's book *Permanent Partners:*

> It is no longer a matter of making up my mind if I want to be with her or not. It is a matter of acknowledging and accepting the differences between us, rather than seeing them as plots against my sanity or precursors of the demise of the relationship. I know now that there are certain parts of me that she will never understand no matter how long I talk or what lengths I go to in an effort to introduce her to these corners of my being. I know she will always object

to certain things I do because she believes them to be fundamentally wrong and there are beliefs and behaviors of hers that offend me and probably always will [p. 37].

All couples must adjust to, and accept, their differences if they are going to live side by side in a respectful manner through the years. In therapy, opposites voice a considerable number of complaints. They also share their concerns about whether they will be able to transcend their differences and form a lasting union.

It is through these common everyday complaints that their differences are best illustrated. It is also through these gripes that you can most easily identify yourself and your partner. These complaints are universal, but at the time you may think you and your partner are the only ones who have such problems. It is important to keep this goal in mind: bridging your differences in order to create a more mutually satisfying love relationship. In later chapters specific topics, such as conflict, communication, and affection, will be addressed, along with specific techniques for addressing problems. Below are some common complaints of RB and LB partners. Again, remember that you may, or may not, identify more with one list than the other.

COMMON RB COMPLAINTS ABOUT AN LB PARTNER

- Is emotionally unavailable to me
- Is preoccupied when we are together; obsessive
- Is not in the here and now; always in the past or future
- Is too inhibited; can't let go and play
- Is insensitive; too blunt
- Is self-centered, introverted, antisocial
- Does not need me
- Won't talk about feelings
- Isn't romantic; should intuitively know what to do; doesn't merge emotionally during lovemaking
- Doesn't demonstrate caring about me
- Is boring in conversation; doesn't like to chat
- Is too invested in routine

COMMON LB COMPLAINTS ABOUT AN RB PARTNER

- Gets too emotional when talking about problems
- Wants too much of my companionship
- Is too extroverted; draws attention
- Won't stay on one topic
- Does not take a logical approach to problem solving
- Personalizes things; too sensitive
- Doesn't have enough interests; needs to be entertained
- Jumps to conclusions about my behavior (i.e., silence does not necessarily mean unhappiness)
- Isn't direct about wants/needs; expects me to "know"; places too much emphasis on becoming "one"
- Doesn't appreciate and devalues the ways I demonstrate my caring
- Utters too many irrelevancies in conversation
- Doesn't pay enough attention to details; is careless

All of us have *some* of these characteristics because we operate from both sides of our brain. Problems develop when we lose our balance as a couple and become polarized in our behavior with no sense of how to, or no willingness to, make that difficult trip to meet in the middle. Yet this is the key to opposites maintaining long-term, healthy relationships, as we shall see later.

Differences are very important to relationships. Only through exercising individual differences is the true strength of a relationship tested. Respect for your own, and your partner's, way of being is vital to the health of your union.

The problems that opposites have are usually in two main areas: Either the couple is in trouble because of the way each interprets the other's behavior, or the partners are expending too much energy trying to change each other so that they will be more similar. Of course each partner believes that his or her way is the "correct" one. Being more right brain or left brain is central to one's identity as a person. It dictates a person's values, how a man or woman approaches life, sets priorities, responds, creates, and even how he or she is described by others. When that identity is threatened by one's partner insisting on change, it is only natural that one becomes defensive.

The challenge has always been to accept one's partner as he or she is. This does not mean, however, to ignore unmet needs. Some of your needs are dependent on your partner's involvement, and it is necessary to address any areas of neglect. You will frequently have differing needs—sometimes conflicting needs—because you are two separate and unique individuals.

There is an old rule of thumb: *The person whose needs are being met has no desire to change.* This makes sense. Why fix something that works? One person may prefer to keep the status quo rather than tinker around with a relationship that is, from his or her point of view, just fine. This leaves the other mate feeling helpless about the situation. This sense of impotence eventually translates into resentment and anger, which is directed inward (depression, eating disorders, insomnia) or at the partner (chronic criticism, daily conflict, lack of sexual desire) or at the relationship (abandonment threats, infidelity).

Professionals who specialize in counseling couples are very familiar with a particular scenario: One partner has "dragged" the other into therapy. It is painfully obvious that these are desperate hours and that psychotherapy is perceived as CPR for a seriously ill relationship. In many cases like this, the couple arrives too late, with only one of them invested in the outcome.

In Chapter 11 we will look more fully at what you can expect in counseling. Love relationships are too valuable to neglect, and they are certainly too precious to abandon unnecessarily. By the end of this book you should be able to identify the specific RB/LB problems in your relationship, have some ideas about how to address them, and have developed a sense of the direction you want to take.

3

FACTS AND FEELINGS: BECOMING A "BILINGUAL" COUPLE

There are two ways of spreading light: to be
The candle or the mirror that reflects it.
—EDITH WHARTON

I am writing a rough draft of this chapter, yellow legal pad in hand. At my fingertips are piles of sorted research notes, a steaming cup of tea, and a stash of my favorite pens. In the background Mozart soothes my rough edges.

My loving husband steps into the room to see how I am doing. I tell him that I feel "under the gun" with so many projects going at the same time. I share my fear that I might not carry this particular one off, that writing a book is far more time-consuming than I anticipated. I let him know that some days I think I must be crazy to be doing this. My self-doubt floods the room. He looks at me thoughtfully for a minute, taking it all in. I can tell he is searching for something to say in the face of my pessimism.

This is shaky territory. He's been here before. Should he be encouraging? Sympathetic? What if he sounds condescending or paternal? What would be the right thing to say? He heads for more familiar territory, and his response is in the form of inquiry: Why am I writing in longhand when a perfectly good word processor is parked on my desk? Has a problem developed? A computer malfunction? Can he help? Oh—glancing at my tea—by the way, I should make sure I keep liquids away from the keyboard.

How can I reject all that advice and concern without rejecting him? I try to explain that what he has walked into is not a disaster area, that I am not a victim of chaos but rather that I have carefully created an environment which attends to all my senses and promotes—in my world—productivity. I tell him that for me words are not merely tools to be manipulated to achieve precision, that I actually have a *relationship* with them. I say that I find joy in forming their shapes on paper and that a keyboard short-circuits the process and robs me of the pleasure of "drawing" what I have to say.

I convey this as best I can and see that it makes absolutely no sense to him. He can't resist a forlorn glance at the dust that has accumulated on my underutilized printer. He tries to appreciate the essence of my message, but I notice something else forming on his face: his "tutorial" expression. He is going to make another attempt to mediate between the "wonderful world of technology" and me. Instead of empathy I'm going to get unsolicited instruction. We are—as are most opposite couples—a work in progress, and this is never more evident than in our communication.

COMMUNICATION AND COUPLES

As researchers have long observed, one cannot *not* communicate. This is especially true for couples. Although the most common complaint I hear in my practice is "We don't communicate" or "My partner won't communicate with me," I know that's impossible. There is no such thing as lack of communication in a relationship. The absence of an anticipated letter in the mail, a forgotten phone call, a closed door, a silent, sulking lover, a slap in the face: each of these seemingly noncommunicative acts sends a message.

Communication is learned, and the most influential teachers are parents or whoever else has the role of caregiver. These adult figures pass on what they themselves learned in their own childhood.

Consequently, many of us were taught to communicate poorly by well-intentioned adults. We learned certain patterns that create problems for us and for our partners as well. These patterns include: being superficial (instead of inviting authentic dialogue), erecting facades (rather than revealing our true selves), playing interpersonal games (in lieu of being direct about our needs), and manipulating through language (eliminating the possibility of equality).

Sending and receiving both verbal and nonverbal messages is the essence of communication. We communicate to survive, to give and get information, to persuade others, to establish and maintain power, to express our imaginations, to satisfy physical needs, to make decisions, to make sense of the world, and to establish relationships.

Human beings communicate in order to have relationships with others, so they can satisfy emotional needs, feel secure, valued, and connected. Virginia Satir, a therapist whose lifework focused on relationships among family members, summarized in *People Making* the role of communication:

> Once a human being has arrived on this earth, communication is the largest single factor determining what kinds of relationships he makes with others and what happens to him in the world about him. How he manages his survival, how he develops intimacy, how productive he is, how he makes sense, how he connects with his own divinity—all are largely dependent on his communication skills [p. 30].

In close relationships information about one's partner is essential. This information is obtained in stages, starting with superficial, descriptive, surface knowledge and evolving into more predictive knowledge, which is arrived at through time and many shared experiences. As intimacy grows, communication expands to include a third kind of knowing: making sense of one's partner's behavior.

An intimate relationship is a privilege because intimacy is earned through trust. The most intimate kind of contact with another person is allowing him or her access to your inner reality, your hopes, dreams, fears, and doubts. This can be done only through open, authentic, undefensive communication.

Over time intimate couples develop a private language of their own. It consists of special names, terms of endearment, and personal references derived from many shared experiences—good and bad. This private language is both verbal and nonverbal and serves two important functions. First, it enables the partners to communicate intimately in the presence of others. Secondly, it contributes to their identity as a couple by creating a boundary between them and those who do not share their language.

Rapport between partners is dependent upon trust and open, authentic communication. Observing a couple with good rapport is like watching a ballet. There is a distinctive rhythm, with each dancing in and out of the conversation freely, an occasional pas de deux interwoven among alternating solos.

In order to establish rapport with your partner, you must first regard him as a separate, unique human being whom you believe to be your equal. Rapport is about relating, as the theologian Martin Buber phrased it, on an I-Thou level. On this plane one's partner is not an object to be used to meet one's needs (I-It) but rather a path to a *shared* knowledge. I-Thou communication is about "between," which is the essence of rapport.

When we relate to others, how we see ourselves affects our communication style. People develop their self-images through relationships, through being "mirrored" by others. Each of us holds within us an "ideal" image of what we want to be and how we want to be seen by others. The gap between this mental picture and the actual self is fertile ground for distorting communication and creates blocks in our attempts to connect. Self-image is a mental impression of the self. Self-esteem is how we feel about that impression. Both the internal image and our opinion of that image contribute to problems we encounter when attempting to communicate—with ourselves as well as others.

This self-image is combined with our perception of the other person. As we engage someone in conversation, we begin to form judgments and opinions. These are of a prejudicial nature, based on stereotype. We have not gotten to know the person before we jump to global conclusions about his or her nature, intentions, attributes, and credibility. We try to "read" others, and we then make guesses about their feelings for us.

This tendency leads to significant difficulties in love relationships because of our emotional investment in, and dependency on, the partnership. We distort the information our mate sends us. We do this by projecting our wishes, seeing what we want to see, hearing what we want to hear, jumping to conclusions, making assumptions, and allowing our first impression of what people say to influence our opinion, in spite of contrary data.

Most of us hope to establish a rewarding, satisfying relationship with someone special. We may have all the desire, motivation, and time but lack relational skills. Without these skills we end up living parallel lives, which include proximity but little or no intimacy and in which blocked communication leads to the eventual destruction of any bond.

Ineffective communication creates interpersonal frustration, dissatisfaction, and stress. Chronic dysfunctional communication causes a pervasive sense of isolation from one's mate and feelings of alienation and loneliness. This loneliness or "emptiness" is a growing complaint not only in therapists' offices but throughout our culture at large. It seems as though the increasing materialism in our society is but a search for solace in *things* rather than *people,* and things do not require communication. The "me" generation is now discovering that having the most toys just isn't enough, not if you don't have anyone to play with.

Lack of intimate communication diminishes one's sense of self. The most troubled couples I see in my practice are those who have individually failed to achieve good human contact *prior* to establishing relationships with one another.

We can't really fully develop without linking ourselves to others and interacting in some meaningful way. Later, when another soul invites us into his or her life, not only are we offered a connection, but we are also presented with the challenge of balancing *self*-love against love for the *other.* Without a history of friendships, the partners lack "practice" in the art of give-and-take, making reciprocity difficult.

Communication is the life force in all relationships; when that force is blocked, the relationship weakens; with chronic neglect, it eventually dies. Love relationships are fragile and particularly dependent on healthy communication. As Aaron Beck observes in

Love Is Never Enough, ". . . aside from their sexual relationship, [a couple's] most intimate exchanges occur when they are engaged in conversation. Since they spend far more time talking together than making love, their conversations are crucial for the survival and growth of their rapport [p. 214]."

SENDING A MESSAGE: TWO DIFFERENT LANGUAGES

Every communication has a content and a relationship aspect. Each event (fact) triggers an emotion (feeling). These two "languages," facts (LB) and feelings (RB), are spoken by all opposite couples. Problems develop when each person is fluent in only one language, believes that to be the "true" language, and is not interested in learning the partner's. Or, as the saying goes, "He who is good with a hammer tends to think everything is a nail."

When partners *aren't* opposites, they speak the same language and use communication for the same purpose. They therefore have fewer problems with communication and less misunderstanding. Two RBs, for instance, will communicate in order to feel more connected, using intimate language to explore each other's experience at a feeling level.

Sarah and Len, two RBs, have been together seven years. Sarah is an art teacher, and Len works with physically challenged adolescents. They describe themselves as "exceptionally close" and frequently finish each other's sentences as they sit in my office describing the redecorating they are attempting on their own. Their language is joining, colorful, lively, and rich with metaphors. Both are animated as they share a recent decision-making process around the issue of choosing a fabric for a secondhand sofa Len has inherited from his aunt.

LEN: (RB) Sarah and I had shopped for fabric, and I found five or six really beautiful patterns that I could envision looking great at home.

SARAH: (RB) Yeah. Unfortunately I found about six more that I liked, so we sat down on the floor in the living room surrounded by this rainbow of a dozen or more choices and immediately realized it was an impossible task—

LEN:—so we started talking about each one: why we had chosen it and what it touched in us, you know, why it was beautiful and all.

SARAH: After an hour or so I could tell that Len was drawn to a particular one that I hadn't liked—

LEN:—so she asked me why it appealed to me. She wanted to understand my choice. I told her a story about my aunt's house and how that particular color combination triggered in me a memory of my aunt's sunroom and the times I played there—

SARAH:—and since this was his aunt's sofa, he thought that would be a good choice.

THERAPIST: So did you choose that one?

LEN: No. We're still going back and forth on this. Sarah has two or three that really strike her as "perfect."

SARAH: That's why we're here. This whole thing has lost its appeal. In the beginning we loved talking about what we liked and why, but now we can't make a decision, and we've begun personalizing it. Len says I don't like his aunt, and I'm accusing him of having no sense of color."

Problem solving is difficult for two RBs. Two LBs, however, have less difficulty communicating when a solution is sought. In addition, they have little need for intimate knowledge of each other and instead prefer language that is grounded in solid logic. Because of their avoidance of feelings, arguments remain between positions and never become personalized. An LB/LB couple prefers to problem solve *within* the relationship and usually has great success doing so. For these reasons therapists seldom see two LBs in their offices.

The following couple was a rare example of such a consultation. Maureen and Robert both are health care workers. Maureen is a laboratory technician, and Robert a biochemist. They met while on a river-rafting trip that focused on local geological formations. Robert was the coleader, charged with giving minilectures along the way.

Their office visit was precipitated by an unplanned pregnancy (also rare with two LBs), which had plunged both partners into a deeper level of emotional focus than they were comfortable with. Their reliance on hard data and logic did them no good at a time when mutual support and the intimate language of feelings might have served them better.

MAUREEN: (LB) As I said on the phone, this is not what we had planned on. I have done some research, and there is a failure rate of two percent with the type of birth control I use. I guess I've become a statistic.

THERAPIST: How do you feel about being pregnant?

MAUREEN: I just don't understand how it happened. We're always very responsible.

THERAPIST: Robert, what are your feelings about Maureen's having conceived?

ROBERT: (LB) I think some of the studies I've seen quoted higher rates than two percent.

THERAPIST: Maureen, are *you* aware of any feelings about this sudden event?

MAUREEN: I plan to get back on track at work. I've taken a week off because I'm having trouble concentrating. That's why I'm here. I can't afford to make mistakes in my job.

THERAPIST: Robert, why are *you* here?

ROBERT: I'm always open to suggestions, new information, anything that might help. This will mean some major changes for us, which we have to talk about.

Maureen and Robert, unaccustomed to focusing on their feelings, prefer to limit themselves to the facts about the situation. Both LBs, they speak the same language and use communication for the same purpose.

If you are partnered with an opposite, it won't come as a surprise that the entire *purpose* of communication is different for an RB from what it is for an LB. RBs regard communication as a means of arousing interest, as a way to experience solidarity, and as an opportunity to engage their partners on a path toward intimacy, whereas LBs perceive communication as a forum for achieving precision in their understanding, solving problems, and making joint decisions. Consequently, RBs associate talking about their relationships as a way to stay *connected,* and LBs associate talking about their relationships as a *sign of problems.*

During any given discussion your opposite will interpret you, what you are trying to communicate, and most of the things that occur primarily in terms of his or her own experience, understanding, and language—*as will you.* This is a natural process but can create a polarization that diminishes satisfaction for both partners.

In healthy relationships, differences are regarded as a strength and not as something to be eliminated. There is an appreciation that truth is not absolute and that human behavior is complex and can be explained in many ways.

In *Successful Marriage,* family therapist Robert Beavers points out that much of a couple's disagreement is about ambivalence and that partners must understand this is human nature, especially with regard to "anything finite and yet needed—such as loved ones [p. 71]."

Differences need not stand in the way of good communication. They actually provide an opportunity for an altered sense of what is possible, opening the partners up to avenues they have never considered. It is differences—the ability to balance reason and emotion—that make interdependence possible.

Partners cannot work together when emotions overwhelm their ability to problem solve, yet logic alone is not sufficient for solving problems between lovers because many aspects of any relationship simply are not rational.

As important as accuracy is in communication, in love relationships most people seek connection as well. In *Getting Together,* Roger Fisher and Scott Brown inform us: "Emotions can convey important information, help us marshal our resources and inspire us to action. Wisdom is seldom found without them. . . . We need both reason informed by emotion and emotion guided and tempered by reason [p. 10]."

An LB finds it difficult to talk with an RB who refers to intuition or other mysterious insight and "privileged" knowledge, is overly emotional, excuses inconsistency, and is frequently illogical. This approach makes problem-solving discussions impossible and problem solving is necessary for conflict resolution.

Darren and Ryan have lived together eight years, including six as business partners in a small advertising agency. Darren takes care of the nuts and bolts of daily operations, while Ryan is responsible for marketing, public relations, and socializing with clients. Ryan is a "natural" with people, conversing with ease and entertaining them with humorous stories.

At the office the responsibilities are easily divided with clear lines distinguishing each partner's area of operation. At home it is more difficult to make decisions. At a recent session they were asked to discuss a decision they had to make. Darren turned to Ryan and began:

DARREN: (LB) We should sell the condo. We just don't ski enough to justify holding on to it.

RYAN: (RB) But I love going there. I love that big fireplace on a cold night.

DARREN: It just isn't practical to keep making the payments, while it sits empty so much of the time.

RYAN: I can't believe you want to do this. Doesn't it mean anything to you that we have spent every anniversary there?

DARREN: I know that, but we've got to cut back on expenses. This last quarter we barely made a profit. The condo is the most obvious choice.

RYAN: To you it's just a figure on paper. What about all the great times we've had there? You're just flushing them away!

DARREN: Give me a break! I'm trying to figure out how we can reduce our expenses and you're talking about me as if I'm ending our relationship. How did we jump to *that* topic?

RYAN: Never mind. I can see what your *real* priorities are.

DARREN: Look, Ryan, I don't want to sell it, but I can't see any other way.

RYAN: Just hold on to it. I *know* we'll do much better this quarter.

DARREN: What is that based on? The figures I've seen so far don't indicate that.

RYAN: I have a real good feeling about the Woods account. I can't tell you why, but I have a sense that it is going to expand beyond belief.

DARREN: You have a good *feeling*?

It is equally frustrating for an RB to try to talk to an LB who insists on a rational approach to all topics and retains a totally objective stance, never revealing a bias, an opinion, or a feeling about a subject. This approach makes intimacy impossible, and intimacy is the heart of all love relationships.

Nora and Evan have been together for three years. Nora is a computer programmer, and Evan is a social worker for a rehabilitation hospital. They are in counseling because Evan is frustrated with trying to communicate with Nora. Nora brings a pragmatism and logic to their conversations that squelch Evan's attempts to share intimately. This frustrates Evan, who then attacks Nora for not caring. Nora responds defensively, as she rejects the notion that she is uncaring. Long silences follow these aborted efforts to communicate. Now, sitting in my office, I ask them to start with their last argument:

EVAN: (RB) I came home complaining about the mountain of paperwork I had and how each patient generates an entire forest's worth of forms.

THERAPIST: What did you want that comment to trigger in Nora? What were you hoping for?

EVAN: Some connection, some sense of knowing the frustration I was feeling.

THERAPIST: What did you get?

EVAN: I got a speech about the necessity of tracking patients so they can be properly billed and the purpose of all those forms. The kind of thing I might get from my own unit manager!

NORA: (LB) I think I said something like "I'm sure all those forms are necessary, even though there are so many."

EVAN: It wasn't just what you said, but the *way* you said it that made me feel lousy. I was all crazy and slamming my briefcase down and going on about being buried under paper. Then you, in that very controlled way, said something about the hospital having reasons.

THERAPIST: What was that like for you, Evan?

EVAN: I felt like Nora had thrown ice water on me. Totally unconnected. Cut off. Like a switch had been flipped. That happens a lot. I'll be expecting her to say something that will make me feel better, but I end up feeling worse.

THERAPIST: Nora, what are you thinking as you hear Evan retell the situation?

NORA: Well, I don't feel any different. I still think it's true that all those forms are necessary. I'm not really sure of what I'm *supposed* to say. What I said made perfect sense to me.

Each partner is deeply invested in his or her own way of communicating, often to the detriment of the relationship. The magic words "Let me see if I really understand what you are trying to tell me" are foreign. I am indebted to Stephen Covey's following story from *The 7 Habits of Highly Effective People* to illustrate this:

> Suppose you've been having trouble with your eyes and you decide to go to an optometrist for help. After briefly listening to your complaint, he takes off his glasses and hands them to you and suggests that you wear them. He says, "I've worn these glasses for ten years and they've really helped me. I have an extra pair, you can keep those." But when you look through them, your vision is worse. You say, "I can't see a thing." He says, "What's wrong with you? They worked great for me. Try harder [p. 236]."

Mary Field Belenky and her colleagues, while doing research for their book, *Women's Ways of Knowing,* discovered that although many women conceptualize and communicate in ways that are related to traditional socialization, *gender is not always a predictor.* Contrary to myth, women do not always arrive at knowledge in the same way; just being female does not dictate how you think, problem solve, or communicate with others. Belenky called some of the women in her study, "connected knowers" and others "separate knowers": "Separate and connected knowing are not gender specific. Each of the women interviewed in the study . . . tipped toward one orientation or the other [pp. 102–03]."

A connected knower, as Belenky describes her, is very similar to what is referred to in this book as an RB, and a separate knower is what is being called an LB. Like the RB and LB in conversation, the connected and separate knowers not only use different languages but use communication for different purposes as well.

The most important discovery of Belenky and her colleagues that is relevant to our discussion is the realization that connected (right-brain) knowing is just as *procedural* as separate (left-brain) knowing. In our culture, where right-brain thinking is considered less "legitimate" than left-brain, this is good news for RBs, who have long sought validation for their way of conceptualizing and communicating.

Connected knowers (RBs) regard personal experience as the most trustworthy source of knowledge, far superior to authority alone. Because they believe that access to knowledge is through the experiences of others, communication in relationships is the way they come to understand another person's ideas. They attach to that which they seek to understand. Their conversation is peppered with questions, not because they are attempting to detect the steps in another's logic but rather because they are interested in how experience leads to a person's perspective.

The other women in the study, separate knowers (LBs), prefer *impersonal* reasoning. At the heart of their process is critical thinking, the search for loopholes and flaws. These LBs rely on their analyzing and evaluating skills, taking pride in a willingness to explore the validity of their own ideas as well as those of others.

LBs, or separate knowers, believe it is far more important to know the rules (leading to a rational conclusion) than to know the person. Unlike an RB, who considers a person's personality a rich addition to the process of understanding, an LB regards personality as not only extraneous but detracting from the purpose of communication: the pursuit of "truth," through the presentation of facts, in precise language.

LBs speak a nonintimate language of objectivity. Their intention is to remove any bias, which means that they eliminate the "self" from their communication in order to take as impersonal a stance as possible. This is why they have difficulty engaging in intimate conversations, which by their nature, require a diving into subjectivity and then making that subjectivity public. Many LBs are unskilled in this process, because they lack a vocabulary for doing so. (The Exercises Section contains a "Feelings Vocabulary" which may be of help.)

Harriet Goldhor Lerner, in *The Dance of Anger,* discusses couples one partner of which is much more comfortable with feelings than the other: "Opposites do attract, but they do not always live happily ever after . . . it is reassuring to live with someone who will express parts of one's own self that one is afraid to acknowledge; yet the arrangement has its inevitable costs . . . [p. 49]." Addressing nonexpressive partners, she goes on to warn that when one partner relies on the other to do the "feeling work," he or she loses touch with this important part of himself or herself. A typical opposites exchange reflects this dilemma:

RB: We don't talk much about us, have you noticed? We always seem to talk about *things*. I feel like we're growing apart because I don't feel connected to you. I never know what you're thinking or feeling. It scares me when I realize how little I know about you.

LB: What is it you want to know?

RB: I don't know. Anything!

LB: Anything about *what?* Could you be more specific?

RB: You're impossible.

The tendency for LBs to ignore feelings is based on the idea that in order to analyze a situation, one needs to make it as impersonal as possible, divorcing oneself from any beliefs and emotions and relying on pragmatism as a guide. Belenky informs us that separate knowers deplore the "egocentricity" of connected knowers, believing that an RB's emotions are blinding and that any conclusion arrived at under the influence of subjectivity and the absence of "hard" data is at best a "half-baked truth." An LB will abandon even his or her own position, if unable to support it with nothing more than subjective data (feelings).

Unfortunately, when an LB eliminates feelings from communication, that includes dismissing those of the RB partner, leaving the RB "defenseless." If relationship is about connecting, and communication within intimate relationships is entirely objective, this creates a distance between the partners and subtracts from the overall satisfaction.

In order to communicate as partners, opposites must come to appreciate the separate languages they speak. The LB's language concerns itself with facts; the structure of that language is logic. It is essentially binary, with things being either black or white, in order to be as precise as possible and eliminate the possibility of being misunderstood.

THE LB'S LANGUAGE OF FACTS

- Is precise
- Uses authoritarian, rational vocabulary
- Emphasizes separation, independence
- Reference is logic
- Uses communication as clarification process
- Heart of communication is critical thinking
- Uses impersonal language of objectivity
- Has goal of presenting facts through rational procedure
- Uses questions as tools to understand the other's logic (what kind of reasoning has gotten my partner from A to B?)
- When problem solving, uses language to guide another to the "correct" solution; has role of mentor

The RB's language is one of feelings and therefore not as precise as that of the LB. It is closer to what is known in the world of computers as fuzzy logic. There is a logic to it, but not in the classical sense. It is less like math and more like a movie, full of images and attending emotions. Its goal is to engage the other person into relationship, to achieve rapport.

THE RB'S LANGUAGE OF FEELINGS

- Is ambiguous
- Uses empathic, emotional vocabulary
- Emphasizes attachment, interdependence
- Uses symbolic references, metaphors
- Regards communication as connecting process
- Heart of communication is shared experiences
- Has intimate language of subjective knowledge
- Has goal of making interior contact with another through common experience
- Uses questions as tools to determine how experience has led to

current perspective (what has happened to my partner that has gotten him/her from A to B?) [This is what Belenky terms experiential logic]

■ When problem-solving, uses language to assist another in coming to his/her own solution; role of midwife

Although "opposites" approach the truth in different ways, they do share, as Belenky phrases it, their ability to "get out from behind their own eyes and use a different lens [p. 115]." Connected knowers (RBs) do this through empathic communication of feelings, stepping out of their own experience to imagine the experience of the other. Separate knowers (LBs) accomplish it through an objective presentation of facts, leaving personal bias behind.

When they come together as partners, there is, as a consequence, a marriage of these two different procedural processes or "languages," one emphasizing shared experiences and the other based on an entirely impersonal process. This is nowhere more evident than during an argument between opposites. The RB perceives the disagreement as being between the *partners,* but the LB identifies the same transaction as existing between *positions.*

LB: This election is going to be close. Both candidates have strong backing. But in spite of that, I think our organization needs someone with experience and that's Jackson.

RB: Jackson? You've got to be kidding! He's history. He got himself into a real mess with that Orlando deal.

LB: I disagree. His explanation for the missing funds was quite credible. He was never formally charged.

RB: *[I can't believe he's siding with Jackson.]* Don't you remember the time he came up to me at that party and hit on me?

LB: What does that have to do with his ability to lead?

RB: *[He's not even supporting me in this.]* I'm going with Emory. She's far more capable. Besides, she's a much nicer person.

LB: What does her personality have to do with her ability to lead?

RB: *[He's really picking a fight with me.]* I happen to like her. Do you mind?

LB: I just think you're straying from the facts, and the facts support Jackson.

RB: *[I hate him when he gets this way. I feel a million miles apart.]* I don't want to talk about this any longer, and I've decided I don't want to go to the movie either.

LB: What? Where did *that* come from?

RB: We're just miles apart on this. I don't feel close to you, so I don't want to spend time together right now.

If these partners appreciate that this is the nature of their relationship and not due to a defect in either of them, they can begin to move toward a more bilingual existence, which requires a balance of the two and creates a need for "cross-cultural" education.

To make this commitment, partners need to understand that good communication occurs when the effect of a partner's message is exactly as he or she intended. Interdependence is necessary for this to occur: The "sending" partner must communicate in an unambiguous manner, *and* the "receiving" partner must not distort the message. This shared responsibility rests *between* the partners. When it is neglected, miscommunication and misunderstanding result.

4

TALKING TO YOUR PARTNER

*Tact is the art of making a point
without making an enemy.*

—*T. H. WHITE*

You've been communicating for years. From the beginning of your life you've been reaching out in an effort to connect, to make yourself known, and to understand those around you. On any given day you may find yourself talking business, wiggling out of a traffic ticket, ordering a delicious meal, or delivering a speech. You regard yourself as a good communicator; people seem to grasp what you mean without much effort.

Yet as an otherwise articulate person you find that you often become completely ineffective when attempting to communicate with your opposite. An attempt is made and intentions are good, but misunderstandings and hurt feelings occur. The most significant culprit is the two different "languages" you speak, but even if you become bilingual, communication can fail.

When you realize how many things can get in the way of communicating to your partner, it may seem that nothing short of a miracle could achieve the desired results. Listed below are common barriers to sending a message. *All* of these present problems for couples, but those which are especially problematic for "opposites" are in boldface. As you read through them, your tendency will be to note the ones that are your partner's. Stretch yourself, and identify the ways that *you* contribute to your communication problems as a couple. (Checkoff lists are provided for you and your partner under "Talking," in the Exercises Section.)

BARRIERS TO SENDING A MESSAGE

- **Lack of trust**
- **Failure to include your partner**
- **One-way communication**
- **Sending mixed signals**
- **Lack of self-awareness**
- Aggressive/abusive language
- Abstract language/indirect communication
- Topic avoidance
- Withholding
- **"Mechanical" problems**
- **Monopolizing**
- Stress
- Alcohol and drugs
- **Competition/power struggle**
- Inability to remain in present
- **Personalization**
- Blaming

LACK OF TRUST. Trust is essential for the development of intimate communication. In order to voice an opinion, risk sharing a feeling, or suggest a solution, you must have two things; a belief that your relationship is strong enough to support honest, authentic communication, and some idea of how your mate will respond. If either of these is missing, one or both partners will remain guarded, and meaningful, satisfying dialogue will not be possible. LBs often have difficulty trusting RBs because an RB's behavior is not predictable, and his or her response is frequently disarming. An RB can help by being aware that his or her style creates an "unsafe" climate for an LB and realize the value in thinking something through before commenting on it.

FAILURE TO INCLUDE YOUR PARTNER. Unfortunately a climate of trust is not enough. Even if it is "safe" to talk, an LB may not discuss something because it doesn't occur to him to do so; his mind is focused on the content, not on who should be included. More likely, he perceives consulting with his partner as "seeking permission" because he is more invested in his autonomy than in promoting good communication.

LB: It seemed more important just to get it done than to ask you. It really didn't occur to me that you might care.

RBs also fail to bring their mates into the decision-making process but for a different reason. An RB believes she can predict her mate's response and therefore sees no need to communicate with him or her.

RB: I took the liberty of choosing blue for the new carpet because I knew you'd like it.

Not seeking out one's partner and discussing a situation prior to making a decision create untrustworthiness and alienation, especially if the decision will have an impact on the partner. It is not enough to announce a decision after the fact. When one partner decides a matter without consulting the other, he or she is communicating that the partner is not being considered and that the partner's needs and feelings are of little or no interest to him or her.

ONE-WAY COMMUNICATION. Once two people get together, communication breaks down if it is only in one direction. An LB tends to "talk at" others while focusing only on the facts and his or her observations about those facts. Forgetting to listen, the LB cuts off the chance to learn his RB's reaction and therefore discourages a dialogue. Not being invited to contribute and realizing that feedback is not truly welcome, his RB will eventually learn to "tune him out." LBs need to entertain questions and invite comment in order to promote two-way discussions.

LBs often become annoyed when interrupted and will return to the interrupted thought as if no one else had ever spoken, often following this with a "rewind" of the salient points that might have gotten missed. All this is done as a security measure, so the LB will be able to make a point as clearly as possible. Unfortunately this effort can be counterproductive because it diminishes the RB's interest and increases his or her frustration. Remember the LB's goal in communication is to be precise. The RB's goal is to create a connection, which is what the interruptions are about. Conflict between opposites is frequently rooted in frustrated communication.

SENDING MIXED SIGNALS. Partners must be careful not to be ambiguous. Ambiguity occurs when behavior does not match the words, or thoughts on a single topic are not consistent from day to day. Although RBs are comfortable with inconsistency, they must be sensitive to how this confuses an LB partner, who does not shift gears easily.

LACK OF SELF-AWARENESS. Communication is fuzzy when the sender has failed to communicate with himself first. For LBs, communications with the "self" is in the form of a debate or a lecture; rarely does it focus on feelings:

LB: I should be spending more time on this project, but how? There's no time left. I've taken on too much. How can I maximize my efforts on this and still leave time for that meeting tonight? Something has to go. I won't eat dinner. That'll give me another hour.

The RB's inner communication is saturated with feelings about the self and the self in relation to others:

RB: I wonder what Phil's going to say when I tell him I have to stay late again. I hope he understands. I'm worried that this is causing problems for us. I feel overwhelmed with all this work. I feel really alone in this. It never seems to end. I notice that Phil's tired of it, too. He's been withdrawing when I get home, just as I need him to be close and supportive.

There are a variety of reasons why a partner may not be aware of feelings or, if aware, not communicate them freely: being raised by nonexpressive parents (two LBs), belonging to a minority group, and possessing a particular personality that inhibits expression.

A partner who has grown up in a nonexpressive family may resent the "push" by her mate to open up and talk. She may resist in direct proportion to her mate's effort to be encouraging, resulting in a childish power struggle and a lack of intimacy between them.

Don Clark, in *Loving Someone Gay,* reminds us that gays and lesbians have an additional communication problem imposed by the straight world. From their first attempts to discuss their awareness that they were "different" from other kids, their feelings have been invalidated by others. In response to this experience some have cut themselves off from their internal state, while others have developed a heightened sensitivity as the result of their struggle to be heard.

Psychiatrist Irvin Yalom notes that some adults have personalities that make it difficult for them to differentiate between various emotional states. They cannot localize internal responses within their body, and they rarely have fantasies related to any of their feelings. He has observed that significant problems arise in relationships for these people because partners can never tell how they are feeling. They are often described as unspontaneous, wooden, heavy, lifeless, and boring.

Not only is the emotional landscape barren for these people, but their relationship with their own bodies is also lacking. Their movements are deliberate, forced, and blocked. They are often criticized for being wooden in their speech as well because nothing of feeling "shines through." They tend to be overly self-conscious, ponderous, serious and fail to make good playmates as adults. All these observations could also be used to describe a partner who is *extremely* left brain.

Feelings are important to identify and communicate because they add dimension to the facts. Emotions are about the relationship of the event to the self, and information about the self is the heart of intimate communication. When information about a partner's internal state is not available, the mate becomes drained in the relationship by becoming overly responsible and expressing all the feelings for both of them.

Aggressive/abusive language. Abusive language *always* over-powers the message. This is why aggressive partners are often un-able to get their points across; the language becomes the listener's focus, and the information buried beneath the offending language is lost. The mate has no problem *hearing* but will probably stop *lis-tening.*

When a person is angry at his partner, he is in a particular frame of mind that magnifies his partner's flaws and negative traits. In an adversarial state, positive aspects are forgotten. Yet an RB of-ten believes that only in highly emotional states are true feelings re-vealed. The fact is that in extreme states of affect, partners are *least* likely to express their genuine thoughts. An out-of-control partner invites anger and alienation—or withdrawal—from an overwhelmed lover or spouse.

Abstract language/indirect communication. Even those more in touch with their emotions may at times mask their feelings and hide behind intellectual analysis. "We're just too different to make it" is an example of "terminal" language and presents a dead end. When a partner has come to a conclusion, it is important to share not only that opinion but the series of thoughts or experiences that led to that position as well. Words are imprecise, but the more ambiguous a message is, the less likely it will be understood.

The majority of us were raised to be unassertive and indirect when communicating our needs. For this reason our messages of-ten need to be "decoded" by our partner. Since this involves guess-work, the burden then swings from the sender to the receiver, who must seek clarification to avoid a misinterpretation or misunder-standing. Partners frequently fail to do this, and this creates unnec-essary problems.

Topic avoidance. Another way we are indirect is in our effort to avoid certain topics that feel "unsafe." Like testing the water with our toes before plunging in, we send a message out, wait to see the response, and then alter the message, if necessary, so that it is more acceptable to our partner. This prevents conflict, keeps us in his or her favor, but makes authentic communication—especially inti-macy—impossible. The price for a "safe" relationship is superficial talk that never touches on those things that are in need of deep dis-cussion.

All couples have "hot" topics (most common: sex, finances, parenting, religion, politics, and in-laws), but not all manage to transcend the discomfort and possible conflict in order to discuss them. In relationships with a lot of avoidance, there is an air of tension and an absence of spontaneity, lending a lifeless quality to the communication.

Withholding. In an attempt to protect herself in awkward moments, a partner may hold back information (lie by omission) or distort information (lie by commission). There may *seem* to be intimacy, but it is unauthentic, between one partner and the "false self" of the other.

"MECHANICAL" PROBLEMS. All partners must adjust to each other's timing and pacing. When to initiate a discussion depends on several factors; if these are ignored, your partner may not be receptive to your request. You cannot be taken seriously if you are not heard, and you won't be listened to if you fail to notice that your partner is preoccupied (either mentally or physically), stressed, worried, tired, under the influence of alcohol or drugs, or deep in concentration.

How many times have you found yourself heading into an all-nighter or marathon discussion just as the two of you are getting into bed? RBs are far better equipped for these and are frequently *energized* by talking for hours, achieving a stronger sense of connection with the LB through greater insight and understanding.

LBs avoid these marathons, if possible, because they hold little pleasure for them. Instead of walking away from an extraordinarily long discussion feeling a greater bond with the RB, the LB finds the experience draining. Just as the RB is getting his or her second wind, the LB enters a comalike state. As long as they are talking, the RB considers the relationship a satisfying one; as long as they have to *keep* talking, the LB considers the relationship problematic.

Different speech patterns create problems between opposites. An LB's speech is precise but without passion, often flat and sober in tone. This can lead to an erroneous assumption by the RB that the LB is displeased or angry. The RB tends to have a variation of inflection, but with expression often dominating the content, so that the LB is often distracted from the point the RB is trying to make by having to wade through all the dramatics.

The LB prefers to formulate thoughts and present them in a slow, methodical, logical, and uninterrupted sequence, while the RB partner jumps in with half-formed ideas and conflicting emotions, plowing on ahead at warp speed. This discrepancy in the delivery is the focus of many an argument until they adapt to each other's unique, if troublesome, method.

LB: I want to discuss a problem with the present plan for switching cars before I leave for my trip on Friday. The way we have arranged things is not going to work after all. . . .

RB: Why not come by my office and do it there?

LB: The present plan is not going to work because we are operating with two different time frames and—

RB: Well, I'm willing to go home first, if that is what you want.

LB:—these different time frames are causing us a problem. That's what I need to talk about.

MONOPOLIZING. When partners operate at different speeds, it can be frustrating for both. Equally upsetting is the LB's domination of the conversation by creating an overly detailed monologue and blocking any true exchange. An LB often fears not being able to make himself clear enough and keeps adding examples and related bits in hope of becoming more precise, but the exact opposite happens. Instead of helping the RB focus on salient points, the LB's repetitiveness and overinclusiveness turn the RB's interest (and ability to listen) off. However, if the LB allows his RB partner to interject, he will realize that either things are already perfectly clear or he will know exactly what needs to be clarified. An LB is not so much trying to dominate the other person as to control the mechanics of the communication process itself. LBs seem to be guided by the idea that "The more I talk, the more you have to listen to me. The more you have to listen to me, the better able you will be to grasp the soundness of my arguments or the necessity of following my wishes." They repeat themselves over and over in an effort to be precise and establish understanding.

Stress. We all become defensive when we are under pressure and feel "up against the wall." Times of stress are the least productive—because partners either become too emotional (RBs) or withdrawn (LBs)—but communication can't stop. This is the time to table problem-solving talks and shift into mutual support. Under stress, when the territory is painfully familiar because you've been talking in circles, it may be more effective to stop any discussion and take some action—even if it is to "agree to disagree."

Alcohol and drugs. Mind-altering substances are self-serving, contribute to aggression or withdrawal, and result in one or both partners' not being fully available for conversation. Some partners believe that alcohol actually helps the process along by eliminating fear of rejection, failure, and other inhibitions, but authentic communication between partners is not possible with these feelings being artificially eliminated. It can occur only when both are willing to talk in spite of their discomforts. Intimacy requires the courage to risk; true courage is eliminated when a person is under the influence.

Alcohol and drugs close off possibility, distort self-image and perceptions of others, increase objectification of people, make intimate contact difficult, and prevent attentive listening. The person who is high is overly focused on himself and has little or no interest in how his behavior is impacting on his partner and the quality of the relationship.

COMPETITION/POWER STRUGGLE. In relationships where discussions are always arguments, and one partner must win while the other loses, open and honest communication is not possible. Opposites must realize that it is possible for them *both* to be right while holding very different perspectives.

Inability to remain in the present. Relationships are fragile and require protection from certain harmful elements. One of these is the past. When two partners are in dialogue, it is important to stay current and to resist dragging in elements from a former life in order to make a point. The future is also a barrier when it comes in the form of threats. Lodged between what has already happened and may be deeply regretted and what is yet to happen and cannot be known, partners may find it challenging to stay in the present.

Not only is the past a problem, but jumping into the future is also. RBs must be careful to control their tendency to leap to conclusions and begin taking action before all the data are in. LBs must learn to anchor themselves in the intimacy of the discussion by maintaining eye contact with their RB partners. Without eye contact, the RB drifts off into unrelated thoughts because there is no connection.

PERSONALIZATION. Differences in love relationships are, for obvious reasons, more threatening than differences in other relationships. An RB (who is focused on connecting) often becomes anxious when her LB mate voices a conflicting position, especially a totally opposite view. An RB has difficulty separating "opinions" from the "person" and confuses rejection of her ideas with rejection of herself. Dissension is threatening because it requires, if only briefly, a separation. So invested is the RB in "merging" with her LB in order to understand, the discovery of his or her opposing view may be experienced as a betrayal.

RB: I think it's great that we both like camping. I can't get anybody else to go out into the desert with me.

LB: Most people don't want to leave their television sets. I like to camp, but I hate the desert. The high country is the place to go. There's nothing like being up in the mountains.

RB: But you've been talking about how we can go camping together. I pictured us near a favorite cave of mine.

LB: I haven't changed my mind about camping. I just don't want to camp in the desert.

RB: What else have I suggested that you hate? You don't really want to go camping with me at all, do you?

It is far better for the relationship if partners *expect* to disagree and not jump to conclusions about what that disagreement means. Opposing stands are no stranger to opposites, but they need not let that affect the quality of their communication. Many couples learn that there are certain topics about which the partners simply "agree to disagree" in order to maintain the relationship. This allows differences to exist without jeopardizing their bond. Each can remain true to his or her own personal beliefs and principles. Even though RBs often feel misunderstood, when in fact they are only being disagreed with, partners do not have to become of one mind in order to remain satisfied with each other and their relationship.

Blaming. Blaming is a terminal process that blocks further communication and prevents resolution of the problem. Either partner may hold the other responsible for some action or inaction, but that alone will not encourage forward progress.

NONVERBAL COMMUNICATION

According to Robert Bolton in his book *People Skills*, the degree of communication derived from words alone is only from 7 to 35 percent. Words are best for communicating facts, but body language, or nonverbal communication (NVC), telegraphs our feelings, the degree of intensity, and how well we are coping. Nonverbal communication consists of the placement of one's body in relationship to another person, facial expressions, gestures, and even the degree of eye contact. *When the content of the verbal and nonverbal aspects of a message are inconsistent, the nonverbal clue carries more weight, is more genuine, and has greater impact.* NVC serves a number of functions:

- It signals interpersonal attitudes. These include how much a person likes another, how he or she perceives his or her status in the relationship, and the degree of interest in the other.
- It reveals emotion behind our words; our face registers which feeling we are expressing; the rest of our body manifests the degree to which we are feeling it.
- It serves as elaboration and exaggeration when we need to emphasize verbal expression.
- It provides rituals for saying hello, good-bye, and congratulations.
- It acts as a substitute when words are inadequate.
- It makes it possible to insert emotion into the conversation without interrupting the flow of the speaker's words.
- It gives us a way of communicating what might be considered

rude if vocalized: yawning instead of saying, "You're boring me."

- It creates a "shorthand" when time does not allow a lengthy discussion.
- It provides impact, adding punch to our words.
- It allows communication at a distance, when hearing is impossible—or not desirable (as with the infamous "finger salute").

Because NVC is associated with feelings, LBs, who prefer not to have their feelings revealed, work overtime to control it. Camouflaging works to a degree but eventually undermines any relationship, because too much energy is spent in suppressing reactions and gestures that might provide "leakage" of emotions. This prevents an LB from being fully present, eliminates spontaneity, and diminishes intimacy.

After one lives with a person over the years, that person becomes more transparent. This, in addition to an increased sense of security, leads extremely guarded people eventually to shed their armor. Unfortunately their mates often abandon these relationships out of frustration before any metamorphosis occurs.

Nonverbal communication is not taught; we learn it by modeling ourselves on those who raised us. If a person was raised in a nonexpressive home—for instance, by two LBs—he or she got a "loud" message that there is something unsafe or undesirable in revealing oneself to others. When a child in this family does so, as is the nature of healthy children, he or she is reprimanded until the lesson is clear: Who you are is not acceptable and should be kept "under wraps." The child begins a process of stopping natural responses and thus short-circuiting energy that would, if left to free expression, result in a more spontaneous, expressive, and invigorated adult.

When a child is allowed to develop undisturbed, touch plays an important role in communication. Reaching out to others is a healthy response, which is stifled in families where more emphasis is placed on conforming to group expectations and adhering to rigid standards for what is proper than on self-expression. LBs frequently report histories of diminished expressiveness because of profound parental disapproval.

For other adult partners, a reluctance to touch others may be related to childhood abuse, which is a manifestation of what Martin Buber termed an I-It relationship. Adults who were treated as objects in their childhood have different relationships with touch from those who were not. Partners must always remain sensitive to the fact that although there are times when only touch can communicate effectively, "adult survivors" may not feel comfortable with it.

Even at times when words are not spoken, because of nonverbal communication, a message can still be sent. The next time you hear yourself saying, "My partner just won't communicate with me," ask yourself, "What does his silence (passivity, absence, avoidance) tell me?" The answer is there and may become painfully obvious, if you have the courage to explore it.

Herb Goldberg, in *The New Male,* tells us that couples can survive communications hazards if they develop "an acceptance of their inevitability and a commitment to working them through when they arise, rather than fleeing to a new utopia." He goes on to suggest that communication problems can be transcended "if the relationship is composed of partners who are committed to their own growth and are willing and able to experience the anxiety and assume the risks inherent in the process [pp. 137–38]."

The natural tendency is to identify the ways your partner fails to communicate. However, it is more effective to know which of *your own* behaviors create barriers and begin to work on changing them. These are the only ones in your control. An even greater challenge is to ask your partner to complete the checklist on "Talking" in the Exercises Section, which will give you feedback on what he or she considers your blocks to effective communication. Start working on the ones that *both* you and your partner agree on as being problematic.

It is not easy to change ways of relating after a lifetime of one preferred modality. But at least it is possible, whereas changing your partner's style is not. And the beauty of it is that if only one of you changes, the relationship will automatically change.

If you decide to change your habitual way of communicating in order to become more effective, there will be a series of stages you will go through. You will first identify what it is you want to alter and then adopt new skills to replace the old. Until your proficiency increases, you will feel awkward, then less self-conscious, and finally—with enough practice—your improved version will become second nature.

Even if you don't change your communication style, your relationship will change. It will get either weaker or stronger, but it is a living force and cannot remain the same.

5

THE GIFT

OF

LISTENING

Some things can be sensed
but not understood.

—*CHINESE PROVERB*

Whether negative or positive, it is not how a message is *intended* that determines its effect but rather how it is *received*. As Robert Bolton tells us in *People Skills,* the distinction between *hearing* and *listening* is important. Hearing refers to the physiological process of receiving auditory sensations. Listening is more complex and involves the interpretation and understanding of those signals. You can hear a person without ever listening to him or her. Whether or not we can actually listen—and be listened to—plays an important role in the quality of our lives: our satisfaction with friendships, the cohesiveness in our families, and our effectiveness at work.

However, there is far more to listening than just keeping quiet, although we all have been taught that this is the polite thing to do. Simply sitting in silence is not enough; this "passive" form of listening contributes to misunderstandings between partners. There is an art to listening, and there is a responsibility for the receiving partner to listen as actively as possible, just as there is a responsibility for the "sending" partner to be as clear as possible with the message he or she is sending.

Active listening is an attitude, demonstrating concern, respect, interest—and even love. It isn't easy for some partners, reports Dr. Carlfred Broderick in his book *Couples*. He tells us: "In that moment you lose your status as chief expert on what your spouse really thinks, wants and feels. Instead your spouse takes over as the final authority on his or her own feelings [p. 41]."

Active listening carries an element of personal risk because "in that moment" we are very close to seeing the situation the way our partner does, and it can be threatening to abandon our own position and adopt our partner's, even briefly. It is important to note that the more absolute or rigid our position is, the more likely it is based on fear or a threat to our personal integrity.

Listening undefensively to your partner means letting go of your investment in your own position long enough to be available to consider hers. Intimacy is dependent upon you and your partner's being able to do this. If you do all the talking, you can't do any of the learning, and intimacy is about learning.

Learning through skilled listening requires a great amount of energy because the tendency is to do what "comes naturally"; for many people this is to be either passively silent or aggressively competitive while someone else is talking. Skilled listening begins with creating a climate in which there is concern and respect for what the speaker has to say. This is done through two conscious, intentional acts: *attending* and *fostering*. These two skills are the first ones a psychotherapist learns. If you and your partner are able to develop them within your relationship, you will have 80 percent of what professional counseling provides without having to pay the fee!

Attending is achieved when the listener is willing to invest himself or herself as fully as possible in the moment, focusing attention on the speaker and clearing his or her mind of any preoccupations. Effective attending is powerful: It sends a message that the speaker is important, that what she or he has to say is of interest and concern to the listener, and it provides lubrication for a smoother flow of information.

Attending is achieved through the listener's nonverbal presence. Body language speaks louder than any of our words because it is unconscious and therefore unmonitored or uncensored. If I say, "I'm listening," but my nose is in a book or my attention is captured by the television, then I am really saying, "I can hear you, but you have my divided attention." (Therefore, I'm not listening.) There are times when this doesn't matter, when the need for a partner really to *listen* is not acute and just being heard will suffice. However, for those times when our partner wants our attention, we need to be fully available, not merely provide a "pseudo" attendance.

The most significant way we can demonstrate our interest is with eye contact, which increases arousal and expands intimacy, as reflected in the saying "The eyes are the windows to the soul." It is a way of saying, "I'm with you," while remaining silent, as is the use of touch. A hand resting on an arm or knee is another way of maintaining contact during silence.

In addition to attending, skilled listeners contribute to a climate of effective communication by fostering. Fostering occurs in two stages: prior to and during an actual discussion. Prior to coming together to talk, one partner may sense that the other is worried yet isn't talking about what might be bothering him. Extending an invitation to discuss it is the first step in fostering:

- Acknowledge that you have observed your partner and that he or she "looks worried."
- Extend an offer to listen: "I'm here if you want to talk about it."
- Maintain a connection (through either eye contact or touch) while you provide a silence during which your invitation can be considered.
- Respond to the first rejection with "I really do have the time" or "I would like to help."
- Respond to the second rejection with a respectful "If you change your mind, you know where to find me."

Partners who do not accept the second no and continue to pursue in order to make sure things get talked about eventually find themselves in the role of a "pursuer" chasing an "avoider." When this happens, the listening partner takes on too much responsibility, working overtime to keep a connection. The listening partner, at that point, is far more invested in creating a conversation than the partner who looked worried. It's safe to say: *When you want your partner to talk about something more than he or she wants to, it probably won't happen.* Or if it does happen, despite protest, your partner may feel pressured and resentful.

An invitation to share a concern is like a tap on the door: slightly intrusive but respectful of the boundary between you and the other person. When you ignore the first no and offer your support, it is an ever-so-light push on the door, appreciating that we all are ambivalent at times. If your partner rejects your suggestion a second time, don't put your foot in the door and insist, unless not talking is potentially dangerous to either one of you or the relationship itself.

Following are common barriers to effective listening. Again, remember that it is more productive to identify the ways that *you* contribute to your communication problems rather than search for those ways that reflect your partner. Remember, too, that these barriers are common to all couples, but the ones in boldface are often a source of conflict for opposites. (Checkoff lists are provided for you and a partner under "Listening" in the Exercises Section.)

BARRIERS TO LISTENING

- **Unsolicited advice**
- **Polarization**
- **Poorly timed logic**
- **Passive silence/playing it safe**
- **Rigidity**
- Blind spots
- Loss of attention
- Triggers
- Poor self-esteem
- Failure to clarify
- **Withholding/overwhelming feedback**
- **Lack of curiosity**

- **Degree of self-disclosure**
- Failure to allow silence
- **Failure to interrupt**
- **Preconceived notions**
- **Misdirected focus**
- **Internal distraction**
- Ill-timed reassurance
- Selective listening
- Criticizing and judging
- Name-calling and labeling
- Diagnosing
- Strategizing
- Deflecting

UNSOLICITED ADVICE. Of all the barriers to receiving messages, the most problematic one for opposites is the tendency for RBs to seek empathic responses, while LB partners offer advice. Feeling wounded, an RB fails to appreciate that the advice arises out of true concern for his or her welfare. An RB, although disappointed with an LB, needs to be more gracious about what *is* offered.

Empathy is both projective and receptive: It involves using one's own similar experiences as a template, as well as being open to whatever experience the other person is describing. Empathy is required for skilled listening because emotions can't be separated from facts without altering the partner's message. Contrary to what some partners may believe, emotion is not a sign that something is wrong; it is part of the message that is being communicated.

While the goal of empathic listening is to emphasize the feelings woven into the message, LBs prefer what might be termed deliberate listening. This is a process of sorting out the acceptable and unacceptable elements of the message. Statements are responded to in a dichotomous manner, the LB partner either advising or saying nothing. Neither one of these meets the need for the RB to be empathized with and contributes to chronic frustration with the LB partner and eventual dissatisfaction with the relationship itself.

LBs take pride in their ability to problem solve and describe this as one of their strengths in relationships. It is therefore difficult for them to understand why this service is not appreciated by their RB partners. Taking on the role of solving the partner's presenting problem may mean any of the following: giving advice, offering simple logic, preaching ("shoulds"), ordering, and even threatening. The last three are demoralizing and almost always result in conflict.

RB: I don't want to teach anymore. It isn't satisfying. I want to try another field, but I'm worried that I'm too old to start over. I don't even know what else I could do.

Nonempathic response
LB: I think you should stay where you are. This isn't any time to change jobs. (*Unsolicited advice/giving information.*)
Empathic response
LB: You sound like you don't enjoy your work anymore. I've felt that way. What has changed for you? (*Empathy/seeking information and showing interest/identifying with.*)

RB: I spend more time being a security guard than I do teaching. The kids don't really care about learning. It just seems like a waste of time.

Nonempathic response
LB: Some of those kids need a security guard. (*Logic/giving information.*)
Empathic response
LB: You're really disenchanted with the whole thing. When did you realize this? (*Empathy/seeking information.*)

RB: I've been thinking about leaving for at least a year. I'm flirting with the idea of real estate.

Nonempathic response
LB: Are you crazy! You don't have any idea what you're getting into. Talk to Dave. He'll tell you. (*Labeling, preaching, advising.*)
Empathic response
LB: I had no idea you'd been unhappy for so long. Why real estate? What interests you about that? (*Empathy/seeking information.*)

Many LBs do not appreciate that discussions need not be con-clusive; as natural solution seekers they feel like fish out of water if they are asked just to listen. LBs frequently have occupations that focus on problem solving, and therefore, they don't always recog-nize there are alternative ways to relate to someone troubled. They undervalue the benefits of simply serving as sounding boards and providing an opportunity for their partners to leave a conversation with greater insight and additional alternatives, but not necessarily a solution. Being result-oriented, an LB assumes this is the ultimate goal for an RB as well.

A guideline for opposites who wrestle with this problem of em-pathy versus advice is: *The person with the problem is the best person to solve that problem.* The partner with the concern has more of the data, is the one having to take the risks and suffer the conse-quences, and ultimately must implement whatever solution is cho-sen. When the LB rushes in to offer advice and provide guidance, this diminishes the RB's confidence and creates a dependency on the LB. When the LB continues to be the source of advice, and rarely the recipient, a particular dynamic evolves: a hierarchy that prevents a relationship of equality and thereby eliminates the possi-bility of intimacy.

Even though an LB may consider advice the most helpful gift when his mate is distressed, advice giving is often a basic insult to the RB's intelligence. The unstated message from the LB is: "The solution is immediately apparent to me. Why hasn't it occurred to you?" There is an implication that the person does not have the ca-pacity to think of solutions. It also demonstrates a lack of confi-dence in the partner's ability to cope effectively with the situation in her own way. The advising LB, below, does not appreciate the big picture and is overly focused on one piece of a much larger puzzle.

RB: I'm very upset. I finally got up the nerve to write to my sister and tell her what she did that made me so mad and why I did not go there for Thanksgiving. It was really hard just to come out and say it. I sent the letter over a week ago, and I haven't heard from her yet. It had a check in it, too. I owed her some money.

LB: You'd better call the post office right away and trace it. Call your sister to see if she got it. You can stop payment on the check, if she didn't.

(NOTE: All of these ideas have occurred to the RB 99 percent of the time.)

If the LB couldn't resist focusing on the facts, then he or she could have asked, "What have you done about that?" or "Is there anything I can do to help?" This is, however, not a substitute for empathy and is best received if delivered *after* a response such as "That was a real risky thing to tell her. No wonder you're upset."

POLARIZATION. When a mate *does* seek a solution, problems remain unsolvable as long as the partners remain stuck in one hemisphere or the other. Problem solving is a creative process that actually requires both. The first stage occurs in the left brain, where the actual problem is formulated. In the second stage the problem or concern may be "set aside" in the unconscious, imaginative, "incubating" right brain, while the person goes about his day, focusing attention elsewhere. At some point a solution will surface, unexpectedly in the form of an "aha!" If the problem remains in the logical left brain, where it is overly analyzed and put to every test, creativity will be suppressed. This is true for problems between lovers as well.

The goal is to encourage whole brain thinking, using both hemispheres, to arrive at a solution. Western culture perpetuates the illusion of a split world: right/wrong, good/evil. We have been conditioned to perceive our environment in a dualistic, polarized either/or way. It is only through appreciation of Eastern thought that we gain another possibility: both/and. That perception is not a matter of elimination but rather one of inclusion.

POORLY TIMED LOGIC. Logic serves a very important function in discussions between partners, but there are times when it is not only inappropriate but damaging because it contributes to a sense of alienation when a partner is seeking connection through empathy. Logic is not helpful, for instance, when a partner is under stress unless the stress is directly related to an unsolved problem. An LB, in her effort to sort things out, separates the partner from the problem and, in doing so, narrows her lens. This leaves the RB feeling like a nonperson—and worse, a nonperson alone with his or her unacknowledged feelings.

RB: I'm late because some kid backed his truck into me as I was leaving the office. I wanted to have time to go home and change, but I couldn't and get here before dinner. So, sorry I'm late . . . and overdressed for a barbecue. I feel really stupid in these clothes. Everyone is going to think I—

LB: Did you get his license number? *(Completely ignoring the fact that this person is upset and embarrassed.)* You should call your insurance company right now.

The primary purpose of actively listening is to facilitate the process of sorting out thoughts, feelings, and ideas. The listener makes that possible not by jumping in and offering solutions but by attending, fostering, and providing feedback. Those who prefer to avoid their own feelings and the feelings of others tend to offer up logic at the worst moments. Logic focuses on the facts of a situation, but when a person is emotionally troubled, feelings are the issue. When logic is attempted, and an emotional involvement is avoided, distance is created at a time when the upset partner needs closeness.

A common misconception between opposites is the idea that only logical LBs utilize reasoning in their thinking and decision-making process. A more accurate observation is that LBs use deductive reasoning and RBs prefer inductive. LBs break information down into smaller units to comprehend it and are more comfortable with "absolute," while RBs build from specific to general and are more comfortable with "probable."

PASSIVE SILENCE/PLAYING IT SAFE. Because of their preference for offering advice, LB partners are at a loss when asked to cease the search for solutions and simply to listen. When instruction and guidance are not an option, LBs fall into silence, which RBs interpret as lack of interest. The LB's fear of saying the wrong thing leads him or her into silence, but silence can easily lapse into uninvolvement, indifference, and apathy. Soon the listening partner is not even participating in the process.

A technique known as bridging prevents this from happening. Bridging is accomplished by the utterance of phrases that in essence promote progress, ease the flow, and demonstrate connection at the same time. Your invitation to talk begins the fostering process, but it is maintained through bridging. Common bridging terms are: "uh-huh," "um-hmm," "yes," "right," "go on," "then?," "tell me more," and "really?" The beauty of bridging phrases is that they offer the listening partner a mechanism with which to encourage his partner to continue without his having to construct a lengthy response or even agree with what is being said. By periodically uttering one of these, the listening partner is saying, "I am following you. You have my full attention. Your words are being received."

Although it is frustrating for the RB who is speaking, it is easy to understand why an LB partner might choose to remain silent. If he or she attempts to add to the speaker's comments or augment understanding, the LB might say something inaccurate. If the LB is not willing to risk that and does not know about bridging, no response at all is obviously the safest choice from his or her point of view. As an alternative, LBs can learn the art and science of mirroring. This is a technique that satisfies one's need to *do something* while at the same time avoids advising.

To mirror one's partner, it is important that the listening spouse be able to infer the speaker's feelings. This may seem risky at first because it appears to be in the arena of "intuition," which is not natural territory for an LB. Actually it is the exact opposite; it is coming to a conclusion based on evidence. The challenge is to recognize and accept the data, which are "soft."

Information regarding the internal state of the speaker is available in two forms: observing the speaker's body language and the *listener's* own internal state. When a partner is talking and at the same time slumped over, looking at the floor, the listening partner can recall what was going on in his life when he has found himself in a similar position. Does he associate such posture with dejection or joy, with helplessness or celebration?

Additional clues are acquired by the listener's turning inward and asking, "What would I be feeling if what my partner is describing had happened to me? Have I had a similar event in my life? Anything close to it? What was my response?" Of course, there is no guarantee that the response is identical, but it is a beginning.

LBs tend to wait until they are absolutely sure before taking action, but it is best not to try to play it so safe, because intimacy is impossible without risk. If an LB is unable to identify any similar situation and can't detect any clues in the RB partner's body language to guide him, then the most compassionate (and honest) thing to do, in order to demonstrate attending, is to say, "I can't imagine how that must have felt." By mirroring what we have heard our partner say, we are demonstrating that the words are being taken seriously and that an attempt is being made to look through his or her lens. Mirroring is a difficult and learned process; it requires skill and, when applied, gets dramatic results. Nothing feels quite as good as being truly understood.

RIGIDITY. LBs tend to be more structured in their thinking because of their preference for that which is certain. Therefore they may have greater difficulty compromising, because this requires them to violate certain self-imposed rules. Such a violation registers at one level as "very wrong." When an LB is asked to consider an RB's position which is not framed in terms of absolute truth, the LB, in accepting it, may feel he or she is abandoning a deeply held principle. LBs can avoid this discomfort by appreciating that they need only be open to *considering* a mate's differing perspective, but that does not have to mean agreement with it.

In conversations between opposites the LB emphasizes the facts. Facts are important, but there is always a relationship between any event and the person experiencing it: the person's reaction to the event. These are feelings—feelings about facts—and should be considered as data, even though they may be regarded as soft. Too often LB partners dismiss this, believing that only hard (measurable) data are legitimate, and since the RB, or connected knower, relies heavily on experience—and feelings about that experience—when the LB makes decisions, this rejection of experiential data translates into: The data are nonexistent, the position is unsupported, and the partner's concern is not to be taken seriously.

RBs lean the other way and ignore hard facts, preferring to study the person rather than the situation. An RB can become overly emotional at a time when it is important to focus on the message, not the messenger. Just as the LB has difficulty accepting data that are not measurable or provable, so the RB does not give weight to data that have not been derived from someone's experience. This, too, is a rigid posture.

Within opposite couples, the debate between hard and soft data is a familiar ritual; the process of determining what counts is no small task. Physicist Timothy Ferris contributes to our discussion by noting:

> To the naive realist, every view that does not fit the official model is dismissed as imaginary . . . to set one's self up as the sole judge of what is actual, is to taste the delights of godlike power. . . . Once the realist settles on a single representation of reality, the gate slams shut behind him, and he is doomed to live thereafter in the university to which he has pledged allegiance.
>
> We may feel more comfortable with our own frame of reference than with that of others, assume it to be more valid, but the frames are there nonetheless. There's no escaping them.
>
> . . . various minds take varying views of reality—in terms, say, of spatial relationships versus language, or of sentimental versus rational education—I can no more legitimately impose a single model on myself than I can expect to impose it on others [pp. 6–7).

Paul Watzlawick echoes this thought in his book *How Real Is Real?*: "Our everyday, traditional ideas of reality are delusions, which we spend substantial parts of our daily lives shoring up, even at the considerable risk of trying to force facts to fit our definition of reality instead of vice versa. And the most dangerous delusion of all is that there is only one reality [p. 1]." Opposites know all too well the number of hours spent in trying to understand each other's world, but it can't be done as long as partners continue to view it through the same old lenses—their own perspectives.

Blind spots. We all have blind spots, which play a large role in our failure to communicate effectively with our mates. A blind spot exists when a person is unable to see or acknowledge something in himself that is obvious to others. This is one of the benefits of an authentic and safe relationship: the opportunity to be guided gently into awareness by a trusted companion.

There is an art to the science of confrontation. When your partner has shared something with you, and it seems to you that a blind spot is possibly operating, it is a sensitive moment. You can use the opportunity to reflect back to your mate an inconsistency that is preventing you from fully understanding her. It is important to appreciate that blind spots are a form of self-defense. The human mind filters out anything that is ego-threatening (i.e., unpleasant, painful, potentially shaming, etc.). We may fear rejection and erect a wall, which prevents us from communicating effectively and, worse, makes us seem insensitive, when in fact, it is our *hypersensitivity* that creates the barrier.

We all need to protect ourselves, but some methods, like blind spots, work against us. It is important to learn how to protect oneself adequately while remaining as undefensive as possible.

Common discrepancies are between what your mate is saying and what he or she is actually doing, or between the contents of two conflicting messages. Examples of gentle confrontations are:

You say you want to quit your job, but at least three times this week you've come home and said how satisfying it was to be part of that team. You seem to have mixed feelings. *(Conflicting thoughts.)*

You say you don't really mind if I go to the dance without you, but it looks like you're about to cry. I think we need to talk some more about this. *(Conflict between words and body language.)*

You say you want to spend more time together as a couple, but you continue to use all the time on weekends to work on your hobby. I'm confused. You're saying one thing but doing another. I'd like to understand this, but you're communicating two different things to me. *(Conflict between words and action.)*

You say you don't care, but you've been talking about this for an hour. It seems you care very much. Would you rather talk some more or go on to the movie? *(Conflict between behavior and expressed feeling.)*

You say you don't have a problem with drinking, but you can't make it through a day without a shot. We need to talk. *(Conflict between words and reality.)*

Remember we *all* have blind spots. So the first step is to ask yourself, "How would I like someone to bring this to *my* attention, realizing I'd rather not know?"

Loss of attention. Even if the words and actions and body language all match, and there is nothing to confront, the listener still has an obligation to attend. We speak at a rate of between 125 and 175 words per minute, but our ability to listen is three or four times faster; therefore, sometimes we find ourselves, while listening, with empty "air" time. When an LB is speaking slowly and in a monotone, there is an almost hypnotic quality to the communication, which makes it even more of a challenge for an RB to stay fully in tune. When an RB listener becomes preoccupied or "checks out," important information can be missed, creating later misunderstanding.

An LB loses attention when an RB floods the conversation with highly charged feelings. This makes it difficult for the LB to track. Remember, an LB is looking for the main point of the discussion, something to hang on to if things get bumpy. When the focus of the discussion is lost, so is his or her attention.

Effective listening is hard work and more demanding than talking. It is an active process which requires all your attention. This means you must be able to ignore, or at least to resist, both external and internal distractions which prevent concentration.

Pretending to listen, in order to be polite, will do no good. Comprehension is impossible if your energy is going into "looking" as if you are listening instead of actually attending. Eventually you will find yourself in the uncomfortable position of trying to discuss something you have not fully understood.

If you find your mind wandering, you are beginning to leave the here and now. Bring yourself back by tuning in to your senses.

Do whatever you have to do to keep yourself attending in the moment and not allow yourself to be seduced by competing, internal thoughts, which might take you forward or backward in time and leave your partner abandoned.

Take responsibility for your own inability to listen any longer rather than place it on your partner for not keeping you alert. All you need to do is admit that you are no longer an effective listener, emphasize your interest, and request that the conversation be continued later. To demonstrate your interest, take the initiative, and seek out your partner when the opportunity to continue comes around. Better yet, create the opportunity.

Triggers. We all have emotional filters which distort communication, but each of us has our own version. One particular word or phrase may trigger in me immediate strong feelings, while you may remain neutral about it. Words are in themselves only symbols, but we assign meaning to them based not only on what we've been taught by others but on our own experiences, our own history.

When certain words are used during a talk with your partner, you may unexpectedly react, and your partner may be surprised, not knowing what happened. You, too, may be shocked by the strength of your response.

Poor self-esteem. In addition to emotional connotations, we can distort what we hear through the lens of self-image or self-esteem. Our attitude toward the person speaking significantly affects how we feel about what he or she is saying, his or her credibility and authority. How we feel about ourselves has equal impact on how well we receive messages. A secure person will hear and interpret a communication differently from an insecure one. A partner riddled with self-doubt and lacking self-trust, and trust in his or her mate, will distort communication by personalizing it, often creating a relationship between the words and himself when none exists.

PARTNER 1: I think I'll go into the study and read for an hour or two. I feel like being alone.
PARTNER 2: You might as well go ahead and say it.
PARTNER 1: What?
PARTNER 2: You don't like spending time with me.

Failure to clarify. It is important to seek clarification any time you find that you simply do not understand what your partner is trying to tell you. If you fake understanding, you will discover that much of your energy is being sapped and you are unable to attend. Problems can be avoided if couples take more time to clarify what has been said and heard, even if they *think* they've understood. Failure to do so results in a pseudo understanding.

This is most problematic when a decision has been made and each partner begins operating with a different conclusion, assuming they agree when, in fact, they do not.

Despite the childhood prohibition about interrupting, a very good time to interrupt is when you first realize you have not understood what your mate is trying to convey. You are actually facilitating communication when you do this. A simple phrase can do it: "Excuse me, but I'm not sure what you mean by . . ." This is an information-seeking technique that fosters the discussion. This type of interruption should not be confused with the tendency to interrupt out of disagreement or defensiveness. Often this is done under the guise of misunderstanding: "Excuse me, but I don't understand how you can say . . ." (This is not an attempt to facilitate; it is an invitation to debate.)

You may need to seek clarification because the speaker was ambiguous, or you may seek it because you found your attention wandering. If the latter is true, it is important to address that, as your partner probably suspects it anyway. You can do this with a "Wait, I missed that last sentence. I'm sorry, but I lost my concentration for a moment. Would you please repeat it? I'm truly interested." If you have a mature and gracious partner, you will get another chance, and you will probably be closer because of it.

It is a risk to let a speaker know you have lost track; it takes no courage to pretend you are still attending until you catch up. Emotional risks build intimacy. By admitting your lack of attention and asking for clarification and declaring your interest, you have built a bridge in a moment of potential alienation.

WITHHOLDING/OVERWHELMING FEEDBACK. By definition a conversation is an exchange of information. If the speaking partner does not get feedback from her mate, she will wonder if he or she is really listening, is uninterested or preoccupied. This can lead to misunderstanding and even hurt feelings when, in fact, the partner *was* listening. A speaker without feedback feels out on a limb, not knowing what, if any, impact her words are having. Feedback encourages the speaker to continue, except in the case of RBs, who can easily overwhelm an LB with too much to consider at once. Withholding feedback confuses the speaker, especially an RB who uses feedback to feel connected to the speaker and through that connection remains interested in what he or she has to say.

It is helpful if the listener offering feedback can also reflect the speaker's tone. If your partner is telling you something disgusting, respond with similar disgust. If he is enthusiastic, respond excitedly. A listener who responds in a dull monotone may be accurate regarding the content but will not be perceived as fully understanding the speaker. Reflective expressiveness is a powerful way of saying, "I know exactly what you mean."

Many LBs lack "rhythm" when they speak, making it difficult to mirror any particular tone. They have a habit of speaking in a guarded fashion, eliminating spontaneity. LBs, who painfully consider the validity of each statement before offering it and who may spend hours at work immersed in the logic of bureaucratic jargon, develop a monotone which erases any trace of their uniqueness. Consequently, their conversation is not as lively as it could be, and this makes it difficult to hold an RB's attention.

LACK OF CURIOSITY. Sometimes feedback is in the form of questioning. One of the ways I can let you know that I have been listening is to ask a related question. This also tells you that I am interested enough to want to know more. The way a question is asked and the timing of a question both contribute to either facilitating discussion or shutting down the process.

Desiring a connected knowing, RBs ask questions as a way of maintaining their investment in relationships. To them curiosity creates a feeling of "between" because it facilitates the flow of information about the person, and that increases the degree of intimacy. This is reflected in the focus of the questions that RBs ask: The emphasis is not on the facts as much as on how the facts impact on the person, the person's relationship to the event, and his or her expectations and disappointments. RBs regard asking questions as a sign of interest, a way of understanding what makes the other person tick.

SPEAKER: I'm going to go to Europe alone for two weeks. I've finally decided if I don't go now, I never will, even though Ellen might change her mind someday.

RB'S QUESTION: Are you afraid to travel alone?

RB'S QUESTION: What will it be like without Ellen?

LB'S QUESTION: What countries are you seeing?

LB'S QUESTION: What airline are you flying?

If an LB seems out of contact with her feelings, the RB may respond by trying to probe. This is often perceived by the LB as an invasion and is usually defended against.

RB: Are you worried about the party? Would you rather I not invite so many people?

LB: I don't know. I haven't given it that much thought. I don't have time to think about it now.

RB: But every time I mention it, instead of getting excited, you seem to look irritated. Are you angry with me for giving you the party? I know how you hate them.

LB: No. I don't think so. I really haven't thought about it.

RB: Well, could you think about it now? How do you feel about my giving you a party and inviting fifty people?

LB *(angry):* I said I don't know. Why do you keep asking me? Just give the damn party!

LBs often regard inquiry as meddling or intrusive rather than as an expression of caring. An LB tends to think, "If my partner wants to tell me something, he'll do it. I don't have to ask." Because of this, LBs don't ask many questions of their RB partners, and this can leave the RB feeling unimportant, uninteresting, and uncared about.

RB: I got another offer today. Now I have three. I'm not sure which one to take.

LB: Umm. Sounds like you've been busy. *(Does not expand the dis-*

cussion by seeking more information and showing an interest in knowing more.)

When an LB asks a question, it is likely to be "why?" because of his need to make sense out of what his partner is saying. Questioning is an attempt to pin his partner down when he can't figure out the rationale for the partner's behavior. It is also a way to sneak in unsolicited advice:

LB: Why are you taking more art classes when you know there aren't any jobs out there for set designers?
RB: I just like them. I get a lot of pleasure doing the sketches and presenting ideas.
LB: Why don't you learn about computer graphics? That way you could train for a *real* job.

However, "why" questions do not facilitate intimacy as much as they trigger defensive reactions. Although couched in an attempt to "understand," this type of question is often a challenge and the beginning of a debate. This happens when the LB is more invested in *his* need than in his partner's; he is more interested in pointing out the flaw in his partner's logic than in "joining" his partner through empathy. The "illogical" RB ends up feeling not only misunderstood but "trapped."

Not asking questions can lead to problems as well because too little information is exchanged. RBs ask questions to clarify the degree of relatedness between the partners; LBs ask questions to remove ambiguity. The RB is constructing a bigger picture, a theme; the LB is breaking information down into smaller bits. *Both* are attempting to understand.

Marital therapist Richard Stuart suggests that one way of demonstrating genuine interest in what your mate is saying is to ask *two* questions:

(old, one-question approach)
RUTH: "How did the job interview go?"
SUSAN: "Well, I think I did O.K."
RUTH: "It's hard to tell sometimes."

(two-question approach)

RUTH: "How did the job interview go?"

SUSAN: "Well, I think I did O.K."

RUTH: "It's hard to tell sometimes. What do they have to offer that appeals to you?"

DEGREE OF SELF-DISCLOSURE. Directly asking each other is one way to learn, but self-disclosed information is another. It is only through reciprocal self-disclosure that intimacy can be achieved. The effective listener will occasionally share related material about herself not as a shift in focus but as a way of demonstrating connection with the speaker's concerns. Revealing this kind of information expands the authenticity of the relationship. An LB often fails to volunteer intimate information, believing that if the partner wants to know, he or she will ask. An RB often discloses too much too soon, overloading the LB's system, which processes data one piece at a time.

During courtship there is a high level of curiosity, mutual questioning, and revealing. Later, unless partners keep the curiosity alive, indifference settles in and questioning is relegated to heated moments of adversarial discussion.

Failure to allow silence. "Attentive" silence occurs when the listening partner allows the speaker time to go deeper into himself and to pace his remarks at a comfortable rate. This is difficult for partners who are uneasy with silence because they are then forced to focus on their own inner states. This happens when the speaker is experiencing a feeling that is difficult for the listening partner to keep separate from herself. Because RBs tend to be more sensitive to what others are feeling, they often find it very difficult to tolerate silence at a time when strong emotion is present.

For a partner who finds silence difficult, it helps to refocus his or her attention during that period away from himself or herself and on to the speaker. This is time to ponder what has been said so far: What has this all meant to the speaker? What might it be like for him to be talking about it now? The speaking partner is the one with the concern, so if he or she needs to be silent, silence is how the listening partner can be supportive.

Total silence, as noted earlier, is not part of skilled listening because feedback is vital to a speaker. However, silence does have a function. It allows the speaker to reformulate her thoughts, to think about exactly what she wants to communicate. Silence is a demonstration of respect for that process.

One of the difficulties partners experience around silence is that each has his or her own history with silence and brings those memories along. Some adults as children were punished with silence, their parents refusing to speak until certain conditions were met. This is similar to the act of shunning in certain groups. Others in childhood were ignored or told not to speak unless spoken to. The symbolic meaning of silence probably means something different for your partner from what it means for you. Discuss it before it becomes an issue.

FAILURE TO INTERRUPT. A listener should not hesitate to interrupt because listening is about getting information. If the speaker no longer makes sense and the listener says nothing, soon the listener will drift off, triggering a major conflict by conversation's end, when the speaking partner realizes that nothing was absorbed. Timely interruptions demonstrate active listening and engagement and facilitate the flow of information.

The listening partner, while attending to the mate as he or she is speaking, may notice that the speaker is talking in circles or meandering all over the place, making it difficult to follow what is being said. If the partner stops listening and jumps in and says, "Get to the point!" that is sure to end any discussion. The listening partner, however, *can* facilitate the process by helping the speaker become more concrete. This is done by asking a simple question like "Can you give me an example of what you mean?" or "Exactly what did he say to you?"

Some speakers lose their trains of thought and need assistance in getting back on track. This can be gently noted to the speaker: "I'm sorry to interrupt, but you were talking about Tom, and now you're talking about your vegetable garden, and I've totally missed the connection." (Notice the listener takes responsibility for "missing" the connection, rather than accuse the speaker of not making any sense. This is part of compassionate partnering.)

Sometimes a listener will struggle to make sense out of seemingly unrelated events. This is especially true for LBs, who present information in a more logical, sequential fashion than RBs. If the LB is patient, he or she may eventually appreciate the "theme" the RB is presenting, but often the connections are less than obvious, and the LB has to seek clarification.

RB: I really needed you yesterday, when I was working on the taxes and you were playing tennis.

LB: I'm sorry. You know I had that planned a month ago. I put it on the calendar.

RB: The dog still needs to go to the vet.

LB *(Thinking: "Where did that come from?")*: I know.

RB: If you don't want to plan the trip with me, just say so.

LB *(totally confused)*: What? I was still thinking about the dog.

RB: You don't ever listen to me. I don't think you really care. Just look at you . . . the taxes, the dog, the trip.

LB: Wait a minute. I'm confused. What are we talking about here?

RB: I can't count on you. You always say you'll help, but then you're off and doing other things. *(Theme)*

PRECONCEIVED NOTIONS. Any communication, intimate or not, is less effective when it is burdened with prejudice; when the listener has formed a mind-set. Listeners erect barriers when they are unable to set aside their feelings about the speakers' words and reject the words because they are uninteresting, too simple, too complicated, or already known. Authentic discussions between partners require the shedding of preconceived notions in order to be fully present.

LB: I want to talk about last night.

RB: I already know what you're going to say.

LB: I don't think you understood what I was trying to say.

RB: You don't have to say anything. I know how you feel about my brother visiting.

LB: Well, I don't think I made myself clear because we ended up in a fight, and that was not my intention.

RB: What good is it going to do for you to repeat yourself? I knew how you were going to react before I ever opened my mouth. I knew exactly what you would say.

This RB is unable (unwilling) to set aside any thoughts of "knowing" what the LB partner is going to say and just let it flow. This partner is too invested in having his or her intuition confirmed. Is it so important to be right? What do you think your relationship needs more: one more "right" person in it or the opportunity for each partner to be fully heard? This means one has to let go of rigid, long-held thoughts and try to approach each discussion as "new."

MISDIRECTED FOCUS. LBs make poor listeners when they become overly focused on rules. In doing so, they completely devalue the messenger as well as the message. Instead of attending to what a partner has to say, the LB is targeting poor grammar, logic, syntax, or an underdeveloped vocabulary.

RB: I am completely snowed under at work. If they don't hire some support staff soon, there's going to be a total meltdown, and we'll all be up the creek without a paddle. *(Loaded with images, this partner's message is one of urgency and panic.)*

LB: Don't mix your metaphors. *(This pedantic approach completely misses the purpose of the communication, the RB's cry of distress.)*

The speaker is the one trying to communicate, the one on whom attention should be focused. At times the listening partner may redirect the focus to his own concerns, never returning to the speaker's original concern. Redirecting the focus can also happen when the listener is very uncomfortable with the topic and cannot tolerate a discussion. For instance, an LB may engage an RB in hope of exploring alternative solutions to a problem the RB has been complaining about:

LB: I've been thinking about where you could invest your money. Here are some brochures I picked up at a seminar I attended last week.

RB: No way. I'm not going to read these. I don't even want to think about numbers. The very thought of having to make decisions about money overwhelms me. Get those out of here! Let's talk about what movie we want to see tonight.

Redirecting the attention and redirecting the topic are barriers to effective listening because both sabotage the speaker's original intent.

INTERNAL DISTRACTION. LBs, because of their discomfort with spontaneity and the risk of saying something idiotic, frequently spend energy preparing their next comments, while at the same time attempting to stay tuned in to their partners.

RB: What did you think of the movie? Didn't you love the part where he jumps into her arms? It reminded me . . .

LB *(thinking): "What am I supposed to say?* Was *it a good movie? What if I say I liked it and she hated it? What part about the jumping? I don't remember any jumping business. I seem to have missed the most significant scene.*

RB: . . . of when I tried to do that and we both fell off the dock. I'll never forget that. Remember?

LB: It was OK. *(At this point there are too many questions to construct answers—and each one requires thought—and now she is asking another one.)*

RB: *What* was OK? Falling off the dock?

LB: *What* dock? I thought you asked me about the movie? I thought the movie was OK.

RB: Are you still thinking about *that?* I'm not even talking about that anymore.

Equally disconcerting is the listener who, rather than remain fully engaged in what the speaker is saying, begins creating responses, rebuttals, and countermessages. This takes energy and makes attending impossible. Although most people who do this claim they are actually listening, they are usually only *hearing,* for their attention is far too divided to be truly present.

This is selective listening, which focuses only on the factual content, because it takes extra energy to listen beyond the words to the feelings about the words, and the LB is using that extra energy to construct. This eventually diminishes the quality of the contact between the opposite partners, and the RB senses the loss.

RB: I'm concerned that we are drifting apart. I'm not feeling as connected to you. On Wednesday, you totally ignored me.

LB *(feeling defensive/constructing countermessage):* *"What's wrong now? What does he mean about Wednesday? Doesn't he know I've been swamped with this project?"* Yeah. Well, I've been swamped in case you didn't notice. *(Ignore the "big picture" of alienation and focus instead on the specific of Wednesday.)*

RB: It seems like we never talk anymore, and when we do talk, your mind is elsewhere. Isn't our relationship important to you anymore?

LB *(constructing a response):* *"Talk? What does he want to talk about? Why doesn't he just tell me if there's something he wants to talk about?"* Well, you're not talking either. *(Misses the concern and fear in the RB's message.)*

Ill-timed reassurance. This barrier to listening may not even seem like a barrier at first. It is the listening partner's tendency to reassure. Now, most of you will consider reassurance a sign of support, and that is true, but used at certain times, it prevents effective communication from occurring. Reassuring statements often leave a person feeling isolated in his or her position and not fully understood:

DAVID: I'm going to fail that test tomorrow. I just know it.

ELLEN: No, you're not. You will be one of the top scores.

Essentially Ellen, although trying to be comforting, is saying, "Your perception of yourself is wrong. You don't know what you're talking about." This adds to David's sense of inadequacy. This type of reassurance does not allow him to feel comforted because he is being *corrected.* Reassuring remarks are ill timed when used by partners who don't want to experience the emotions behind their partners' messages.

Human beings, once they get an image of themselves, are very resistant to altering that image. Partners who find themselves in the position of feeling the need to reassure can do so while at the same time honoring the perspectives their partners hold. This could be done by Ellen's simply saying, "I know you feel that way, although I see you very differently. Would you like to talk about it?" This eliminates a contest between the two opposing perspectives and opens the door to communication.

Several barriers come under the term "defensive listening." These include selective listening, criticizing and judging, name-calling and labeling, diagnosing, strategizing, and deflecting.

Selective listening. The listening partner doesn't want to hear what is being said when the message is too shaming, too painful, or too overwhelming or simply does not fit the listening partner's self-image.

Listening selectively means that the partner is choosing what he or she wants to hear, agrees with, or is able to take in.

Criticizing and judging. Criticism, in general, is not negative; much can be gained from listening to someone who knows you very well. Criticism serves a healthy purpose when it is done in a caring and respectful manner. The danger comes when one or both partners are constantly on a fault-finding mission.

Name-calling and labeling. A label is a stereotype and nothing more: "You're a jerk." It is fired out of hurt, anger, or frustration, and little thought is given to the whole person. The partner doing it, rather than be authentic and identify what he or she is feeling at the time, takes a shortcut and targets the other person. Apologies may follow, but the sting lasts much longer.

Diagnosing. Another example of defensive listening is diagnosing. Just as the criticizer is on a fault-finding mission, so the partner who diagnoses is on a hidden-motive safari. Never taking what is said at face value, this partner believes that there is something behind, under, and masking over everything her mate is communicating.

The problem is that a diagnosing partner is not listening. Time and energy are being spent digging, rather than in being in the here and now. When a partner begins the hunt for a motive, she is either in the past, trying to piece together a theme which will then support a hypothesis, or in the future, predicting what will happen on the basis of her "knowing" her mate.

Both labeling and diagnosing are insulting, and both use terminal language, which creates a no-win situation and constructs a hierarchy, eliminating the opportunity for understanding through equality. This can be demonstrated using Freud's diagnostic labels and an everyday situation:

- If you come to a party late, you are *hostile.*
- If you come to a party early, you are *anxious.*
- If you come to a party on time, you are *compulsive.*

Strategizing. A person cannot listen and strategize at the same time. When a partner begins to build a response, create a clever comeback or plot a defense, he or she has stopped listening. That person has left the moment and is projecting into the future. When this happens, the speaker will often notice and ask, "Are you listening to me?"

Deflecting. The last example of defensive listening, deflecting, occurs when one partner compliments the other, and as a result, the other feels embarrassed or self-conscious and responds by rejecting the praise.

Partners with low self-esteem, or partners who in childhood were not permitted self-celebration, experience emotional discomfort in moments of praise and, in an attempt to rid themselves of that discomfort, will fail to embrace the compliment. If you recognize yourself as such a partner, you can increase the quality of the communication in your relationship by learning to reply with a simple "thank you." A compliment is a gift; it is an insult to return it unopened.

You love each other, but you are only human. No partners can always be there fully for each other. Accurate listening takes a great deal of energy and involves a commitment to the moment, rejecting all distractions. To be able to be there for your partner, you must be mature, open, and able to see past your own current needs. When this happens, and your partner *knows* you have given him or her this gift, it can be an extremely satisfying moment for both of you.

*   *   *

Learning to communicate well is not all that complex; it is *unlearning* poor methods and old habits that presents a challenge. These habits are related to problems with both "sending" and "receiving" messages. This unlearning, coupled with a greater understanding of what makes your RB or LB tick, will serve to create a more loving environment as well as more successful problem solving.

6

CONFLICT: YOU'RE BOTH RIGHT!

We have met the enemy,
and they is us.

—POGO

As an RB I like to express myself freely and spontaneously when the urge strikes me. As an LB my husband, Rick, likes to express himself as well, but he prefers to do so when he is clear about what is expected of him, knows what the "rules" are, and has some reassurance that he won't make a mistake. Consequently, we often find ourselves in conflict in the most unlikely places.

Take the dance floor, for instance. One minute we are gliding around, and the next minute we are standing still.

RICK: What was *that?*
ME: What was *what?*
RICK: That little bump you just did with your hips.
ME: I don't know. I got caught up in the music, and it just happened. I didn't really plan it.

RICK: This is a rhumba. You aren't supposed to bump so much. You
    got me off count.

ME: I think it's dumb to be counting so much. I just like to move.

RICK: It doesn't work that way. You have to do certain things on cer-
    tain beats. This is ballroom dancing. You can't just move when
    you want to. I wish you'd understand this.

ME: I think that takes all the romance out. And by the way, why do
    you keep pushing me, insisting we go this way or that? I feel
    like a shopping cart.

RICK: It's called leading. It's what the man's supposed to do. What
    does that have to do with keeping count?

ME: It feels like pushing to me. No self-respecting feminist should al-
    low it. What if *I* want to go someplace else? Why do they call us
    partners if the power isn't evenly distributed?

RICK: I don't know. I didn't make the rules about keeping count or
    about leading. Do you want to dance, or what?

At this point I don't want to dance anymore; the fun's gone out
of it for me. I no longer have images of Fred and Ginger in my
head. Rick's no longer enjoying the evening either. He's become derailed by my impulsiveness, is very frustrated, and now needs to
collect himself.

He is *right* about the need to keep count, especially for begin-
ners like us. I am *right* about sacrificing the romance. We are each
having our own personal difficulty with this moment. There is no
need to debate or argue until one of us wins. Even though we are
experiencing very different feelings about different aspects of this
encounter, we are, in fact, *both* right. We must appreciate this in order to prevent escalation in the moment and to ensure a mutually
rewarding relationship through the years.

To prevent this scene from repeating itself over and over again,
I, as an RB, will need to become more sensitive to his preference for
guidelines and the security they bring him in any new situation, especially one that has an aspect of performance. As an LB Rick will
contribute to peace by remembering that he fell in love with, and
even admired, my spontaneity. In order to keep it alive, he will
need to be more flexible about it . . . or it will wither.

Ballroom dancing has a mathematical, sequential precision to it which appeals to the left brain. It also offers the opportunity to be dramatic and exhibit oneself, which is anchored in the right brain. If you watch professional dancers, you will notice this merging. On one level they are monitoring and calculating; on another they are thoroughly free, enjoying the feeling that comes with self-expression. To enjoy a committed relationship, opposites must do the same. There must be a constant awareness of, and respect for, both levels, both ways of being in the world, for they are equally valid.

Opposites who have not yet reached this understanding find themselves in chronic conflict. Their perceptions of problems (and each other) are insufficient, their resolution strategies inadequate. They argue over preferences, attitudes, priorities, philosophies, tastes, beliefs, sensitivities, values, and perspectives. Even the most mundane issue is blown out of proportion as they dig in their heels and jockey for position. The power struggle is evident in their inflexibility. Each is absolutely convinced of his or her position; each believes that an offering of "I could be wrong" would be "losing the battle."

Chronic conflict can be demoralizing to a couple: Their deepest needs go unsatisfied, and they lose sight of the purpose in their being together. Each partner is more invested in promoting his or her perspective—believing it to be the *right* one—than in a willingness to acknowledge the other's. To be able to problem solve rather than engage in chronic conflict, opposites must learn the *art* (RB) and the *science* (LB) of meeting in the middle.

Although happy couples report that they quarrel less often and consider separation less frequently than unhappy couples, no truly intimate love relationship is free of dissension. It is a myth that conflict is the sign of a poor relationship; it does not deserve the bad reputation it has earned.

The truth is all couples live with some "irreconcilable differences" because no two partners are exactly alike. It is how those differences are interpreted and coped with that's important when one predicts couple satisfaction. If they make a partner feel separate and alone or create the misconception that togetherness is impossible, problems can erupt. If, on the other hand, the differences are relished and treated as opportunities to stretch oneself through an exchange of strengths, then the relationship runs more smoothly. To help you identify specifically how your differences as a couple impact on you, turn to the Exercises Section and complete "Inevitable Differences."

The crucial point is not that dissimilar ways exist but rather that there exists simultaneously a desire to integrate those different ways—and an appreciation that friction may be necessary for integration to occur.

The truth is that friction serves a vital function, since no two partners can be continually in sync, have identical needs, and agree on every aspect of cohabitation. When couples who report that they "never argue" are interviewed separately, one partner frequently admits that he or she has developed a pattern of "peace at any price" and the price is usually the loss of self.

A nonconflictual relationship continues in a formal sense but lacks vitality. Conflict is a refusal to let a relationship die of apathy. A good relationship is one worth fighting for.

Individuals bring to any relationship personal histories that dictate their experience of, comfort with, and skill at conflict and conflict resolution. If an adult was raised in a family with two LB partners (or parent figures), conflict means something entirely different from what it does to an adult raised in a family with either two RB parents or parents who were opposites (RB/LB).

In an LB/LB family there would have been rational and civilized discussions, avoidance of strong emotion, and a high regard for problem-solving (and possibly debating) skills. Conflict in an RB/RB home might have resembled a dramatic play with lots of emoting but very little resolution. Solving the problem was not the priority in an RB/RB home: talking (yelling, crying) about it was. In a family of opposites (RB/LB parents), all the above is possible.

Our expectations of what conflict involves are largely based on what we witnessed growing up. This image is what we bring with us into our adult relationships, the one we are most familiar with, and as adults we tend to fall into behavior that is familiar, no matter how sincerely we want to try something else. This is especially true in times of stress. Each of us thinks we see things as they are, but we see things as we are conditioned to see them. None of us is as objective as we would like to think. What we see is highly related to how we see.

In relationships of inequality this fact is ignored; in a hierarchical structure one partner speaks as an infallible authority, and there is no room for subjectivity. But the language of subjectivity bridges differences, and in egalitarian relationships there is no need for a "winner" or a "loser." Power is not the issue, but rather arriving at a mutual understanding—if not agreement—is. By offering "the way I remember it" or "from my perspective," a partner demonstrates an assumption that there are alternatives and thereby honors his or her partner's view as equally valid.

In a committed relationship, if either partner has a problem, it deserves time for discussion. To be able to have a discussion rather than an argument, both partners must remember that two very different perspectives will be presented and that they both are valid points of view. With RB/LB partners, conflict is not so much related to what is happening *within* the individuals as it is to what is happening *between* them, when their differing ways clash.

Information comes through our senses and experiences as well as through cognitive processes. As mentioned in Chapter 1, there is more than one way of knowing, more than one way to express reality. Although we have been taught that "real" truth comes from hard data, intuition plays a major role in interpreting such data in meaningful ways. When you and your partner sit down to discuss an issue, this is very important to remember. Each must respect that your individual way of collecting information is not better or worse than your partner's; it's only different.

In his book *Getting to Yes,* Roger Fisher reminds us that conflict is not something that exists independently; it exists in people's heads:

> Truth is simply one more argument . . . for dealing with difference. The difference itself exists because it exists in our thinking. Fears, even if ill-founded, are real fears. . . . Facts, even if established, may do nothing to solve the problem. . . . As useful as looking for objective reality can

be, it is ultimately the reality as each side sees it that con-stitutes the problem . . . and opens the way to a solution.

Before you engage your partner in an argument, be sure you know what you expect to accomplish. There are many reasons for initiating conflict. These include:

- Venting stored-up feelings (resentment, anger, frustration).
- Getting your point across.
- Shaking things up (when the relationship has become too sober or too predictable or boring).
- Scoring a victory (needing to prove you are right).
- Attempting to change your partner's behavior or perspective.
- Wanting to be taken seriously.
- Trying to be understood.
- Evening the score from a past hurt.
- Justifying your behavior. (If you get your partner mad at you, you will have a good excuse to drink or eat.)
- Avoiding intimacy. (If we have a fight, we won't make love, and I don't want to, but I don't want to say so.)
- Avoiding responsibility. (If we fight, I won't have to clean out the garage.)
- Getting attention when feeling neglected.
- Solving a problem.
- Getting your partner to open up and talk.
- Exerting power over your partner.
- Advocating for your relationship. (Help! We're in trouble.)

Whatever your reason, think about the possibility of a non-conflictual way to achieve what you want. You may have already tried several alternatives which have failed, and now you are frustrated. Identify those times, and discuss them with your partner. Sometimes those attempts have gone unrecognized, and merely describing them brings to your partner's attention how important this particular issue is to you, and how desperate you are to talk.

Following are a few guidelines to keep in mind as you consider how to approach conflict as opposites:

- Issues must be presented in terms of the facts and the feelings about those facts.
- Discuss both the concrete and the emotional impact of any solution.
- Conflict resolution in a committed relationship is a team effort.
- No two adults can do more damage to each other than those who are intimate partners.

Issues must be presented in terms of the facts and the feelings about those facts.

Diane is a thirty-nine-year-old attorney who has been living with Tony for almost a year. She was recently given a very difficult case to handle, one which has the potential to affect significantly her chances for partnership. When she sits down to tell Tony, an elementary school teacher, the information results in a huge fight and Tony's threatening to move out. By the time they make an appointment for therapy, each has decided that they are absolutely wrong for each other and indicate they want to use this "one-time visit" to work out the ending of their four-year relationship.

DIANE: I really can't take this anymore. Every time I try to explain to Tony about my work schedule, he just blows up. I can't get him to understand long hours are the nature of my business. I've explained this until I'm blue in the face.

TONY: What I *don't* need is another explanation. I'm not stupid. I understand perfectly well why she's not home. I just hate not being together in the evenings.

THERAPIST: What are the facts around this issue?

DIANE: Well, I'm trying to earn partnership, and that not only means increasing billable hours, but also means impressing certain parties. The reality is that you have to be very visible and very active to get noticed in a large firm.

THERAPIST: Tony, are there any facts you would like to add? From your end?

TONY: One fact is we have a relationship. Another one is we spend very little time together.

THERAPIST: I'm sure you both have more facts that will come up later, as we begin to look more closely at the situation, but for now let's move on to the feelings you have about the facts you've mentioned.

DIANE: Well, I feel my future's on the line. At work and at home.

THERAPIST: Diane, that's a thought. Try to stay with that thought until you become more aware of how you *feel* about your shaky future.

DIANE: Um . . . well . . . I worry. I'm afraid I'll wake up some morning, and I won't be a partner and I won't have Tony either. I'm worried about losing everything.

THERAPIST: Stay with it. What does it feel like to imagine working so long and hard and not being rewarded for it?

DIANE: I don't know . . . uh . . . it's frustrating, I guess . . . disappointment . . . I even feel angry about all this.

THERAPIST: Angry about what part?

DIANE: Angry at Tony, because he *knew* what my hours were like when he met me. We had to jockey our schedules even back then.

THERAPIST: Tony, what feelings do you have about the facts presented here?

TONY: I'm angry, too. I'm angry at Diane for changing her priorities. When we met, she said she wanted a relationship and she knew she could manage both. But she doesn't care about the relationship now.

DIANE: That's not true!

THERAPIST: Diane, this is where we get into the hard stuff. From Tony's perspective, this *is* true. I want you to listen to how he comes to this conclusion. It's very important that you validate things from his perspective, even though you may not agree with how he derives his data. *(Turning to Tony.)* Tony, how have you come to the conclusion that Diane doesn't care anymore?

TONY: She dashes off in the morning without even kissing me good-bye. From the time she gets up, her mind is preoccupied. I might as well be invisible. At night, when I ask her about her day, she doesn't want to talk. She just isn't connecting with me.

THERAPIST: Diane, Tony is using his experience of himself in your presence; he is aware that you are not as tuned in to him and that your energy seems to be directed to work, leaving him feeling isolated within the relationship. Can you *hear* this separate from whether or not you agree with it?

DIANE: Not exactly, but I'm trying.

THERAPIST: Diane, try telling Tony how you feel about your situation at work.

DIANE: I worry a lot. I worry all the time. Every morning I start thinking about my day long before I get out of bed. By the time you realize I'm awake, I'm already out the door in my head. When I get home at night, I just want to turn all thoughts off. I wish I had a switch. I would really like that. You want to talk, and I want to disconnect.

Diane and Tony represent thousands of couples who bring to each other important information about themselves in hopes of gaining understanding, sometimes solutions, and often comfort. Unfortunately, because they conceptualize the issues differently, problem solve differently, and have differing styles while under stress, they are frequently unable to meet each other's needs.

If Diane and Tony were able to address this issue by "meeting in the middle", it would sound like this:

DIANE: There are some things I need for you to know. I'm being considered for partnership, and it means very much to me. You know how hard I've worked.

(facts about the issue) I've just been given a case that could seal it for me. I really need your support at this time. I'm going to be gone for long periods of time, and I just can't be as socially involved with you as you would like.

(feelings) I'm afraid this is my last chance; so many new hotshots are joining the firm. I'm feeling insecure about being able to keep up this pace. I'm also worried about how this is going to impact on us, and I'm afraid that you might leave me when it gets too lonely for you. That really scares me.

TONY: *(facts)* I come home at night and pop a dinner in the microwave and grade papers. I don't make plans to go out in case you call to say you're coming home sooner than you thought. I try to stay up so we can talk and be close when you get home, but you come in the door, pour a glass of wine, and tell me you'd rather talk in the morning. In the morning I reach for you in bed, and you're already on the phone.

(feelings) I feel lonely most of the time. I wonder why am I in a relationship when I don't have a partner. I get angry because I transferred to another school so we could be closer to your law firm, but I would not have done that if I'd known we weren't going to have time together. I feel cheated. I'm afraid. I'm afraid we can't make it together, and I want to, but sometimes I can't remember why.

DIANE: I didn't fully understand what it was like for you. I thought you had it made, getting off work so early. I envy all that free time you have alone.

(meeting in the middle) What can I do to make this change easier for you?

TONY: I didn't realize how much you worried about us. I thought you cared only about your job. I always see you as so confident I never imagined that you doubted your future there.

(meeting in the middle) What can I do to make this time easier for you?

Diane and Tony would then go on to the next step: They must be willing to enter into trade-offs. That is, Diane would make a few suggestions, and Tony would follow with some of his own, until they agreed on one or two that would answer, "What would make it easier for you?" Diane might be willing to take breaks at certain times, when Tony could meet her to go out to eat, or he could bring takeout to the office and join her. That would mean Diane would have to give up working straight through, so that Tony could get his need for companionship met.

Diane could trade for down time when she first got home, time that is hers alone, without any interruptions from Tony. That would be what Tony would be willing to do in order for Diane to meet her need to be alone. When two partners are each so stuck in their own interpretation of the problem or polarized ideas about solutions, trade-offs can help them move forward.

Discuss both the concrete and the emotional impact of any solution.

Diane and Tony have decided to trade off. Diane is going to set aside time for them to be able to share dinner together; Tony is going to support Diane's efforts to have some transition time alone when she first gets home from the office. These "gifts" to each other are one way they are attending to their relationship. Every change they are making requires a shift in their behavior and an internal shift in how they are interpreting their own, as well as the other's, actions. They will also need to take into account how they feel about the proposed solution(s).

DIANE: *(facts)* If you are going to come to the office so we can eat together, call me first. That way I will have time to pace myself, so I won't be in the middle of something with another attorney. I need at least thirty minutes' warning.
(feelings) I feel closer to you since we've decided to do this, but I'm also worried about how you will react if I really can't get away. I know that's going to happen occasionally.
TONY:*(facts)* I'm prepared for that, but if our plan doesn't seem to be working, I'll talk to you about it. Also, it's not convenient for me always to be the one arranging where and what we eat. I want that responsibility shared.
(feelings) I'm excited about being able to have dinner tonight. I'm also anxious about this working out. We've tried things before, and I'm afraid that this might not work either.
DIANE: *(facts)* I'll block out time on my calendar for us to do this. I will do what I can to protect that time, even though I may need it for work. In turn, I want an hour alone in the evening to unwind in my own way.
(feelings) I find that without some kind of transition time between work and home, I don't feel like connecting with you. By having this time alone, I will feel less stress and closer to you.

TONY: *(facts)* I'm willing to step back and give you room when you get home, but I want a hug and a kiss before you withdraw.

(feelings) If you come home and immediately withdraw without greeting me, I feel hurt and rejected. With a hug, I'll feel you care, even though you're dashing off to be alone.

Conflict resolution in a committed relationship is a team effort.

This requires an occasional shift from individual desires to what is in the best interest of the partnership. A partnership cannot survive without each individual attending to it.

In the traditional heterosexual relationship of the fifties and sixties, as interpreted through couples like Ward and June Cleaver, the responsibility of monitoring the pulse of the marriage, of keeping the flame tended, fell to the wife. As the women's liberation movement made its mark, more women entered the workforce and took on all the problems and associated stresses that men have lived with for years.

More and more couples are discovering that although there are rewards for all those long hours at the office, care of the relationship has been abandoned; attending to it now and then, as two-career couples (especially those with children) do, isn't enough.

There will be times when one partner has a personal need that is in conflict with the relationship itself, a need that could possibly have a negative effect. Without discussing this with his or her partner, without thinking through the ramifications of his or her actions on the health of the relationship, this person is placing the partnership in jeopardy.

This does not mean that individual needs can never override relationship needs, but to ignore the existence of such a bond and to act unilaterally without considering the impact, disregards the commitment the two partners have made to each other. Relationships require nurturing, because they are fragile; they are not immune to human desires, human error, and human neglect.

One way to nurture a partnership is to accept more personal responsibility for problems and their resolution, rather than place that burden on the relationship, hoping things will "work themselves out." This can be done by a shift in individual perspective. Ask yourself why you are so invested in the views you have. What would it take to consider another? Try to stretch to at least three ways of looking at any situation. This moves you out of individual stubbornness and into readiness for negotiation.

One of the reasons LB/LB couples are seldom seen in couples therapy is that they possess problem-solving skills. With low levels of emotionality involved, they address issues between them as they would an issue at work. Marriages between scientists, for example, report negotiating as their primary problem-solving technique.

No two adults can do more damage to each other than those who are intimate partners.

Intimacy involves an exchange of sensitive information. It is through revealing our deepest thoughts, dreams, fears, and failures that we come to be bonded closely to other people. This bond is rooted in the trust that this same information will not be used as ammunition during an argument.

Intimacy is a paradox; it provides an avenue by which partners simultaneously increase their sense of closeness as well as their sense of vulnerability. If partners know each other well enough, they have the capacity to do great harm. It takes a mature individual not to take advantage of such information.

Each opposite partner has areas of strength. In Chapter 7 you will see how RBs are better at keeping romance alive and what LBs can do to improve their efforts in that area. However, when we discuss conflict resolution, LBs are the ones who shine. Outlined below are ways that RBs can increase their capacity in this important area of communication.

HOW AN RB CAN BE BETTER AT CONFLICT RESOLUTION (AND WHY HE OR SHE ISN'T)

- If you have something to discuss that may lead to conflict, be sensitive in your timing. Don't "spring" it on your LB.
  (RBs rarely think things through ahead of time, and therefore, they often scare off LBs who otherwise might have listened.)

- Focus on one issue at a time, and get resolution on that one before jumping to another.
  (RBs make mysterious connections between issues that to them justify stringing several together in a single argument.)
- Tolerate facts. They do not erase your feelings, and they are a key factor to any problem-solving situation.
  (RBs are offended by facts being thrown at them while they are in the middle of their angst. Facts actually *distract* an RB.)
- Try to walk through the process sequentially rather than jump all over the place; that is extremely disconcerting to an LB.
  (There is no logical sequence for feelings, so an RB is unaccustomed to having to order events.)
- Have patience with an LB's desire to replay events methodically until they make sense to him or her.
  (RBs would rather deal with the "surface" of a problem, skimming over the facts of a situation. Digging deeper into detail is uninteresting to an RB, unless it provides great emotional release.)
- Inform your LB if you are getting so worked up that you are no longer processing what he or she is saying.
  (RBs can't believe it when LBs fail to stop everything and attend to the RBs' overflowing emotions. An RB expects an LB to take notice and say, "I can see that this discussion is really upsetting you. Let's talk about your feelings for a while.")
- Do not assume anything. Check out things for clarification. Do you have the same idea of what the problem is? What alternative solutions are available? Have you agreed on a solution? Are you sure?
  (RBs jump to conclusions and operate on the assumption that those conclusions are not only valid but shared by the LB!)

In addition to the general guidelines above, it is important to be aware of how the characteristics of being right brain or left brain dominant contribute to both conflict and conflict resolution. By studying these factors, you can see how easily an argument can start, how rapidly misunderstanding can occur, and how difficult it can be to agree on a solution.

HOW OPPOSITES CONTRIBUTE TO CONFLICT AND RESOLUTION

- LBs prefer to avoid conflict. They will do almost anything to prevent getting into it with their RB partners. Conflict presents the possibility of losing control, especially emotional control, and this is very uncomfortable for LBs. An LB avoids talking about and expressing feelings, because he or she isn't sure what to *do* with them. To an LB feelings are inconvenient, an impediment to progress toward a solution. To an RB feelings are the avenue to resolution. For one partner they are a nuisance; to the other they are a necessity; no wonder the topic of feelings alone is enough to ignite an argument. For this reason, if you are an RB and there is a highly emotional issue that needs to be addressed, you should expect that you will probably be the one to initiate any discussion of it.

- LBs take a logical, rational approach to problem solving, preferring a slower, intentional style to shouting, screaming, and crying. Even so, because of a fear of making mistakes or appearing foolish (even though they may have solid arguments), their response times are slower. They frequently become too methodical in their effort to cover all the bases so as not to be misunderstood. This creates two problems: First, this places them in a one-down position against their faster-thinking, faster-talking RB partners, and second, it frustrates the RBs, who lack the patience to listen to all the details from the LBs.

- LBs fear being put on the spot, being asked to do something unfamiliar or not yet mastered. A spontaneous request from an RB triggers performance expectations and all the attending anxiety. RBs can avoid conflict by not "springing" things on their LB partners, by not expecting immediate responses to requests (give an LB time to decide whether he or she really wants to do something), and by not doing anything that puts their LB partners in a spotlight. LBs can avoid conflict by lightening up a little and not taking spontaneous requests so seriously. They need to learn to respond with "Let me think about that" or "I don't know" or "I need some time to decide." Just because an RB asks a question or makes a request (let's dance!), an LB doesn't have to respond to it immediately.

■ LBs prefer to have issues addressed one at a time and resent having old and seemingly unrelated problems thrown into arguments by RBs. RBs, because they think in patterns and relationships, are able to connect the most remotely related events in ways that makes perfect sense to them. They stay attentive to any hint that this experience is similar to a previous situation. To an RB each example serves to illustrate and *support* the central issue. To an LB "dragging in the kitchen sink" is an attempt to *divert* from the central issue. Just because an LB doesn't make the connections doesn't mean they don't exist. When an LB thinks the "kitchen sink" has just arrived, he or she should ask, "How does this relate to what we are talking about?" and then *listen*. An RB needs to stay issue-focused and describe what is wanted rather than what is wrong; what is desired, not what is missing.

■ RBs get caught up in their feelings about topics and lose sight of the facts. They often fail to get their points across because they are buried in an avalanche of emotion, which overwhelms their LB partners, who then have difficulty digging through to the message. Being uncomfortable with emotional displays, the LB, instead of listening, focuses his or her energy on maintaining whatever control is left. As the RB becomes progressively more emotional, the LB becomes more rational and determined to be reasonable. These polarized positions can drive the partners nuts. A good rule of thumb is never to make decisions that affect the relationship while you are in a highly emotional state (either positive or negative). These decisions should be made during a rational discussion to avoid the regrets that often accompany impulsive behavior.

■ RBs lack patience when communicating with their LB partners, who are more methodical. An LB does not want to leave any important detail out for fear of being misunderstood or, worse, incorrect. Listening to everything an LB has to say about any given topic can be a tedious ordeal. (For this reason LBs are sometimes described as boring.) Often, unable to wait, an RB will interrupt, responding to a single phrase or a fragment of a sentence without allowing the LB to finish. (For this reason RBs are sometimes described as rude.) In their impulsiveness RBs frequently jump to erroneous conclusions and take things personally without checking with the LBs to see if they've misunderstood.

- When communicating, LBs want to be precise, whereas RBs want to arouse interest and establish rapport with other people. These different goals can create conflict, no matter what the issue. LBs, because they want to be precise, demand precision in other people. They have difficulty communicating in metaphors, visions, guesses, insinuations, implications, and assumptions. Yet an RB frequently thinks in symbolic meanings that go far beneath the surface realities. Everything, to an RB, has the potential to reveal something else. At various points during an argument, the LB may need to ask, "What do you mean? What are you saying? What do you want?" because it really isn't clear to him. This can exasperate an RB, who believes he or she has been perfectly clear all along.

- RBs process bits of information simultaneously. LBs process sequentially. When this difference is not remembered and respected, and misunderstandings arise, issues may not get resolved. There is an order to things in the LB's mind; there is also an order to things in the RB's mind, but it's not as obvious. When an RB begins to throw out several things at a time, an LB will become flustered and will try to sort them in some manner before making sense of it all. An RB who is not aware of this will be unwittingly contributing to the conflict.

- LBs prefer to break down thoughts and separate them (analyze). RBs prefer to combine thoughts into patterns (synthesize). At certain times during conflict each partner will be going in a different direction. The LB is using deductive reasoning: going from the general to the specific. The RB partner is using inductive reasoning: building from specifics to the general.

When my husband (LB) and I (RB) are in conflict, he focuses on a specific incident, dissecting it, trying to understand the different parts. I take everything in, searching for similarities, until I have a theme. The flaw in his approach is that his conclusion may be limited by tunnel vision. The flaw in mine is that I may construct generalities. To eliminate these problems, he needs to appreciate the big picture; I need to be cautious about making sweeping statements.

- LBs are very literal and can be blunt. It is important for them to keep an awareness of their capacity to hurt an RB's feelings. RBs say whatever comes to mind and must also be aware that their impulsiveness can harm. Many conflicts are fueled by the insensitivity of the partners.

- Because LBs are more concrete in their thinking, they are more explicit in their communications. RBs are more implicit, and this can lead to misunderstanding when there is an assumption that both partners are interpreting the same event in the same way. It is therefore important to check out each other's understanding before doing anything. This applies to things like where to meet, when to meet, who's invited, what to bring, what's wrong, and what do you want. Save yourself a headache; get it clear before you act on it.

- RBs initiate conversations in order to connect with their partners. When concerned or upset about an event, they turn to their partners for empathy. LBs, when presented with a concern, immediately frame it as a problem to be solved. This kicks in the LB's natural tendency to advise. Because the RB partner is looking for understanding, conflict often results. The RB feels unloved when advice—rather than empathy—is offered. The LB feels rejected when the advice is scorned.

Every couple must stretch and grow if their bond is to survive. This requires many uncomfortable, anxious, and even painful moments as each partner takes risks and goes into previously unexplored territory. There will be conflict as long as there are two partners who respect their individual needs as well as those of the relationship. There is no single way to argue that can be offered to all couples, but there is a single goal all couples can aspire to: to achieve a win-win outcome.

Judith Jordan through her work with the Stone Center at Wellesley College emphasizes the role that conflict plays in *healthy* partnerships:

A relational perspective, an interest in the well-being of the relationship facilitates movement into what Jean Baker Miller calls "good conflict." When in conflict, people often perceive their realities or personal goals to be completely opposed. I am not using the term *conflict* to indicate a fight or a battle. Rather I am suggesting it is an interruption of confluence or harmony in a relationship, caused by disruptive difference. . . . The goal in *good conflict* is not to eradicate difference but to move beyond mere tolerance of existing difference to the creation of new opportunities [p. 4].

Through conflict, in addition to problems being resolved, information that adds to one partner's understanding of the other is often exchanged. This new material serves to strengthen and enrich the relationship by illuminating a corner previously out of awareness.

A committed relationship is *not* a fixed institution but rather a potent force in constant flux. Committed couples know that change often brings conflict. They also know the value of confronting problems head-on.

7

THE ART (RB)
AND SCIENCE (LB)
OF LOVING

Love is the triumph of
imagination over intelligence.

—H.L. MENCKEN

Love appears in many forms. It is precisely this that is so important to remember when opposites come together. For it is in their very different ways of loving—and preferring to be loved—that hurt is often born.

Throughout this book it is important to remember that we all move back and forth between our right and left hemispheres. The less movement—the more polarized a couple's positions—the more they tend to have problems. Each of us can move more toward the middle, toward balance, by making a conscious act to do the opposite of what we seem to do naturally. Couples who adapt to their differences experience less conflict and far greater love.

Several months ago I was working with a couple, Sharon and David, who entered marital therapy in order to decide whether or not they should divorce. It was painful watching them as they shared their history with me. As each spoke, it became obvious that they did not actually want a divorce but had come to the conclusion that it was inevitable.

They described their love for each other, which seemed genuine and mutual, yet here they sat considering separation. Their frustration filled the room, as did abundant evidence that they had worked hard to stay together in spite of their differences. If they loved each other so much, if they had worked hard at saving their marriage, *what brought them to my office?* Listening to Sharon and David, I became aware of a theme, a central issue woven throughout their years together:

THERAPIST: I'm curious. You seem to be very sure that you love each other. What do *you* think is the problem?

SHARON: We can't figure it out. I talk to David all the time and let him know what I'm feeling. I ask him about what is going on for him at work. I include him in activities I'm involved in, and I buy him special presents . . . little things I know he would really like.

THERAPIST: David, what do you do for Sharon?

DAVID: Well . . . I give Sharon a lot of freedom. I don't pry. I repair things for her.

THERAPIST: Your intentions are golden, yet I get the feeling that you're both missing the mark in some way. Sharon, you've let me know that you love David very much, but I'm wondering . . . do you feel loved in return?

SHARON *(starting to weep):* I know this sounds crazy . . . David does all those things he just said. I know he loves me, but I don't feel loved.

THERAPIST: What about you, David?

DAVID: You mean, do I think Sharon loves me?

THERAPIST: No. I mean, do you feel loved by her?

DAVID: Well, I never really think about it in that way. I suppose so.

THERAPIST: It's possible you two aren't feeling loved, despite your individual efforts, because you never learned how your partner wants to be loved. When we don't have that information about our partner, we automatically demonstrate our love in ways that *we* want to be loved. Our partner ends up feeling unloved, and we feel unappreciated and rejected. Sharon, what could David do that would help you feel more connected . . . to feel his love?

SHARON: He could talk to me more, especially about his feelings. Ask me to do things with him. Take a real interest in things that I like. And he could show me he is thinking of me in little ways . . . like leaving me notes or giving me little presents for no reason at all. He is usually so preoccupied. I think that his silence makes me feel he doesn't care.

THERAPIST: David, how could Sharon show you she loves you in ways that fit for you?

DAVID: She could give me some free time alone on the weekends instead of expecting us to spend it all doing things together.

THERAPIST: That isn't very much. Anything else?

DAVID: No, not really. Sharon does a good job. I can't think of anything else. I just feel bad that things aren't working out for her. I'm not as dissatisfied.

THERAPIST: What if she complimented you . . . noted when you had done something that pleased her . . . instead of criticizing you when you didn't. Would that help?

DAVID: I sure wouldn't discourage her!

THERAPIST: If you remember, as both of you were describing how you showed your love for each other, you mentioned that you did certain things. These things are based more on how *you* want your partner to love *you* than on how your partner wants to be loved. You'll have to change that pattern by discovering what appeals to your partner and being generous with it.

When they returned two weeks later, I noticed that they were sitting closer together and that David had his hand on Sharon's knee. I was struck by this for two reasons: Sharon had previously felt really "out of touch" with David, and David, being predominantly left brain, was not so public with his affection.

THERAPIST: You look more connected this week.

SHARON: After our last session I asked David to sit down and make a list of all the things I do that he liked best.

THERAPIST: David, you have an interesting smile on your face.

DAVID: I was thinking about how difficult it was for me to do and how patient Sharon was about it . . . and how being patient with me is one of the things I left off the list.

SHARON: He only had *two* things! I started to get upset, thinking he just didn't care enough about us to make the list. Then I remembered what you had said about how left-brain partners hate being put on the spot . . . the pressure to perform and the risk of making a mistake. I didn't personalize it. Instead I suggested that he keep the list in his pocket and when he thought of something, he could take it out and add it.

THERAPIST: Not only did you remember about not putting pressure on him, but you also remembered how helpful lists are. *(Turning to David.)* Did the list grow?

DAVID: Yes. I just can't do anything with someone breathing down my neck. The first couple of days I actually forgot about the list. Then, on Thursday, Sharon did something that felt so good it made me think about the list, and I wrote it down. I think I ended up with seven.

THERAPIST: What did she do?

DAVID: She said she was no longer making plans for us on Saturdays, so I could do whatever I wanted, which was to have time alone to work on a hobby of mine.

THERAPIST: It really doesn't take much time to find out what our partner wants and then become generous with it.

Although partners have every intention of demonstrating their love in ways that will impact on each other, like the couple above, lovers often fail to appreciate that this requires really knowing each other's preferences. "Love Map" in the Exercises Section is designed to help you learn what those are.

True love is not a feeling but rather a thoughtful decision. It is an *active* process, an act of will. It is the transformation of chemistry—over time—into something deeper and more profound. Loving is a conscious choice, more deliberate than the "being swept away" of infatuation.

I find it difficult to capture the essence of "love" in any single statement, so for our purposes I have identified "loving" behaviors that all contribute to a sense of being loved and manifest the loving of another. These are:

- Cherishing
- Offering affection
- Providing support
- Showing respect
- Offering companionship
- Demonstrating concern
- Earning and giving trust
- Protecting relationships
- Accepting imperfection
- Communicating intimately
- Expressing/responding to sexual desire

CHERISHING. To cherish is to hold fondly in one's mind an image or sense of the loved one, to feel a great deal of tenderness toward him or her. Because this occurs in the right brain, RBs are more in touch with this particular way of conferring specialness.

LBs are more likely to think in terms of a particular event that was shared rather than an image unconnected to any real experience. An RB, however, may conjure up this image numerous times throughout the day; the image may float in and out of awareness while she or he is busily working at an unrelated activity. It's just there, a part of the background. An LB may do something that triggers a memory that is connected to the loved one, and that may bring up certain feelings of that person's being special, but this process is activated by an external event. This all seems relatively harmless until the RB partner asks, "Did you think about me today?" This is, of course, a loaded question since an RB considers *not* doing so proof that love does not exist. A covert competition begins: Who thinks about whom most often?

The LB partner is in a bind. The truth may be that there was too much going on at work, that in fact she did not think about her partner today. For an LB conjuring up the image is a much more intentional act because LBs focus on individual bits of information one at a time, each one being replaced by another. If an LB is occupied with a task, he or she is totally occupied; there is no room for un-related thoughts about the partner or anything else.

Unable to understand this, the RB takes it personally, so the LB finds it is safer to say, "Yes, I thought about you," even though he did not. It is the assumptions of the RB that prevent honest communication between the partners: the assumption that the LB is not as much in love, does not cherish the relationship as much, and might even be thinking of leaving . . . all because images of the RB did not take up permanent residence during the day. Remember, to the RB connection (relationship) is everything.

Another aspect of cherishing is being truly interested in your partner, to be awed by his or her talents and strengths and to celebrate how he or she is different from you. In the beginning, when courting, partners naturally exhibit more curiousity about each other. Responsiveness, attention, and wonder are high. Unfortunately, as time passes, that wonder recedes into a background wherein the love object is taken for granted. Couples who report high levels of satisfaction indicate that they make sure this does not happen. They understand that it is arrogant to believe that one knows everything there is to know about another, even after fifty years. They also appreciate that not being curious about one's part-ner demonstrates an indifference at a very intimate level.

RBs, in their ongoing effort to connect, frequently use curiosity as the bridge. This is often met with rejection, defensiveness, and even hostility. LBs are extremely private and guarded individuals; energy is directed to *not* revealing intimate details about themselves. If an RB spontaneously asks a question—especially a personal one—it is a moment of vulnerability for the LB, and all internal forces gather to prevent a sudden exposure. The RB, meanwhile, is innocently attempting to know more about his or her LB partner, who experiences the curiosity as invasive and a threat to emotional safety.

Only time together and consistent nonjudgmental acceptance of what the LB shares will help the LB feel more comfortable with such situations. The RB can also keep in mind that timing is im-portant. A question sprung on an unsuspecting LB will not receive the same consideration as one that is presented in a way that al-lows time for the LB to organize her thoughts and lessen the risk of seeming inadequate. For instance, an RB could say, "I've al-ways wondered what it was like for you when your parents gave your dog away. Would you be willing to think about that and tell me on our walk tomorrow?"

The RB is attempting to increase intimacy, but this can't be done in a vacuum; cooperation by the LB is necessary. The LB still has the option of saying, while they are walking, "I've thought about it, and I find it too unpleasant to talk about. Can you understand?" At this point the RB has the choice of taking it personally (why *can't* he talk to me?) or accepting it (he feels it would hurt too much and he might not be able to stop the pain).

Acceptance is a form of cherishing that instills a sense of trust and security in the partner being accepted. Needless to say, the RB *also* needs to be accepted as attempting to connect through curios-ity, rather than criticized—or shunned—for invading the LB's private world.

Valuing the relationship is manifested in whether or not the partnership is treated as a priority. Because RBs look at the world through an interconnected lens, they take responsibility for main-taining the priority status of their bond. This includes making sure there is enough couple time and time set aside to talk about the re-lationship. This is often an unpopular role, for it can seem to the LB as if he or she is being nagged into doing things together when in fact, the RB is providing a necessary service. If neither partner takes the time to check on the health of their bond, it will die of apathy or neglect.

RBs create couple memories through rituals and celebrations as well as record events in letters and picture albums. They regard their significant relationships as living entities, deserving attention and nurturance. Unlike LBs, who are more grounded in the present, RBs often spend blocks of time thinking about the past—the earlier times together, for this was when romance was in full bloom—or about the future, as they grow old together.

OFFERING AFFECTION. This is the area in which there are the most complaints and which seems to create the most conflict. Opposites have a very difficult time agreeing on how to communicate affec-tion, both verbally and physically. Of primary concern is the RB's requirement for romance and the discomfort with things romantic on the part of the LB, who prefers a practical approach to relationships.

Despite the potency and obsessive nature of romantic love, it isn't sufficient to sustain a long-term commitment. The eventual awareness by the RB that the LB is different from the RB's idealized image is felt like a betrayal. The struggle to get the LB to conform to the cherished fantasy contributes to alienation between the two partners, for the LB wants only to be accepted as is.

With the passage of time it becomes apparent that the "ideal" partner and one's actual partner are not the same. The LB, being more practical, is not as shocked by this revelation as the RB. The LB has a clearer sense of the function of courting behavior as a way to attract in order to *initiate* a relationship: the RB considers courting behavior a way to *maintain* relationship. For the LB, it loses its purpose once the relationship has been established.

Initial infatuation is a state of strong attraction to another person based on resemblance to a fantasy. Millions of people attempt to make the reality of their partners conform to the unreality of their romantic ideals, leaving both frustrated. Marital experts agree that friendship is an infinitely more stabilizing basis for a long-term partnership than romance. Sam Keen, in his book *Fire in the Belly,* cautions:

> If you consider marriage a lifelong romance, you are certain to be disillusioned. . . . Marriage is designed to allow two people to fall out of love and into reality. . . . Romance is all "yes" . . . built around the illusion of unbroken affirmation. Marriage is "yes" and "no" and "maybe"—a relationship of trust that is steeped in the primal ambivalence of love and hate [p. 220].

However, so important is romance to an RB that many couples break up over nothing more serious than the fact that courting behavior has ceased. This makes no sense to the LB sitting shattered in my office. He was responsible, faithful, constant, and loving (by his definition). Yet here he is, abandoned. When I talk to his RB partner, I am told he is cold, distant, uninterested in her, and unloving (by her definition). When we get together to discuss what happened, it becomes evident that the culprit was romance—or rather the absence of romance—and that this left the RB feeling alone, unconnected, and unloved—a very common story among opposites.

Because an RB has a rich fantasy life, he or she may bring certain expectations into courtship. An RB dreams of being swept away, overwhelmed by passion, and blinded by the light in her partner's eyes. Relying heavily on intuition, a "gut" response is as good as documentation that this is the right partner. An RB will describe a variety of somatic (physical) responses: racing heart, tingling all over, shaky knees, light-headedness, etc. All these cues are interpreted as a green light. The greater the feeling of losing control over oneself, the greater the belief that this is Ms. or Mr. Right.

RBs are more in tune with their senses, and this translates into their preference for creating a "mood." Candlelight, flowers, incense, satin sheets, and music all are avenues to an RB. This wouldn't be a problem, except that an RB expects his or her LB partner to feel this way, too, and create just the right environment—or at least respond to it. An RB calls this "romantic" and is frequently disappointed to discover that his or her LB has no such need . . . or interest.

TERRY (RB): I was really excited. I fixed the apartment up like it was Valentine's Day, even though it was July. Red everywhere. A terrific album was playing, and I lit a bunch of candles.

LYNN (LB): My first thought was that I couldn't see where I was going. And then I found the music very distracting. I didn't want to say anything, because I knew the mood was important to Terry. But it didn't really do anything for me. I just like being with Terry. I don't need all that extra stuff.

There's nothing wrong with creating what you want, but don't expect your partner to need or want the same thing. Most LBs prefer more predictable approaches to things and can become very uncomfortable when the unexpected is thrust upon them. They do not tire of routine as readily as their counterparts and often describe the everyday rituals in the relationship as part of what contributes to their satisfaction. To an LB routine means security, but to an RB it screams boredom.

RBs want to be courted *throughout* the marriage or relationship. This seems like a simple request, but instead it becomes a point of contention. Why? What is so difficult about being romantic? In order to understand more fully an LB's reluctance, here are some suggestions for LBs and accompanying explanations for RBs as to why these behaviors don't already exist in their relationship.

HOW AN LB CAN KEEP ROMANCE ALIVE
(AND WHY HE OR SHE DOESN'T)

- Write poems or little notes, and leave them around the house or apartment.
  (This won't happen if trust is low or the relationship is too shaky; words on paper are open to ridicule; it might seem silly to write little notes; it doesn't make sense to state the obvious.)
- Send cards, but don't just sign your name; add some thoughts or feelings to personalize them; your RB is looking for evidence that you see her or him as special.
  (Fears writing something that might seem too much, too little, wrong, or stupid.)
- Bring flowers (when there is no special occasion), which say you are bringing them just because of who your RB *is* not because of some date on the calendar.
  (Feels his or her love for the RB is obvious, doesn't need flowers to show it. Fears choosing the "wrong" ones.)
- Offer small tokens of caring: a flower picked on a walk, a shell from the beach, a ring from your Cracker Jacks. It is the thought that counts.
  (LBs underestimate the power of small gestures; again, it may seem too silly to indulge in.)
- Personalize your gifts. Anyone can send roses; they're the sign of an amateur romantic. A true romantic selects a gift reflecting the receiver.

(The LB really does not know what the RB is fond of, interested in, prefers. An LB may be too occupied and not see value in intimate data or make the connection between such information and valuing the partner.)

NOTE: My husband (LB) used to agonize over shopping for a gift for me (RB). He was very concerned he might get the "wrong" thing. To protect himself from this, he bought me very generic gifts that anyone would like. Later, as he became more interested in knowing me at an intimate level, he began to present me with things that were more and more special. One of the best gifts was from a camping trip he took in the desert where he discovered a bird's nest that had blown out of a tree during a storm. He knew I collected them and went out of his way to go back and retrieve it and securely pack it for the trip home. By surprising me with that nest, he not only gave me a personalized gift but also let me know that in his absence he had thought of me. That was very important to me as an RB.

- Honor special anniversaries, big and small. If you don't know when they are, ask. "Exactly when did we have our first date?"
  (LBs are more in tune with the major events but, because of ever-present preoccupations, may forget even these without cues such as dates on a calendar.)
- Comment on the value of your RB partner and the relationship to you.
  (Does not see the value in stating the obvious and believes behavior says it all: "I'm here, right?")
- Make special time together at home or away, with romance as the emphasis.
  (Will be reluctant to do so if concerned it will become "heavy" because of lengthy discussions about issues within the relationship; often too preoccupied and self-focused to make couple time; doesn't *occur* to LB; is not as intentional about maintaining health of the relationship.)
- Take more initiative, and be open about your desire, but not blunt. Bluntness can kill romance.

(May prefer to be indirect—"There's nothing good on TV tonight"—taking the risk out of direct rejection. May find it difficult to slip into courting behavior because he or she is more comfortable with the "mechanics" of lovemaking than the "art" of being a good lover.)

- Invite your RB to return to the place where you met, had your first date, consummated your romance, etc. Tell him or her how you were feeling at that time, as you sit there months/years later.

(Does not want to risk going to the wrong place. Seems like a silly thing to do. LB places little value on the symbolic meaning of such an event, so it does not occur to him or her.)

- Be vocal about your passion. Silent lovers are boring lovers. Communicating your own pleasure to your partner is a turn-on for him or her.

(An LB easily becomes self-conscious. May be preoccupied with the mechanics of sex and withdraw into himself or herself in order to concentrate on correct moves or on not losing control. Hates to be out of control.)

- Spontaneously demonstrate your affection in public. This is a very romantic thing to do. You might just take your RB in your arms for a kiss or lean over and tell the person next to you that you are crazy about your RB. This is not a time to be concerned about your image or the approval of others. Romantics are unpredictable people.

(Will be reluctant to bring focus to self in a moment of vulnerability. Seems far too silly to indulge in. Prefers to retain control in all areas, especially in public for fear of judgment by others.)

Romantic, affectionate behavior is both verbal and physical. An LB is often described as being a person "of few words." LBs are often regarded as shy, reluctant, guarded, or even emotionally unavailable. They may have little to say at times, but what they have to say is usually deeply felt. They are much less likely to talk just to hear their own voices. It is often difficult for them to know when their RB partners feel deeply about something because an RB offers up tons of words about everything and the feelings to go with them. This makes it more difficult to know what really matters.

Much of the RB's dissatisfaction has to do with the lack of spontaneity in his or her LB. Spontaneity adds spice to romantic behavior; without it there is a wooden, lifeless, robotic manner that turns an RB off.

Spontaneity is a natural part of being human and is most clearly observed in small children, intoxicated with the freedom to express themselves fully. This freedom is often a pleasure to watch (playing in the surf) but at other times can be embarrassing (sexual curiosity in the grocery line). It applies to those moments when there is no forethought and actions are taken on the spur of the moment. Unplanned, it has a certain shock value that adds spice to everyday life.

It is precisely because of its unrehearsed nature that LBs do not indulge. Spontaneous acts are pregnant with risk. Any situation suddenly becomes a minefield of potential dangers, including rejection, error, disapproval, and the possibility of total humiliation.

Spontaneity requires trust: trust that you will emotionally survive the situation; trust that even if you fall short of your own, and other people's, expectations, you will live to embrace another day. To be spontaneous means you are willing to risk being judged, found ridiculous, and sentenced to the social equivalent of Siberia. It means that you risk being a fool, being wrong, and being criticized.

None of these appeals to an LB. The paltry benefits of an unrehearsed act are outweighed by paralyzing catastrophic fantasies. LBs prefer having a guarantee before getting involved in anything. They have no need to live on the edge. Chance is not as seductive to them as it is to their RB partners.

Because LBs tend toward perfectionism, they are highly rejection-sensitive. They concentrate on the risk in even the most mundane act, such as initiating a conversation. An LB spends so much time analyzing a potential situation that by the time he or she is ready to make a move the opportunity is usually history. It is precisely this intense effort that goes into weighing everything that the RB has difficulty relating to. Behind what seems like a barrier to the

RB is a very sensitive, tenderhearted LB. Don't let the cover fool you. An LB is a book worth reading, but you have to do so one page at a time.

PROVIDING SUPPORT. In committed relationships, closeness serves as a buffer between the couple and the stress, chaos, and craziness of the world. The more authentic their relationship—the better they know each other—the easier it is for them to provide the mutual support they need. Crucial to this process is a shared history of negative experiences and successful negotiation of conflicting needs. Each resolution strengthens the bond.

Support could be defined as the ability to embrace your partner's experience with your own compassion. Support may be offered in the form of empathy, advice, assistance, guidance, encouragement, and nonjudgmental listening. You may not have had a similar incident, you may not agree with your partner's viewpoint, you may not even be able to imagine such a thing, but you can try to put yourself in his or her place and view the world from that perspective. This requires the ability to transcend your own mind-set, to go beyond the familiar and to expand the world as you know it. If you can do this for only a few minutes in the service of your relationship, you will be demonstrating support.

If you can't imagine, if you draw a blank, ask your partner to tell you what the experience was like. Then take a minute to let the description register. If it is impossible for you to get a mental image, you can say, "It sounds so awful I can't even imagine it, but I feel for you . . . for what you went through."

Empathy—identification with another's experience—is a powerful supportive tool. It undergirds the rapport that already exists between two people. For this reason RBs place special emphasis on empathy as a demonstration of understanding and concern. Because empathy requires some mental imagery—actually picturing the situation as the other describes it—it is easier for RBs to provide it. Empathy is about relationship, which is RB territory.

When providing support, LBs offer advice and encouragement in lieu of empathy. Instructions and opinions replace feelings as guidance is given. Because their orientation is toward analyzing situations and identifying problems and solutions, there is less concern with common experience than with fixing things.

All of us, LBs and RBs, need at least one good listener in our lives as part of our support system, but it is difficult to listen when you resist accepting your partner's different way of being. Relationships are demanding, risky, and frustrating. For couples trying to integrate their individual differences, life is complicated. Try to construct ways of caring for each other that do not cripple—but rather enhance—the self. By supporting the "self" of your partner, you are supporting your partnership as well. However, as mentioned earlier, it is important to find out *from your partner* how he or she wants to be supported by you.

SHOWING RESPECT. Love brings together one's self and the mystery of the partner's self. Thus it is important to accept and respect that which is *beyond* understanding or explanation. Successful opposites commit themselves to understanding what makes each other tick; in the spirit of mutual respect they explore each other's way of being in the world. This is based on the desire to appreciate the other's world truly, not to dissect each other in hopes of achieving a psychological victory.

Always assume a need to learn more about your partner. If you want to improve your ability to deal with differences, you should always assume that you do not understand enough. Any situation between two people is the result of two stories coming together; accept your partner's story whether you understand it or not. Respect for another's way of being does not depend upon understanding or agreeing with it; it depends only upon your accepting it as you do your own, *whether you understand it or not.*

For opposites an important question is whether the partners feel *enhanced* or *diminished* by their differences. Satisfied opposites describe an atmosphere that encourages change and growth and—over time—an appreciation of the strengths of the other. Complementary couples demonstrate a generous reciprocity of their talents.

To be successful opposites, it is vital that you develop a healthy respect for the coexistence of love and conflict. You can love someone and disagree with that person without diminishing that love. (If you think you must agree all the time, to be in love, then you are at risk of being a doormat.) The problem is not in the fact that partners disagree but rather in their attitude while disagreeing. Differences that divide a couple can be quite trivial yet can escalate because both believe in the rightness of their interpretation, the universal acceptance of their interpretation, and the universal infallibility of their interpretation. This closed, self-centered perspective is derived from an individual frame of reference, excluding one's partner's reality.

Substantive change in relationships comes not through intense confrontation alone but rather from the decision to apply any insight that is a result of confrontation. Forward movement depends upon that insight, including a recognition of one's own contribution to any problems.

In order to love more fully, it is necessary to value the world of your opposite, even in those moments of confrontation. Ultimately all couples must learn that a true acceptance of the individuality of each partner is the only foundation upon which healthy love can be built. This means that each partner must recognize that he or she has had an image or fantasy of what was desired in a partner and that now that image is being held up for testing against the reality of the person they have chosen. This is often a very difficult moment for RBs. Yet it is through honoring your partner's perspective as fully as you do your own that you bridge the gap between you. Opposites communicate affection, love, intimacy, sexual desire, and passion in dissimilar ways. The more you respect these differences and their inherent strengths, the more likely you will be able to achieve a greater intimacy.

Respect is not an isolated event. It is an attitude woven throughout a loving relationship. This is stated beautifully in the words of Dennis Banks, the executive director of the American Indian Movement:

> For the Indian, "Love" does not begin when the lights go out or when pot or liquor is consumed, and it is not confined to the bedroom or any other hidden place.
>
> The way in which the Indian treats his wife throughout the marriage is the key to making him a superior lover.

His daily acts of kindness, consideration and respect for her demonstrate his love.

OFFERING COMPANIONSHIP. LBs are often accused of being self-centered or self-focused too much of the time. LBs do prefer their own company to the company of others but not necessarily for negative reasons. Able to spend long hours on individual projects, most LBs report childhoods in which they entertained themselves, growing up not associating happiness with companionship. Some preferred to do this from the beginning; others, left to their own company, coped with their loneliness by rejecting the need for friends and playmates. At some point *things* became more reliable, more constant, more interesting, and less of an emotional risk than people. Hobbies, reading, and other solitary activities, therefore, dominate the developmental years of LBs.

This fact creates a wedge in a relationship of opposites because RBs grow up depending upon others to make life more interesting. For them life is best experienced in the company of others or, at the very least, with a single companion. For an RB, companionship magnifies the quality of any experience. Witnessing the same event and then comparing perspectives with an LB partner add dimension to anything they share.

Because of this discrepancy, RBs often become the pursuers as they dog their LBs to join them. The RB is not only more dependent upon companionship to enhance the quality of a situation but also invested in the symbolic value of many events that don't even occur to an LB.

BRAD (RB): Guess what today is.
KEN (LB): I believe it is Tuesday.
(RB): I mean, the date. Think about the date.
(LB) *(looking at the newspaper)*: It's the tenth.
(RB): *Yes!* So I'm making a special dinner for us.
(LB): Because it's the tenth?
(RB): I can't believe you've forgotten.
(LB): Forgotten what? What's the tenth of May?
(RB): You don't know?
(LB): I know what *June* tenth is.

(RB): It's our eleven-month anniversary.

(LB): What does *that* mean? Who celebrates their eleven-month anniversary?

(RB) *(stomping out)*: You're so unromantic!

An LB does not expect taking a walk to be meaningful in itself. A walk can be potentially interesting only if it is going somewhere the LB wants to go or terminates in some activity he or she enjoys. Because an LB does not look at the world through the same interconnected lens of the RB, the metaphoric value of strolling with their lives momentarily intertwined does not register.

BETTY (RB): Let's go for a walk and talk.

PAM (LB): Where do you want to go?

(RB): Anywhere.

(LB): What do you want to talk about?

(RB): Anything.

(LB): Just tell me what you want.

(RB): To be together.

(LB): To do *what?*

(RB): Forget it.

You can see that Betty is frustrated and that Pam is puzzled. Betty (RB) enjoys the simple companionship of a partner on a walk. There is no particular destination because it is the act of being together that is satisfying. Pam (LB) doesn't understand what the problem is. By asking where Betty wants to go and what she wants to talk about, Pam is assessing the *safety* of the situation. Pam does not want to be stranded at the end of a long pier, with no distractions, while Betty begins a litany of all the issues she has with their relationship. Betty says "a walk"; Pam hears "a trap." Betty says "anywhere"; Pam feel anxious. Betty says "anything"; Pam thinks "too open-ended" and feels vulnerable. It is necessary for each to be willing to appreciate how this moment feels *from her partner's perspective,* whether it makes sense or not. It would be a mistake to stop and debate the merits of each position, for each is correct in terms of each partner's reality.

There is great value in just sharing the same space quietly with one's partner, but that value is lost when the LB jumps into her head to think about what she could be doing elsewhere. It is as if thinking, worrying, and obsessing give LBs permission to sit "doing nothing" with their RBs. On the outside they appear to be involved with sharing the moment, but on the inside they are quite busy. Unfortunately this mental activity takes the LB away from the here and now and robs the RB of authentic companionship, leaving only the LB's physical presence and the *illusion* of sharing time together.

To be a good companion, the LB needs to become more comfortable with the concept of nondoing so that time spent just being together is not viewed as wasted because it seems nongoal-oriented or nonproductive. There *is* a goal: companionship. This is too vague for the LB, too ill-defined for his or her understanding, and therefore uninviting. If the LB is a man, he must contend with additional pressures. Male socialization demands that men's time be active and productive; "empty" time is traditionally regarded as female and useless. Female LBs who modeled themselves after their fathers or other male figures may also experience the same internal discomfort with such "idle" activity.

As both men and women grow toward an absence of gender expectations, they are able to reclaim and integrate parts of themselves that were lost in the process of socialization. They can then become more authentic companions. Each partner can look forward to participating in the other's life and will actually become *richer* through engagement with the other, by being introduced to new ideas, experiences, people, and adventures.

DEMONSTRATING CONCERN. Another way of manifesting love is to communicate that what happens to your partner is of interest and concern to you. At those times when your partner falls ill, has bad luck or the blues, share comforting words, words that may have appealed to *you* when you've been in a similar situation.

RBs are usually skilled at voicing concern, related to their ease with empathy. They can deliver it, and they hope for it in return. What they get is often something else. We cannot address the feelings of others any better than those of our own. Because an LB is frequently cut off from his or her emotions, it can be very difficult for him or her to respond appropriately to what an RB is feeling.

LBs, being more comfortable with things than with words, demonstrate their concern in entirely different ways. Some of the most common are: fixing things that are broken and may present a safety hazard (leaking heaters, flat tires, frayed wiring, locks); providing necessities (like batteries, flashlights, smoke detectors, alarms); offering lessons (how to change your oil, tie a good knot); and giving suggestions to increase efficiency (better way of getting from A to B, maximizing software). An LB will repair something or attend to a promised task as a way to say, "I'm sorry . . . forgive me . . . are we OK again?"

Because these gestures involve inanimate objects, RBs do not consider them legitimate ways of demonstrating concern. This results in RBs' feeling unloved or uncared for and LBs' feeling hurt when their offers are rejected or unappreciated. Love, support, and concern take many forms; it is imperative that RBs understand this, or they will continue to feel cut off. Without a sense of caring by each for the other, a gap develops. It is equally important for LBs to learn forms of concern and comfort that involve themselves in more intimate, less practical ways in order to close the gap.

EARNING AND GIVING TRUST. Trust plays a very important role in love relationships. Researchers have found that it is a vital ingredient in sexual satisfaction as well. An individual who believes that his or her partnership is held together by a fragile bond will seek continuous reassurance, usually driving the loved one away. Security, on the other hand, brings the freedom to enjoy the relationship and the ability to "relax into" its embrace. This security frees energy that can be directed to other pursuits, placing less dependence on the relationship for a sense of well-being.

There is a difference between spontaneous and impulsive behavior. Because RBs are more spontaneous than LBs, they are at risk for being more impulsive as well. Like spontaneity, impulsive acts are not thought out. Unlike spontaneity, impulsive behavior is potentially damaging because it does not take into account the effects of the words or the act on other people.

An LB leads a more cautious life. This means that it might at first be difficult for an LB to trust an RB whose behavior is at times disconcerting to the LB. Observing that the RB says whatever he or she thinks, it is frightening to think of one's privacy possibly being shattered by lack of forethought. It is RBs, not LBs, that walk around with a "foot in the mouth."

It is the danger in impulsivity, not healthy spontaneity, that frightens LBs. LBs are less likely to do something on a dare, engage in a one-night stand, or gamble. This is not to say they don't. LBs, like RBs, are not immune to impulsive disorders, shoplifting, alcoholism, gambling, etc. When depressed, LBs, as well as RBs, are at risk for engaging in behaviors they might not consider at other times.

Trust is also an issue for RBs. They do not fear the impromptu dance on a table as much as they fear an LB's "forgetting" old hurts and repeating them. There is an uneasiness that robs them of the freedom to trust their partners fully. Because LBs place less significance on *relationships between things* and assign more importance to *facts about things,* they make the mistake of thinking that when a personal slight, an act of poor judgment, or a harmful gesture is over, it is forgotten.

To an LB, tending to think in polarities, an event either is happening or has ended. There is no gray area, nothing hovering between the two. The most common example would be romantic involvement with someone outside a significant relationship. Once it ends, it ends for the LB. The LB is angered that the topic continues to surface, frustrated that it can't be put to rest, and hurt that what appeared to be forgiveness by the RB seems to have been only a shallow gesture.

Insecurity—the sense of a fragile bond—can arise from within a person who mistrusts *all* relationships, or it can be caused by a partner's devious behavior and dishonesty. People who are lied to become anxious, overreact, and become dependent upon information to keep them apprised of their relative situation. Their partners resent the "interrogation" and cut off the communication, increasing their panic.

If the lying is chronic, as in relationships in which one partner is chemically dependent, a person can become paranoid and believe that he or she is being lied to when that isn't the case. In these relationships insecurity is always present along with a sense of "being crazy" in the partner who is told one thing and observes another. "Sanity" returns when one's partner resumes an authentic, honest relationship.

Lying in intimate relationships is a power play which eventually does permanent damage to the bond. Again, if we use the example of extramarital romantic involvement by an LB, the RB knows the event is in the past but frequently relates it to events in the present. Anything can trigger old feelings in the RB and connect them to current ones. For the RB there is *always a pattern at work,* weaving the past and present into something that he or she can relate to. By looking at it through different lenses and in different seasons of the mind, the RB begins to put it into place to his or her satisfaction.

Opposites need to discuss their feelings about what constitutes a breach of fidelity. Too often they enter into a relationship assuming their partner holds the same set of rules. The discovery of a discrepancy is always a very painful moment for at least one of the partners.

For one couple I worked with, *everyone* outside the marriage was considered a potential lover, and even having dinner alone with someone else was experienced as a betrayal. For another couple, each partner took a separate vacation with the knowledge that explicit, physical, sexual involvement with someone else would be a breach of trust. A third couple had agreed upon boundaries that included having sex with others, but becoming *emotionally* involved was considered an act of unfaithfulness.

Again, each couple has to define for themselves, after discussion, what constitutes their code of fidelity. It is far more important that the partners agree than it is for society to agree with the partners. In some cases one partner will insist on a behavior that is uncomfortable for the other partner either to include or to exclude. This is a serious problem, and counseling is indicated, because in healthy relationships partners aren't expected to compromise their values. Doing so almost always creates a personal crisis.

For trust to exist, freedom must also. There is no value in trust that is never exercised. Like a muscle that atrophies without use, trust is meaningless in a relationship that is bound by rules and regulations and restrictions on each other's lives. This is not to say that most couples don't elect to have monogamous relationships but rather that fidelity loses its value if partners are never in the position of exercising it. If one partner is working in the home and isolated from opportunity, then his or her trustworthiness is not challenged as often as the partner who is in the workplace or may travel frequently. The challenge is in saying no when you have the opportunity to say yes.

Fidelity is something you do for the sake of your relationship, not because your mate requires it. Faithfulness is a decision that is practiced, not just a philosophy about boundaries. The partner who chooses to be faithful is clear that having sexual fantasies and acting on sexual fantasies are two different things. He or she consciously decides which impulses will be engaged and with whom. Of course, drugs and alcohol can cloud this perspective and make responsible decision making an impossibility.

Frank Pittman, in his book *Private Lies: Infidelity and the Betrayal of Intimacy,* tells us: "Honesty is the central factor in intimacy. . . . There is no truth that is as destructive as any lie [p. 281]." He goes on to warn readers that sharing a secret with someone outside a marriage—and keeping that secret from your spouse—are dangerous because they produce a bond between the two who share the secret and distance between the marital partners.

PROTECTING RELATIONSHIPS. Once a relationship or marriage has been established, it can easily be neglected. Almost any excessive habit can seduce us away from time spent with our partner. Drinking, smoking, tennis, watching television, working, gambling, jogging, sailing, cleaning, reading, and even "tinkering out in the garage" all can make it seem as if our partner has a lover who pleases him or her in mysterious ways. In traditional relationships one partner is more responsible for the emotional support of the partnership itself. Couples today are frequently dual-career, with both spending large amounts of time and energy at work. This means that partners must be more *intentional* and protective of couple time.

Protecting your relationship means you must: consider it a priority, create boundaries between you and external stressors (including invasion by friends and relatives), plan its future together, maintain the standards of fidelity you've agreed upon as a couple, and guard against isms such as workaholism, alcoholism, and any other ism that threatens it. Relationships in America are under constant bombardment by outside stressors, as Paul Pearsall, in his book *Super Marital Sex,* informs us: "American marriage is a socially reactive unit more than it is an intimate active relationship that governs itself ... we have become a 'beeperized' culture, never really out of touch as long as a little tone reminds us that a person out there needs us more urgently than the person here with us now [p. 17]."

Sam Keen, again in *Fire in the Belly,* considers the possibility that "marriage may provide the best hospital for our ancient wounds." He reminds us that as children we carry with us an innocent expectation that we are "lovable in our entirety." This, of course, is an illusion, as our parents eventually love us *conditionally.* Keen sees hope, ". . . for unconditional love does not die, it only lies dormant. When we marry it springs to life again . . . The alchemy of unconditional love that heals us only takes place when [partners], knowing the best and worst of each other, finally accept what is unacceptable in the other, burn their bridges, and close off their escape routes [p. 222]."

Daily life is rife with unpleasant events that register on a scale from minor irritation to rage. We cannot express our anger toward our superiors at work; it is impolite to become rude to strangers; our friends might become offended if we let loose. This leaves our significant other—our beloved partner—as the safest target when frustrations mount. It is important to protect your relationship from being used for this purpose, although it is tempting, because our partners are available and in committed bonds with us, which provides an illusion of insurance against abandonment.

In this success-oriented society, we need to protect our significant relationships from our own desires and competitiveness as well as outside pressures. We are reminded of this by Irving and Suzanne Sarnoff in their book *Love-Centered Marriage in a Self-Centered World:*

... lifelong loving requires mates to give much more of themselves than they have ever given to anyone before. It tests to the utmost their courage, empathy, patience, and ability to tolerate psychological ambiguity and stress. It draws without limit on their capacity for insight and their willingness to change. It confronts them with the challenge of constantly finding new ways of augmenting their intimacy—while earning a living, raising children, relating to other people, and absorbing the rapid shifts in social expectations men and women are supposed to enact ... [p. 5].

ACCEPTING IMPERFECTION. G. Peter Fleck, in his book *The Blessings of Imperfection,* quotes Lewis Thomas's book *The Medusa and the Snail.* I present it here for those LBs who find themselves trapped in a prison of perfectionism, bounded by the constricting polarities of good or bad, all or nothing.

We have evolved scientists ... and so we know a lot about DNA, but if our kind of mind had been confronted with the problem of designing a similar replicating molecule ... we'd never have succeeded. We would have made one fatal mistake: our molecule would have been perfect. ... The capacity to blunder slightly is the real marvel of DNA. Without this special attribute we could still be anaerobic bacteria and there would be no music. [p. 3].

We humans are built to make mistakes, coded for error. ... Humans are the only creatures on this earth to whom it is given to be aware of the wrongness, the error, the imperfection in themselves ... [pp. 6–7].

All of us, including our partners, are stuck with living with imperfect people. Successful opposites adjust to this reality. To continue in long-term love relationships, partners must accept the thoughtlessness, selfishness, and pettiness in each other. To give up on a relationship when this reality first hits home is to pass up an opportunity for personal growth and deny the capacity for people to change. Of course, any of these everyday annoyances can be indicators of more serious issues, such as pathological self-interest and emotional abuse. The degree and frequency would need to be determined.

Successful opposites keep in mind that people are limited and finite, that all humans are capable of error. It is precisely because we *are* fallible that honest differences can become an opportunity for growth rather than a needless power struggle. In contrast, those in dysfunctional relationships believe the truth is absolute, that there is only *one* perception, position, memory, conclusion, etc. Thus any differing viewpoint must be challenged; the "wrong" partner must be "corrected."

Healthy couples allow an uncertainty to exist, making it possible for the partners to be differing but "correct," eliminating the need for a power struggle and a victor. Healthy couples tolerate one another's foibles and often use a sense of humor to cope with them on a day-to-day basis. But partners who must maintain an aura of perfection have to protect themselves from being seen, known, understood; in doing so, they lose the capacity for intimacy.

COMMUNICATING INTIMATELY. Erving Polster, writing in *Every Person's Life Is Worth a Novel,* reminds us: "We use stories to join our lives with those of other people [p. 30]." He goes on to demonstrate that we tend to present abstractions to each other—rather than fill in with interesting details—and that in doing so, we do not offer enough to engage our partners. But, he cautions, details are not enough.

Hard data are not what intimate conversation is made of; *details about the self* are what engage and interest. This is why RBs like to flesh out conversation by asking questions. LBs can load their talk with details, but the details are often dry and unrelated to the internal world of the LB. If an LB does not understand this, he or she can spend hours talking and then become hurt when the RB looks bored.

Uninterest in an RB is a signal to the LB that the conversation is losing its intimate quality. A clue for the LB is to ask, "Would I be telling this to just anybody?" If the answer is yes, then it probably isn't intimate, and it probably doesn't meet the RB's requirements for closeness. Look for "Information Exchange" in the Exercises Section. This will help get things rolling.

The goal of an LB when communicating is to be precise; that of an RB is to connect. There is room for both of these desires when people communicate intimately. Loving behavior requires a tolerance for things you do not understand, that you are not in agreement with, and that may not even make sense to you. Intimate communication comes from deep within the self and speaks to a place deep within your partner. To be willing to go to that place, each partner must be flexible enough to look at his or her strengths and weaknesses and be courageous enough to share them.

LBs are at a disadvantage when communicating intimately. The primary problem is not that LBs lack sensitivity but rather that they lack awareness and the vocabulary to describe inner experiences. The Exercises Section contains a "Feelings Vocabulary" which may be of help.

Remember that LBs are "wired" to bypass many of the messages that could be of benefit when relating external experience to internal awareness. Many events simply do not register at a conscious level. For the LB most bits of information do not automatically relate to others. It becomes the responsibility of the LB to look for connections; professional counseling can help this process along.

Experiences, to an LB, are appreciated as singular phenomena to be understood one at a time. For instance, an LB might be dancing to music but will not simultaneously be aware of whether he or she feels sad, nostalgic, or flooded with joy because it is already more than enough to be listening *and* dancing. Later when the couple discuss the experience, since feelings may not have registered, they cannot be communicated to a partner.

To reveal what one fears deeply in her soul or what one feels most in his heart, a partner will need to be willing to risk being vulnerable. If an LB is living in her head, cut off from her senses and feelings, she risks not being fully available in intimate situations. Emotions help promote intimate communication. *Every problem, large or small, has an emotional component to it,* yet strong emotions of any kind can lead to impulsive action and impede a couple's ability to deal with their differences. Even "positive" emotions can damage a relationship. This is the principle behind the current emphasis on "codependent" behavior: giving of oneself to the extreme.

Many partners share a history of alienation from their families of origin and are surprised to discover that in a love relationship old, infantile feelings, needs, and expectations come back. But if an RB is flooded with feeling and is not sensitive to the degree of emotion and the timing of the communication, he is at risk for overwhelming his LB partner. At this point he might want to find a "good ear" outside the relationship. Emotion and reason can coexist, but as with any other extremes, too much emotion clouds judgment, and too much logic impairs intimacy. The solution is a healthy respect for both and a balanced dose of each.

The most important aspect of communicating intimately is that it be done with a respect for the differences in how each partner receives and gives information. Intimacy is impossible without conflict, but for some opposites their cognitive styles and ways of relating are so different that little seems to exist between them but friction, impatience, and irritability. Their *attitude* toward their differences—not their differences—creates a barrier to intimacy. These partners have not found their differences to be mutually enriching, capable of eliciting untapped potential in each other. They do not know how to consider their relationship an adventure into expanded awareness.

Another barrier to intimate communication is erected by adults who become stuck in rigid sex roles and accept culturally prescribed notions about what is male and female. This leads to synthetic relationships between people who are overly invested in their femininity or masculinity. True intimacy frees partners from needing to concern themselves with such issues.

Because RBs show a preference for relationship, intimacy, and empathic communication, couples with a high *combined* level of RB preferences (RB/RB) report the greatest intimacy. Those with a high *combined* level of LB preferences (LB/LB) experience the lowest levels of intimacy, but it is not an issue for them because intimacy is not considered a priority.

In a partnership of opposites lack of intimate communication can contribute to a pervasive sense of loneliness for the RB. This is caused by the LB's inability to disclose personal information and respond appropriately to that which the RB shares. This tendency is most evident in an LB who is characteristically described as "hard to get to know" and who floods conversation with data, never actually revealing his or her inner self. The RB must remember that the LB is not consciously "withholding" but rather that he or she simply doesn't think in those terms; the language of intimacy is a foreign language in the LB's world. Over time, by adopting some of the RB's behavior, an LB can move toward greater intimacy and contribute to increasing the RB's satisfaction.

Successful opposites remember that when they talk with each other not only are facts—and feelings about facts—important, but the choices of words and the timing also play a role. Above all, these partners are respectful of their partners' different way of communicating and regard accommodation to that style a necessary, and loving, behavior.

EXPRESSING/RESPONDING TO SEXUAL DESIRE. According to Lonnie Barbach, in her book *For Each Other,* learning about sex by watching movies or reading romance novels is like learning to be a doctor by watching *General Hospital* or an attorney by watching *Perry Mason*. She tells us that learning through these fantasies raises expectations beyond reality and leads to chronic frustration. She also points out that since negative experiences are never part of fantasies, when one *does* arise for a couple, it can create a needless bout of panic. Of course, in these fantasies the partners are always perfectly in tune with each other. The timing, lights, mood, and weather all are perfect. The partners are energized, excited, well dressed, and well groomed. As disconcerting as they are, these fantasy figures have something in common with you who are opposites.

Because of their different ways of being in the world, opposites often report high levels of chemistry. Each appears to be—in spite of the conflict—truly fascinated with the other. Everything about the partner is a mystery, and mysterious things are sexy. Opposites can present a challenge to each other, as they attempt to move through the stages of sexual intimacy. Yet these couples know a difference that creates conflict outside the bedroom often becomes an asset between the sheets.

Everyone grows up in a household where some type of sexual attitude prevailed. In their book *The Intimate Circle: The Sexual Dynamics of Family Life,* Miriam and Otto Ehrenberg describe four styles parents use. Our parents or parent figures were: (1) *repressed* (the aim was to control all forms of sexual behavior, and a strong sense of shame was associated with any sexual activity); (2) *avoidant* (sex was accepted as part of life but never talked about, giving the impression there was something wrong with it, yet no one ever directly said so); (3) *compulsive* (no boundaries were developed, and uninhibited adults had difficulty controlling their desires; sexual expression may have been forced instead of allowing children to discover it in their own time); or (4) *expressive* (sex was regarded as life-enhancing, and there were age-appropriate discussions).

Most partners share similar attitudes, but what might seem like a minor difference can turn out to be very disruptive. For instance, RBs, being expressive of all their feelings, can be too much for LBs at times. Yet their unpredictable, impulsive, and emotional behavior—often alarming to an LB—can spice up an otherwise boring evening. Given the right circumstances, that expressiveness can be a turn-on for an LB partner.

When the RB's expressiveness comes up against the cautious, guarded, predictable LB, the RB is hoping for some fireworks and the LB is hoping things don't fly out of control. They are at cross-purposes, and unless they can meet in the middle and attend to each other's desires, a mutually satisfying sexual union is not possible. (The key word is "mutually.")

In the early stage of desire and pursuit the LB is at a disadvantage because the role of lover is not a comfortable one for him or her. As noted earlier, it requires creating a fantasy between the two partners, and fantasies develop in the right brain. At this stage the RB's expectations are high for being "swept away." Preferring to remain well grounded in reality, the LB is out on a limb when trying to be someone he or she is not. There is little of the theater in an LB; the act of pretending is foreign (silly) behavior.

A common complaint is that the LB finally says something romantic (after great anguish and simple force of will), but the RB is disturbed because the words sound wooden or unauthentic. At this point the RB must let go of the "ideal" and accept the fact that an LB cannot deliver the right message in the same manner as the lead character in a romance novel. The RB needs to take the message in, appreciate the effort, enjoy the *idea,* and respond as if the world's greatest lover had just uttered it.

If that seems too artificial to the RB, remember that you are asking your LB to be someone he or she is not—a natural seducer—so the RB needs to get into the spirit of pretending, too. This will increase the chances of your hearing more. If the RB criticizes the delivery, that will guarantee that the rejection-sensitive LB will not try again.

Pretending is only one aspect of playing. Another aspect of play is an awareness of, and utilization of, one's senses. LBs spend so much time in rational thought that they are often poorly tuned into the senses of touch, taste, and smell. By giving more attention to these and bringing them into lovemaking, an LB can create a richer experience for an RB. You can bring the senses into bed by: massage, sensuous foods, incense, candles, use of body oils, choice of fabrics, and selection of certain kinds of music.

The greatest stretch or challenge for an LB would be to communicate verbally the pleasure derived in seeing, hearing, touching, smelling, and tasting the RB. The stretch for an RB would be to let the LB do this at the latter's own pace and with words that are comfortable for the LB, without improving on the LB's content or delivery by offering constructive criticism or voicing disappointment. If each continues to do only that which is easy or familiar, nothing changes, and the polarities remain, decreasing the satisfaction for one partner, if not both. When each partner takes on his or her personal challenge, they meet in the middle.

An LB can be too focused on nonerotic thoughts while engaging in lovemaking. These distractive, obsessive messages keep the LB cognitively centered and prevent his or her total involvement. When this happens, the LB needs to refocus on sensations or to shift into right-brain thinking in the form of sexual fantasy. Fantasy is a method of bypassing cognition. It resides in the right brain, where passion waits. Problems arise not because desire is not present but rather because the person learns to turn off at the point when the first erotic sensation is felt or anticipated. For LBs this may be due to "overloading" as they are trying to juggle multiple sensations and messages simultaneously, something that is far easier for the RB to do.

If one partner is always the active one, he or she won't have the chance to enjoy the pleasure of being made love to. If one partner is always passive, that person won't know the erotic experience that comes from his or her partner's response. Successful opposites report they aren't stuck in polarized roles and instead comfortably shift back and forth between them to prevent the boredom that arises from predictable patterns in lovemaking. Our society teaches us that stimulation comes from "out there" (television, alcohol, drugs, pornography). Opposites who report mutually satisfying sexual relationships don't buy into that myth. They indicate that the key is in each partner's taking responsibility within themselves to keep the boredom out.

In her book *Right-Brain Sex,* Carol Wells informs us that: "Boredom in relationships is probably the most extensive and serious challenge facing us. . . . Monogamy, all too often, gets turned into monotony [p. 13]." She reminds us that in the beginning of a relationship—in the courting stage—we function mostly with our right brain and feel overwhelming passion and excitement, but later, after we get settled into our lives, ". . . dual-career couples [have] an even greater need to engage in 'transition' time between the office and the bedroom. This allows one to cross from the left-brain world of work over to the right-brain where erotic images dwell [p. 27]. . . . Really great sex occurs when we allow ourselves to enter a . . . state in which we abandon self-consciousness [p. 35]."

The LB has to work hard to keep intrusive thoughts from interfering with the erotic nature of lovemaking. This can create in the RB a sense that the LB is withdrawing and may cause concern, because RBs seek to "merge" emotionally during sex.

Sexual fantasies are a strong aphrodisiac that triggers arousal. They serve to *maintain* arousal, as they shut off rumination about the office and other nonerotic thoughts. But imaginative and erotic images are products of our right brain and difficult for LB partners to create.

If the LB is a woman, she has other forces working against her. Not until twenty years ago did researchers even realize women had sexual fantasies. Before the sweeping changes brought about by the women's liberation movement, without society's "permission," females had to keep such thoughts to themselves or lose the approval of others. More recent evidence indicates that more than 90 percent of women engage in sexual fantasy. Even with the more liberal attitude people have in general, many women still have difficulty being intentional about their sexuality. Conjuring up fantasies is therefore regarded at a deep level as something "nice girls" don't do.

In actuality, fantasizing itself is not a problem. Problems arise when it interferes with the relationship or spills over into other areas of a person's life. The most serious problems develop when—as with other mind-altering behaviors like drinking or using drugs—there is a compelling need to act on the impulse and an inability to stop.

It is not the content of the fantasy that triggers a problem; it is the function. Sexual fantasy used to augment the satisfaction of lovemaking is healthy. If it is consistently being used to cope with anxiety, stress, depression, to avoid your partner or other things, professional counseling is suggested.

For RBs who are easily threatened by any "disconnect," discovering that their LBs are fantasizing about someone else can trigger an impulsive argument around the old theme of "If you really loved me . . ." In its purest form, romance contains fantasy, but only about the beloved.

Knowing this, an RB may test the relationship by asking, "What are you thinking?" or "Do you think about me when we are making love?" The RB must understand that fantasy does not play as large a role in the life of the LB as in that of the RB and that if fantasy does occur during lovemaking, the RB will benefit because it is keeping the LB tuned in to desire instead of being preoccupied, which is his or her natural state.

Because of their investment in the romantic nature of things, RBs prefer to have partners who can read their minds. The ideal situation for them is to have partners who will automatically know when, how, and where to seduce and satisfy them. Such a fantasized person is imagined to be very confident, sexually savvy, and capable of sweeping the RB away. This places a great deal of responsibility on the LB. An RB needs to remember that just the fact that an LB doesn't glitter doesn't mean the RB hasn't struck gold.

Having to "instruct" partners has no appeal to RBs because they believe that true romantics are very indirect about their needs. But RBs need to appreciate that LBs delight in facts. An LB *wants* information about how and when because this reduces the chance of doing something wrong, which he or she wants to avoid at all cost. Most LBs are willing to learn, since they take a practical approach to lovemaking as they do toward everything else. It makes sense to them that if you want something to happen, it is best to *know* how to make that happen, not to guess. Of course, this gets the cold shoulder from an RB. "If you really loved me, you'd know what I like" is the lament of the RB. "If you really want pleasure, then you'll need to tell me what you like" is the LB's response. It is important that *both* partners let each other in on what they like and don't like, as "unromantic" as that may be.

Another important contribution is using touch in ways that are not goal-oriented. LBs are oriented to solutions. They are linear and like to get from A to B. This is helpful in achieving orgasm, but it isn't always necessary for touch to be productive. Touch for the sake of touch is an important part of lovemaking for both partners. It is soothing, comforting, sensuous, and connecting, without any sense of pressure or performance.

Because LBs prefer to focus on one thing at a time and can be very intense and determined when they do, during lovemaking they can become very involved in the mechanics of sex. There is both an advantage and a disadvantage to this for the RB. It can be extremely pleasurable to have the right buttons punched in the right order and have fireworks result, but it can also seem impersonal and robotlike if the LB doesn't occasionally break the concentration and acknowledge the RB by saying his or her name, looking in the lover's eyes, or expressing pleasure. These gestures create intimacy when things may have become too "technical" because it acknowledges the "wholeness" of each other, rather than remain genitally focused.

This is difficult for an LB to do because it means attempting to do several things simultaneously. This is almost impossible for a *very* left-brain individual. So the LB periodically may need to break away—actually pull back—and "take in" his or her partner "as a person." Because the RB is always focusing on connecting, this is already happening for him or her. Remember that successful opposites combine the science and art of lovemaking.

When making love, because of their tendency to emphasize the symbolic value of events, RBs have a goal of merging with their LBs. The ideal situation is to "become one." LBs, on the other hand, have a very strong sense of independence and prefer a degree of separation to a blending of souls. There is, with an LB, always a little bit held back. This does not in itself need to be a problem, but RBs can create a crisis by insisting that their LBs feel the same way about sex and jumping to the conclusion that an LB's not "merging" is an indication that they are mismatched.

Another concern to partners is the issue of desire. All couples experience a discrepancy in desire at some point in their relationship, either in specific situations or as a pattern. Couples always ask, "What is 'normal' desire?" This is, of course, an entirely individual matter. Yet for RBs it can be a crucial matter because they are so invested in the romantic aspects of connection.

What happens to chemistry over time? The less we know about our partner—in the beginning of the relationship—the easier it is to believe that he or she has the attributes we *want* them to have. After we have shared real experiences on a daily basis over the years, after we have been exposed to all aspects of a partner's personality, it is more difficult to attribute fancied behavior to him or her.

Helen Singer Kaplan, M.D., Ph.D., head of the human sexuality program at the New York Hospital-Cornell Medical Center, has coined the phrase "hot monogamy" to describe fidelity turned way up by chemistry, even after people have spent many years together. Successful opposites know that passion is the best aphrodisiac and that passion within a committed relationship is the best aphrodisiac of all.

Romantic RBs work hard to keep passion (chemistry) alive. They know that "mystery" contributes to chemistry. During the evolution from courtship to everyday life together as partners, layers and layers of information are peeled away, and our lover moves from being an unknown to a known. To become *too* known destroys the mystery: Sharing bathroom time or flossing in each other's company dampens the fires of desire. Build in a little privacy to keep the mystery alive.

Another way to keep chemistry a part of your relationship is to keep aesthetics alive. Beware of the tendency to dress up for work, guests, and social events but to wear the same tattered, stained, and baggy outfit at home alone with your love companion or, worse, when you go out.

It is one thing to look like crud while doing a cruddy job like changing the oil in your car, cleaning the oven, or organizing the attic. It is not necessary to look like crud when being a companion in your home. There is nothing wrong with dressing comfortably after work and on your days off. Find some things that feel and look good; these then become your "play" clothes, into which you change after you've worked all day (in or outside the home).

The diminishment of chemistry is probably not as significant an issue for the LB partner, who finds comfort in the known and predictable aspects of a relationship. But if the RB is concerned about it, certainly both need to discuss the matter. It if matters to one, it matters to the relationship.

The good news is that you don't have to wait for sexual desire in order to initiate or respond. You only have to be willing to be engaged in the process, willing to investigate the possibility, willing to play, to embark on an intimate adventure. Successful opposites don't let their differences stop them from doing just that.

SELECTING
A LIFE
PARTNER

I was so cold
I almost got married.

—*SHELLY WINTERS*

With the proliferation of AIDS, more men and women are seriously seeking monogamous, long-term, committed relationships. Although some individuals say they prefer to continue playing the field, in the privacy of the therapy hour they confess their goal is eventually to find someone special. It seems that most of us want to be part of a twosome; we see the world as an ark.

As society becomes more technologically oriented, people feel alienated, displaced, and even *re*placed. A love relationship is a buffer between a seemingly uncaring society and the individual; it is insurance against the existential reality of separateness, an oasis in a crazy world.

Whether you are an RB or an LB, if you do not have a partner at the present time or you are in the early stages of a relationship, you may be asking yourself how one finds the *right* partner. Romantic mythology tells us that we'll "know" when he or she comes along. We want to believe that love will just find us, that it is some kind of event way beyond our control.

There are two problems with this theory. First, successful relationships are not solely dependent upon connecting with the "right" person, just as breaking up does not necessarily mean he or she was the "wrong" person. There are, however, people who are better candidates for long-term commitment, and this chapter is designed to help you identify them.

The second problem is the belief that love is something that seeks us out, finding us at strange moments. In reality love is something *created* between two people. It is demanding, takes effort to sustain, and is worth every hour.

That other stuff, that swept-away stuff, isn't about love. It's about being "in love," about infatuation, those overwhelming, delicious feelings that invade every pore and occupy every thought in the early days of a relationship. These are the feelings that fuel great poetry, but they are too fragile to support the weight of everyday life. That requires love. And love requires going deep. And going deep takes time.

Opposites *do* attract, but that doesn't mean that every attraction has the potential for a long-term partnership. There are many factors to consider, starting with your own expectations. When I reentered the world of dating following my divorce, I had a "never" list. I was *never* going to go out with a man who, among other things:

- Was younger than I
- Was less educated than I
- Earned less income than I

Having been traditionally socialized, I believed men were supposed to be more of anything I was: taller, older, more experienced, and more confident. This created a problem as I grew older, earned a graduate degree, and became financially independent. With each advance on my part, the pool of potential partners shrank. It became clear that my socialization was a handicap. With each restriction, each "never," I was knocking more and more men out of the running.

One evening, across a crowded room—or rather over chips and

dip—I was introduced to a man named Rick, who was *all* the items on my "never" list. If I had conformed to my socialization, we would never have had these past twelve years together . . . or the next fifty. How sexist I had been. How fortunate that Rick was enlightened enough to help me transcend my tunnel vision.

If you believe there are no good (unattached) men/women left out there, look at your own "never" list. How are you shrinking your own pool of potential partners? What stops you from dating someone younger/older, taller/shorter, disabled/able-bodied, nerdy/cool, obese/skinny or with different racial/ethnic roots? To help you organize your thoughts about seeking a mate, turn to the Exercises Section and complete "Finding a Life Partner."

Once you become serious about a potential life partner, other factors enter into the equation: common values, religious beliefs, life goals, etc. As you begin to explore each other's lives more deeply, mismatches are identified. But you eliminate candidates prematurely by having a rigid "never" list, preventing you from knowing those people beyond their "packaging."

Unfortunately advertising, soap operas, romance novels, movies, and MTV all have contributed to a "romantic ideal," which bears no resemblance to what is desirable in a life partner. The romantic ideal has a brief shelf life, often failing to last beyond the first argument, a serious illness, or an extra ten pounds. This ideal is dependent upon a strict code of behavior, places no value on facts, and creates a chronic sense of dissatisfaction because it is an illusion which cannot survive under the weight of everyday reality. It's terrific icing, but it ain't the cake.

So before you so quickly decide that guy looks too nerdy, that man is too heavy, that blind person wouldn't be much fun, or that woman's too old for you, remember you don't have to eliminate potential partners *before you've even met them.*

We've all observed that some people seem to find just the right persons while others become stuck in a negative cycle of selecting the wrong partners over and over again. Choosing the right partner isn't about luck; it's about information. When you have the right information and you act on it, the negative cycle stops. The information you need when selecting a life partner consists of:

- Facts, feelings, and thoughts about oneself
- Facts, feelings, and thoughts about the other person

When we make any decision, we make it with only partial data. We don't know everything we need to know; we can't make the perfect decision. Instead we make the best one we can. Obviously, the more information we have, the better the chance of making a choice that supports who we are and what we need.

Within every decision are three things to consider: thoughts (which include ideas, beliefs, opinions), facts, and feelings. Missing information about any one of these can create a problem later on. Right-brain partners, being heavily invested in feelings, tend to overlook glaring facts that, had they been noted earlier, might have spared them some pain. Left-brain partners may not realize until too late that they actually felt love for someone.

Information is power; information about *yourself* empowers *you.* There are questions you need to ask if you want to find a life partner with whom you can build a healthy, satisfying relationship. These are difficult questions that require you to look within and take an honest inventory of yourself. In addition, I urge you to ask a close friend to share beliefs, observations, and opinions about you. This might be uncomfortable; some things aren't easy to say—or listen to.

Even though it is risky, a true and intimate friend should be willing to give you the information you are seeking. It may seem odd that I am suggesting you ask someone else for information about *you,* but it is necessary to do so because we all have blind spots. Each of us is constructed in a way that doesn't allow us to be objective about ourselves; sometimes that's what friends are for.

We all have images of ourselves that we go to great lengths to preserve. That is what "defenses" are for. If you tell someone something that does not fit her experience of herself, she will defend against it. This is often true whether the information is positive or negative. If she thinks of herself as unattractive and you pay her a compliment, she will have difficulty taking this piece of information in; there is no place for it in her fixed concept of "self." This is why it is so easy for close friends and lovers to be in conflict over the most minor event. We're often not aware that something we've just said has threatened the other person's self-image. We do not know how others experience themselves but rather only how *we* experience *them*.

First, ask yourself each question, taking notes. Wait a week or so, and let the questions and responses sink in. These questions are only a guide. You may find that they trigger other questions of your own creation. What you ask determines what you discover. Some questions are directed only to you; they depend on your own internal process, to which no one else has access. Others are questions you can ask yourself and your friend as well.

Once you have chosen someone you believe knows you well enough to make informed comments, is courageous enough to take the risk of offending you, and is trusted enough not to hurt you intentionally, then you are ready to ask for feedback. Do whatever you can to make it safe for your friend to share with you. The following may be of help:

- Tell your friend ahead of time that you realize this is a very difficult favor you are asking and you appreciate the risk he or she is taking.
- Advise your friend that you may have strong feelings about the information, that you will take notes about what is shared, but that you will try not to respond to it. (This will be very difficult for some of you, especially if you have a tendency to become defensive or easily feel attacked. Remember, *you asked for this feedback.*)
- Write down a few key words about each piece of information. Tell yourself you are not going to respond to each of these; you are only going to record them and see what you can learn.
- When your friend is through, look at each item, and consider the possibility that your friend is right. Is there a grain of truth in what you've heard?

In talking with hundreds of clients, students, and friends over the years, I have found that the following questions seem important to ask:

- How satisfying have my relationships been? If I have selected partners who have been a good match, how did I contribute to this? If not, what role have I played in the problems that developed? (For a *real* challenge, discuss this with a former partner.)
- What do I hope to gain from a long-term relationship? What do I have to offer?
- How complete do I feel as a person? Am I hoping to find someone who is stronger, wealthier, better-looking, more ambitious, more intelligent, or more educated than I? Why? Am I hoping to find something in someone else that I can't find in myself? Instead of making my own success, am I hoping to share in someone else's? Do I need someone in order to feel whole myself?
- How strong is my identity? Do I hope to find someone so compatible that we can merge into "one"? Or do I fear being so close to someone that I may lose my sense of self?
- What kind of risk taker am I? Do I get involved in unhealthy risks? Do I seem to thrive on the excitement of the unknown, or do I dread the unfamiliar? What's the biggest risk I've taken? Why? What did I learn?
- How difficult is it for me to accept the fact that I can't change anyone else? Why do I feel threatened when others are different from how I would like them to be? What would I like to change about myself?
- How do I get in my own way? What do I do that prevents me from getting what I want? What do I seem to be afraid of? What do I seem to be avoiding?
- Am I still attached to anyone else in a way that prevents me from moving on and connecting again? Do I have ties (either negative or positive) that keep me bound to my past? Do I have any grief or unfinished business with a former partner? What do my past partners have in common? What information about my partners did I have, but chose to ignore, in the beginning of each relationship? Why?
- Do I have any unfinished business with either parent that might prevent me from being fully available to a partner? What do I want to do about this?
- What would be difficult for me to hear about myself, even though it was true? How does this affect the image I have of my-

self? Am I interested in letting go of that image? What would it take to do so?

- How much do I need to control others, the events in my life, and my environment? How does a need for control create problems for me? For others?
- Am I serious about developing a committed relationship? Am I ready? Where is the evidence that I am ready? What feels safe about it? What feels risky?
- Do I tend to look to others for my sense of worth? How much power do I give to others to make or break my day? How much do I need the attention and approval of others? How does this create a problem for me? For others?
- What do I feel shameful about? What do I feel guilty about? What would it take for me to forgive myself?
- Do I have any behaviors that seem to be out of my control? How do these create a problem for me? For others? How much do I want to change? Would I be changing for myself, out of my own need, or for others?
- How flexible am I? Do I have the maturity to negotiate rather than always demand things my way? How rigid is my concept of what men/women can, and should, do?
- How do I get my way? What kind of power do I have: direct (assertive) or indirect (aggressive, passive, manipulative)? Do I see myself as having little or no power in my life? What is the evidence to support this?

Your friend's feedback, combined with your own insight, will serve you well as you continue your search for a life partner. Of all the tools you possess, self-knowledge and self-love are the most important. Without these you will select unhealthy partners and construct unrewarding, possibly even harmful relationships. With self-knowledge, you will be more aware of how you are vulnerable, when you can count on yourself and when you can't, how you give your power away, what you tend to avoid, and what you *should* avoid.

NOTE: When your friend has done her part, if you disagree with her observations and opinions, if what she has shared with you totally fails to match your sense of yourself, one or two problems are operating: Either you bruise too easily and are unable to receive negative information about yourself without becoming blinded by your defenses, or you lack an intimate relationship with your friend and she doesn't really know you.

When selecting a life partner, in addition to facts, feelings, and thoughts about yourself, you need certain information about the other person before you can determine if he or she is a good candidate for a long-term relationship. Some of the above questions could be asked, but since this would seem like an interrogation, simply listening and observing can bring you most of the information you need.

A word of caution: During courtship we are all liars. Human nature dictates that we do whatever we can to attract. This usually means presenting ourselves in only positive terms. If we have a choice between being honest and maintaining another person's interest in us (and do not believe that we can achieve both), we often sacrifice authenticity. So asking questions isn't as helpful as simply watching and noting what we see. The more time we have with the other person, the more we can identify patterns of behavior as opposed to isolated responses. Some of these patterns are extremely important, yet we can become blind to even these, as all ex-partners know when they review their last relationships from a more objective vantage point.

When trying to decide if the person you are dating is a good candidate for life partner, consider the following questions. This process will require you to be more rational than romantic, and that will go against your nature, if you are an RB. However, a rational approach is called for when you are doing something as serious as selecting a life partner, especially if a more romantic, emotional approach has consistently resulted in disaster.

- How intelligent does this person have to be? If intelligence is important to you, don't confuse it with education or occupation. Many highly intelligent people lack college degrees. Some have (and even prefer) blue-collar jobs. Pay attention, instead, to how he thinks, how he expresses himself, and whether he seems interested in a variety of things and multiple viewpoints.

■ Does this person have to be creative? Creativity may also be a factor for you. But you may be looking for it only in the arts. It took me a long time to appreciate the creativity inherent in the process of scientific research, math, computer programming, and engineering. I ignored these professionals and concentrated on more "obvious" creative fields. What I discovered is that there are far more computer programmers than actors (increasing the pool of potentials) and that creativity can be expressed in very different ways.

■ How important is a sense of humor? A sense of humor helps if you're serious about a life partnership. There will be days when it will save you both. This should not be confused with the ability to tell a joke. Great comedy comes out of great pain; humor will help you transcend the minor insults and irritations inflicted by cohabitation. If she's a good candidate, she will use humor in times of stress as an emotional Band-Aid, as a buffer between the two of you and the hardness of life. If she uses it against you, at your expense, this is evidence of low self-esteem. Sarcasm is a form of hostility. Recognize the difference.

■ What do we have in common? It is important to share common interests. Our interests reflect our values. We spend time (and money) on what is important to us. He says he likes to read, but you notice he has only two books in his apartment, and they're both on serial killers. He says he loves pets, but his fish has been floating unnoticed for a week. He believes in doing volunteer work and is "concerned" about the planet, but he never really does anything about this. What you have is someone whose image of himself is all those things, but since life is what we *do,* they really are no part of him. He thinks of himself as more intellectual, more caring, and more involved than he is. No problem—unless you adopt the same belief rather than accept reality.

■ What about respect? She says she is a nice person who really likes people and can "relate to anybody." That sounds promising until you go out to dinner and she treats the waitress like her personal servant. Observe. How does she communicate with those older, younger, disabled, or of a different race, religion, or sexual orientation? How does she talk about them privately? If she seems very judgmental, you can expect her eventually to turn her critical eye on you. It won't matter that you are, by then, her significant other; through *her* lens *everyone* has faults. She is democratic, if nothing else. She describes herself as "real friendly" but "too busy" to make friends. An alarm should go off in your head. (Unfortunately lust/love renders us blind and deaf, so we fail to note these important bulletins.)

- How do you feel in his presence? Do you feel safe enough to let your guard down? Is there an invitation just to be yourself? Or do you feel a subtle pressure to be more or less than you really are? Do you find yourself censoring your behavior and squelching your spontaneity? Does there seem to be permission to express a variety of feelings or moods, or is there an insistence to be "up" or "on"? (Check to see if this pressure is from him or is internally driven, out of your own desire to sparkle.)

- Is there a sense of balance about your interactions, or is one of you consistently doing more than your share of initiating, planning, entertaining, talking, paying, revealing intimate details, apologizing? Look for any pattern that tells you responsibility is not being shared. This may not seem to be a problem for you, but it frequently turns out to be one later on; the information is all there early in the game if you are willing to be open to it.

NOTE: It is very difficult to accept this information if you have a history of failed relationships. That first bit of data that signals "All is not well" is very frightening to acknowledge. A voice says, "Oh, no. I can't believe I've chosen the wrong person again!" This disbelief can cause you to turn away from the evidence, denying what is before you, rather than accept that you may be making another mistake. Even though it is painful, *listen to the voice.* It is your own experience rising to counsel you. If you fear being alone, are desperate to be connected, you will discount its value and walk a well-worn path to a place you've been before . . . and swore you would never return.

- What do I want in a relationship? What is the evidence that it exists with this person? That it does not? If it is very important to you, better to admit it is not there than fool yourself. Time, and attention to patterns, are very important. If you prematurely unite, the missing piece may turn out to be so necessary that the relationship without it is unable to survive.

- Does she seem to like herself? Truly enjoy who she is? (Not so much self-focused as self-accepting.) Or does she seem to be trying to impress you with accomplishments and possessions? Does she appear to have any interests that are outside herself? How much of the conversation is directed to you and your interests? Is she genuinely focused on what you have to say? What is the evidence that she is capable of caring about you?

- Can I trust this person? After you have been together several times, it is important to begin to measure trust. Does he arrive when he says he will (dependability)? Does he remember things that are important to you and respect your request for privacy (confidentiality)? Can you count on his following through on an agreement you have (responsibility)? Is he able to admit when he's wrong (accountability)? Do you find yourself worrying about what he is doing when he's not with you (monogamy)? If he tells you that he can't be trusted or he doesn't trust anybody else, *believe him.* Trying to build a committed relationship with someone who can't trust—or whom *you* can't trust—is like driving a car with the brakes on.

- How dependent does she seem to be? Does she need to spend every hour with you? If you participate in an activity by yourself, does this threaten her? Is she too ready to please, lacking a sense of her own person? How well does she tolerate separations? How much does she want to know about your phone calls, time away from her, etc.?

NOTE: Possessiveness and jealousy are part of the romantic myth, but they have no place in committed long-term relationships. A person who has this much need to be merged with you lacks a strong sense of self. This will always cause a problem later. Being in such demand is terrific for the ego, but you will eventually resent the dependency and probably find it draining. It will be only a matter of time before you are doing all sorts of things to create distance—breathing room—between the two of you.

- How does this person describe himself or herself as a partner in previous relationships? Pay attention to whether he is lumping all his ex-partners into one category. Does he believe that they were all wrong and he has always been the victim? Does he go on and on about how he is always being hurt, dumped, put upon, etc.? Or is he able to appreciate that he participated in both the good and bad aspects of each encounter? What is he willing to admit to? If he claims that he had no clue that a relationship was ending, *believe him.* More important, note that this is a sign of his being invested more in the ideal than in reality, in what he wanted to see rather than in what actually was. It is also a sign of his not being skilled in intimate communication.

- How available is she? How interested is she in a committed long-term relationship? If she says she is "just looking" or "out to party," *believe her.* If she says she has never had much luck with monogamy, take it to heart. If she says she has been burned many times, is not trusting of relationships, and is difficult to love, *listen!* The information is there. You have a choice: To play Red Cross and rescue her from her painful history or to listen and move on. (If you are serious about a life partner, move on. If you are an incurable romantic, you will probably move in, get your heart crushed, and *then* move on.)

- She may be emotionally available, but is she truly free to enter into a relationship with you? Without hiring a private investigator, there is no absolute way of determining if someone is already in another partnership. However, a good test is to make plans for weekends and holidays and occasionally to throw out a spontaneous invitation. If you can't call her, but she can call you, you're probably sharing someone.

NOTE: If you discover that she is indeed already involved, and you are still interested, then you may be fooling yourself into thinking you are ready for a life partner. More likely, you yourself have doubts, and her involvement elsewhere provides a nice "safety net" until you can sort things out. It's not a crime to discover this about yourself, but use the information. Recognize that you are seeking something you're not ready for and that this is unfair not only to yourself but to anyone who connects with you, meanwhile, in hopes of seriously bonding.

- Does his behavior seem out of control? Does he seem impulsive? (NOTE: Being spontaneous is healthy and involves an awareness of, and respect for, others. Impulsive behavior, however, is immature and disregards the ramifications of one's actions.) Does he get violent? Does he consistently drink or use drugs to cope with problems or to alter his experience of himself and others? Does he have to be high to make love? Does he seem to make an exhibition of himself, having an inordinate need for attention? Can he pass up something he can't afford, or does he get deeper in debt with each desirable object? Do you see him as "charming" or "cute" when others think he is a "pain"? Does his life seem out of control, in a constant state of crisis? If any of these are present, is he aware? Is he interested in changing? Is he getting help? If not, is he willing to do so as a condition of your becoming more involved?
- How attached does she seem to be to her ex? Does she keep talking about him or her? A common mistake is to think that if the person is complaining, this means his or her old relationship is really over, and he or she is now ready to love again and reconnect. But she can be *negatively* attached to an ex and be bound as if they were still a couple. The reactivity, the anger, the resentments keep the old relationship alive. Look for a neutrality as opposed to continuing complaints. Anyone who is still obsessed by so many thoughts (good or bad) of an old partner is not ready for the development of a new relationship.

There are only so many questions you can ask and only so many observations you can make when selecting a life partner. At some point you will have to make a decision. Because you will not have *all* the information you need, you will have to make a leap of faith.

Even though I have emphasized the need to pay attention, to listen, and to observe, it is still possible you may fail to detect a significant problem. In some cases people are expert deceivers. At other times a person needs a relationship so badly he or she remains wedded to a distortion of what exists rather than to reality.

Through selective perception, such a person tunes out any information that does not support what he or she wants to believe and discourages anyone from offering conflicting impressions. Best friends, relatives, coworkers, and even strangers may attempt to correct the situation, only to alienate the person they care about.

Even in our most lucid moments, each of us can easily fail to appreciate fully what we are getting into. When we look back to the beginning of a relationship from the vantage point of many years together, it is easier to see how self-deception plays a role in the process of courtship, how we choose to interpret the same behavior more favorably in the embryonic stage of our partnership or marriage than we do later on after we have become secure enough to drop the veil of pretense. His initial shyness is now seen as irritating passivity. Her spunk is now understood as immaturity. His original gift of organization is clearly rigid and obsessive behavior. Her much-admired confidence looks suspiciously like conceit in today's light. His ambition is seen now, unmistakably, as workaholism.

Love *is* blind, but that need not prevent us from helping each other find the way. Having a life partner brings out both the best and the worst in each of us. Every day presents us with the challenge of loving our partner for who he or she is. Those of us who embrace commitment and its immeasurable rewards accept that challenge.

To create a life partnership, you must be willing to go with your new partner into areas that have been unexplored. This leap of faith, taken over and over again within your growing relationship, develops into a bond of trust which is not available at the beginning because it is possible only through multiple, shared experiences. Through these experiences you can come to know each other and build a mutually rewarding union.

9

UNREALISTIC
EXPECTATIONS

When two people love each other,
they don't look at each other,
they look in the same direction.

—GINGER ROGERS

Childhood is a laboratory for life. It is there that we learn through observation what it means to be a woman, a man, an adult, a partner. As we watch those around us, we come to conclusions about how to gain respect, meet our needs, use power, win approval, and find love. Children are curious little sponges, soaking up information wherever it spills around them. They are imitators. And they are believers. To the small child, anything said by an adult is *fact*. Children are not aware that parents, teachers, aunts, neighbors, preachers, etc. are sharing their *opinions* and *biases* about life. Children are also not aware that adults can be wrong, disturbed, and even cruel.

It takes a developed and sophisticated mind to recognize sarcasm, for instance. Hurtful, critical, and toxic comments about us, heard early enough in life, set like concrete. (This is why as adults we continue to believe certain things about ourselves which damage our esteem.) Likewise, those things we witness during our childhood have a profound impact on what we believe about being in the world. Of particular concern to me is the development of unrealistic expectations for relationships, based on what we observed, overheard, and were taught as we formed our ideas about intimacy, love relationships, and marriage.

The following unrealistic expectations have repeated themselves through multiple generations until they now form a body of myths that most of us easily recognize when discussing the lives of others, even though we may be unaware of their presence in our own relationships.

(Before reading further, turn to the Exercises Section and complete "Expectations.")

Love is enough.

The idea is that no matter what problems you may experience (illness, financial disaster, chemical dependency, death of a child), if you love each other enough, you can survive. This is a romantic thought, but that's about all. A committed relationship requires many skills which are unrelated to the emotional bond that exists between two people. This is why many relationships do not survive their first crisis; too much responsibility is placed on love, and it is too fragile to take the load.

Allison, twenty-nine, is recently separated from her husband, Doug, twenty-seven. She sits in a therapy session trying to make sense of the events of the past year. "I don't understand what happened. I thought he loved me." Allison is not looking at the real reasons for the breakup. Doug was an unfaithful partner, but she isn't ready to accept that he has poor impulse control, that he indulges in behavior that places their relationship at risk. She can focus only on the fact that their love for each other was "profound."

Like Allison, many men and women believe that having strong feelings for one's partner eliminates the need for working on a relationship. They regard people who talk about the difficulty in establishing a rewarding marriage as people who are "not really in love."

Conflict is a sign of a bad relationship.

Many people grew up in families that demonstrated extreme responses to conflict: Either they avoided the slightest disagreement or they had to wear flak jackets to the dinner table. *Either* experience can produce the idea that conflict is dangerous. When we enter a significant love relationship, with the intention of its being long-term, we bring with us our childhood images of family conflict, and these inevitably get tested. For some individuals conflict is but one of many ways to express oneself. To others it is absolutely demoralizing and unnecessary. The problem is that the subjects of these two experiences frequently fall in love with each other.

Conflict itself is not a sign that the relationship is a failure. Actually, true intimacy cannot exist without some form of conflict. Conflict is necessary so that individual needs can be addressed and individual growth can be promoted within the context of a shared life. However, when conflict is chronic and nothing is ever resolved—especially if it becomes physical—there is reason for concern.

Marsha and Phillip both came from families that believed it was important "not to rock the boat," so conflict was discouraged. After their first argument Marsha decided that she should never have married Phillip. She began to keep more and more of her feelings inside, in order to prevent more conflicts. Eventually Marsha developed an eating disorder, which she later discovered in a recovery group was related to her inability to express her hurt and anger. She and Phillip are now in marital therapy working on communicating *all* their feelings and learning how to argue in a productive way.

Many partners associate conflict with loss: loss of self, loss of power, loss of relationship. When tension builds, energy is detoured around confrontation, and uncomfortable subjects are never fully addressed. When only "nice" topics are discussed, intimacy is undermined by what looks like diplomacy but is really avoidance. Civility, respect, and tact are certainly called for, but they coexist *alongside* conflict in relationships that are truly healthy.

Unconditional acceptance is necessary.

The belief is that my partner should love me no matter what happens. Love me, love my warts. That works unless your "wart" is the fact that you fail to take responsibility for your part of the relationship, or you prefer to have more than one lover at a time, or you tend to become violent now and then. We are beginning to appreciate that unconditional acceptance is not healthy; it is one of the symptoms of what is popularly known as codependence.

Maria, thirty-three, remembers the early years of her marriage to Thomas. She took pride in her ability to tolerate his unfaithfulness, to adapt to his temper, and to ignore his disrespectful remarks. The harder it was for her to be his wife, the more "accomplished" she felt. Her priest had made that clear the night before the wedding. Now, after twelve years of marriage, Maria is determined to place some conditions on how Thomas treats her. Her motivation comes from observing how their two sons relate to their sister. Maria thinks it is too late to change her own life, but she knows that her daughter is looking to her as she decides how a wife should be. She has made a vow to herself that Thomas's behavior may no longer be unconditionally accepted. In a support group that she recently joined, Maria learns that it is not too late for her to change the quality of her life, and she is encouraged to bring Thomas and join a couples' group starting the next month.

Placing limits on how one is treated in a relationship or on the degree of responsibility one has is a step toward strengthening not only the partner who no longer accepts things unconditionally but the entire relationship as well. A marriage in which "anything goes" is a bond made by children because it is childish to interpret limits as restricting—rather than defining—a relationship.

In healthy relationships partners jointly define what is, and is not, acceptable behavior. If you and your partner are unable to do this, it is due to a conflict in your values and is a serious problem. Partners who are invested in mutually satisfying interactions know the value in defining what is, and is not, acceptable to them. They appreciate that this is a shared responsibility, not something foisted on one's partner that he or she must then adjust to.

I am amazed at how many couples, after being together for years, have never clearly discussed or defined what is acceptable. Each assumes the partner shares certain unspoken beliefs until a crisis, when the discrepancy in their values makes itself known.

While two people are still dating but feel serious enough to consider a life together, perhaps it would be prudent to be more direct: "How do you feel about hitting during an argument?" or "What is your definition of 'infidelity'?"

These questions may seem entirely unnecessary to you, but it is not uncommon to find that within many relationships one partner defines "unfaithful" as being emotionally involved with another, while his or her spouse defines it as being sexually involved. Even when both agree on the latter, couples must go further and discuss what "sexually involved" means. Is it a kiss? Heavy petting? Only intercourse?

A boyfriend or girlfriend may not want to discuss these topics because they obstruct romantic feelings. He or she may always prefer to keep things more on the "light" side; this is impossible if honest communication and intimacy are goals. Although dating is a time when couples have fun and the focus is usually on entertainment and chemistry, when two people begin to project themselves into a shared future, it is certainly appropriate for them to talk about more weighty issues—what's acceptable and what's not—even if it means being uncomfortable at first.

If my partner really loved me, he or she would know what I want without my having to ask.

Growing up, we become used to the adults in our lives anticipating our needs. A young parent takes pride in interpreting an infant's cries before the baby is successfully able to communicate a specific desire. Children get used to adults' telling them what they need. "You look tired, time for a nap." "It's past lunchtime; I bet you're hungry."

We come to adulthood expecting to have that same telepathic relationship duplicated. And we make the mistake of equating it with love. The idea that one adult will always be completely tuned in to the needs of the other is another romantic ideal, but a responsibility that is usually deeply resented.

James and Ruby have been sitting in silence in my office for a very long five minutes. Her arms are folded across her breasts in a defiant, protective way. He looks very puzzled, and near the edges of his eyes is the distinct watering of an inner hurt. Her last question remains unanswered, and I intervene:

THERAPIST: James, what do you make of what Ruby just asked you. Does it make any sense?
JAMES: I hear it all the time. A hundred times a day she says to me, "You know what I want. You just don't care. But you know."
THERAPIST: Has she ever come right out and told you what she wants?

At this point Ruby interjected: "Don't have to. I give him plenty of clues."

It feels terrific when our partner anticipates correctly and responds to an unspoken need of ours, becoming in that moment the good and caring parent to our child self. But it is not a crime if he or she fails to do so.

One of the advantages of a committed relationship is that over time we become more skilled at translating our partner's behavior. Anticipating needs is part of being a considerate partner (for instance, not initiating sex when your partner has lost sleep the night before and appears to want to go to sleep as soon as possible). Things get sticky when the assumption isn't checked out and the suspected need is taken as fact. Better to inquire, "You seem really tired. Would you like to go right to sleep? I can stop reading and turn off the light."

Stating one's *own* needs is the responsible thing to do, but since it isn't part of the romantic picture, those more invested in fictional accounts of marriage than marital reality will continue to wait until a mind reader comes along.

My partner will always feel loving toward me.

This is a common but mistaken belief that couples have. In long-term unions, love is there, but it is not always near the surface. There are times when one or both partners may feel indifferent, disillusioned, disappointed, hostile, and resentful. These are emotions that do not reflect their underlying love for each other. Over the years partners in healthy relationships cycle in and out of these states, but this is not interpreted as a signal that the relationships are failing. Each knows that the other in time will return to feelings like those at the beginning of their romance, even though not of the same intensity.

Lorna and Ray arrived late for their first session. Ray confessed that they had been sitting in their car, arguing about coming for therapy. Lorna felt it was a meaningless gesture since she had "stopped loving" Ray about six months earlier. Ray was hurt and dumbfounded and against ending their nine years together.

RAY: We were going really strong the first couple of years. Then we got so busy in our jobs that we hardly saw each other. Then it was OK again until about a year ago.

LORNA: I don't remember feeling like this before. I don't remember caring this little. I can't believe you think we'll be able to get close again. . . .

RAY: Well, I really didn't like you during that year you spent traveling, and here I am now, fighting for us. I don't expect to think you're terrific all the time. And I don't!

LORNA: Well, I thought you were really someone special until you lost your motivation and started moping around. Now I'm mostly irritated by you, so I think it's clear that whatever was there between us is gone.

One of the most difficult tasks in marriage is the willingness to hang in while feeling irritated, disappointed, or apathetic. It is important to be able to ride out stretches of boredom, minimal sexual desire, and marital fatigue. Doing so challenges the notion that everything must remain shiny and unblemished in order to have appeal. We learn to wait patiently, demonstrating our faith that we will eventually come full circle, back to our joy at being partnered. I am reminded of the words of Anne Morrow Lindbergh:

When you love someone you do not love them [sic] all the time, in exactly the same way, from moment to moment. It is an impossibility. It is even a lie to pretend to. And yet this is exactly what most of us demand. We have so little faith in the ebb and flow of life, of love, of relationships. We leap at the flow of the tide and resist in terror its ebb. We are afraid it will never return.

There needs to be the same level of excitement and chemistry throughout the relationship, or partners will become bored with each other.

There may be continuing excitement about one's partner, but it takes on many forms over the years together. What may have originally been attractive is now blended in with other attributes that may not have been appreciated in the early years or may have developed over time. Couples who have been in mutually rewarding relationships for many years report that sex becomes more intimate, and less mechanical, as time passes. This heightened intimacy and established comfort replace the inflamed loins of dating. Most longtime companions agree that this is trading "up." These seasoned mates respond to their partners' mind, body, and spirit.

Ruben and Lois have been together twenty-seven years. In the beginning Ruben was drawn to Lois's jet black hair and her ability to "really get down on the dance floor." After five children, Lois jokes that now she gets down only to pick up clothes. As she says this, Ruben laughs a hearty laugh and gives her knee a squeeze that says it all. His eyes are dancing as he gazes at this woman with graying hair and a few extra pounds. As I watch them across from me, I am struck by the fact that this couple, although struggling financially and coping with multiple health problems, has struck gold as far as relationships go.

It is each partner's responsibility to continue to be curious about, interested in, and fascinated with his or her mate. These qualities, so evident when dating, do not *naturally* disappear; they are victims of habit, indifference, and apathy. Once you believe that you know everything there is to know about your partner, you become—in that moment—a lousy lover. Stay curious, and you will prevent boredom.

Once you believe that you have revealed everything about yourself, you stop being interesting—as well as self-interested. There is no end to self-knowledge; it is a lifelong journey. We stop forming questions far too early. We treat ourselves as a conclusion rather than a process. Let one discovery about yourself (or your partner) lead to another, and another. The source of your excitement will not always be your partner, but the responsibility for finding excitement in your life will always be *yours*.

Commitment cures loneliness.

There are good and bad reasons for entering into a significant relationship. My work with individuals and couples who are involved in different stages of separation or divorce has reinforced the theory that a significant number of people seek relationships in order to avoid the emptiness of their lives. Many of these same people painfully discover that sometimes marriage is the loneliest place on earth. The hope is that another person can fill your life when you have been unable to.

Those partners who report the most satisfaction in their relationships are people who have either held on to individual interests or developed them as they began to realize their overreliance on their partners and the relationships for identity and purpose in life.

Dennis, forty-one, and Len, thirty-five, have been together for eleven years. Both remember the stormy earlier times when Len was completely dependent on Dennis. Dennis traveled much of the time as a consultant to companies developing computer software. He dreaded leaving, and he dreaded coming home, because of the response either would elicit in Len. As he was leaving, Len would become emotionally distraught, asking Dennis what he was going to do while he was gone. When he returned, Len would withdraw and refuse to talk to Dennis as "punishment" for what he felt was abandonment.

During one of these trips Len developed thoughts of suicide and told Dennis when he returned. Len entered therapy and confronted his emptiness; when Dennis was gone, Len felt that he did not even exist. His identity was dependent on having Dennis to relate to. Now, looking back on that period of time, they laugh, as Dennis refers to its theme: "Len, *get a life!*"

In those relationships in which one partner looks to the other for a sense of self, the other partner frequently feels overburdened and resentful. It is never your partner's job to make life interesting for you or to provide motivation and purpose. To be empowered, one must, above all else, take responsibility for one's own life. If you are not satisfied with the way your life is turning out, if you feel isolated, empty, and bored with your life, look at those things under *your* control and begin there. *Your partner is not one of them.*

My partner will be my friend, and I won't need any other friends.

While they have not always made a conscious decision, it appears that many couples find that over time they have shrunk their world of contacts to include only the immediate family, their coworkers, and possibly an acquaintance in the neighborhood. Somewhere along the way they have loosened their ties to old friends, those who "knew me when."

The first years of a relationship are a great challenge; they are about the business of adjusting, negotiating, compromising, and merging. During this time outside friendships serve a valuable function, keeping us anchored when we feel tossed about. When we are overwhelmed with doubts about our ability to be successful as a partner or when we are feeling unlovable, friends tell us just what we want to hear. The unrealistic expectation is that our partner will satisfy that need to connect with another adult, and if he or she loves us, he or she will want to be only with us. This becomes a thorny problem when a partner develops a friendship with a person with whom there is chemistry or the potential to go beyond friendship.

In healthy, satisfying unions this is not a threat since trust is high. In relationships in which trust is shaky, conflict is often chronic around this issue. The fact is we *all* need friends outside our love relationships. They are only a threat when the significant relationship itself is too fragile to support either partner's expanding his or her world.

* * *

Betsy and Keith both are thirty and have been married only two years, but one of those years has already been spent in marital therapy. Keith grew up with Susan, who has been his closest friend, even during adolescence, when other guys chided him. She has four brothers and has never thought of Keith as anything but another brother. Although Keith briefly entertained the idea of Susan's being a girlfriend, she discouraged him. Their friendship was like a lifeline in college, where they were roommates off campus. Each would demand to meet the other's love interest and then let them know if he or she "approved."

Betsy has never had a male friend. She either regarded men as potential love partners or ignored them. When Keith announced that he was choosing Susan as his "best man" for the wedding, Betsy called my office, and I began working with them as a couple. Betsy was unmovable; she had decided that Keith was in love with Susan and would not explore any alternative explanations. Because she had never experienced the kind of bond that Keith and Susan had, which has no sexual component, she could not allow that it was possible. She couldn't believe that he would want to continue his relationship with Susan after he was married. Their conflict was very typical: She personalized the situation and thought, "I should be all he needs. If she's still that important to him, then I must not be enough."

When we select a life partner, we pick one person over all other potential candidates. The moment that person is elevated to the special status of mate, a different arrangement begins. From then on, the couple will know each other in ways that "outsiders" will not. This creates a boundary around the couple that is necessary to the integrity of their union, as they go about their individual lives. This boundary informs the world that their lives are intertwined through intricate daily experiences known only to them.

The boundary protects them from the demands, expectations, and intrusions of those who want to be part of that inner circle. Yet it can also be harmful. If a couple turns only to each other, the boundary becomes a wall, sealing them off from others, including friends and family who could be helpful during crises, provide alternative companionship, act as playmates, and function as sounding boards.

The longer a partner relies *only* on his or her partner, the more difficult it is to reestablish contact with others. Months and years go by, and soon someone who was once a cherished companion is demoted to being an acquaintance to whom a holiday card is sent once a year.

In my work with couples in distress, countless times I see how a couple has turned in toward each other in the hope of growing closer only to become "pot-bound." Once they are directed outward, to get appropriate needs met elsewhere, they rediscover the richness in their lives that was sacrificed when they bought into the romantic notion that a spouse or mate is all one needs. The key, of course, is in the term "appropriate." Certain needs *should* be met only within the relationship, but not all.

Our partner will have sexual fantasies or sexual desires that include only us.

The truth is that healthy adults frequently have sexual thoughts about people other than their partners. Fantasies alone are not harmful. Problems develop when thoughts turn to obsession or when fantasy about another is translated into behavior. In monogamous relationships, partners entertain any fantasies they like; they may often find themselves feeling sexually attracted to others, but they don't act on these feelings.

Elaine, thirty-six, and Dick, thirty-nine, have had a bumpy life together, but through it all they remain steadfast in their belief that their meeting was "cosmic," and therefore, they should do everything they can to stay together.

Elaine is a massage therapist, and Dick is a personal trainer. Their careers place both of them in a world where they have access to other—often desirable—bodies. They possess a high level of mutual trust, which allows them to work at their individual jobs without threatening their marriage. I asked them how they did this since each day they actually have their hands on fantasy material.

Elaine told me, "It's like window-shopping without my wallet. I look, I may like, but I'm not buying."

Dick offered: "Sure, I think about what it would be like—and those thoughts come in handy sometimes—but I'm not willing to do something that will cause us both a great deal of pain."

Elaine added, "The key is we don't expect to be the only attraction in each other's world."

In a relationship like Elaine and Dick's, certain principles must be in place, and each partner must live those principles on a daily basis. When there is an agreement that sexual experimentation with others is unacceptable and that sexual fantasies about others are part of healthy *mental* gymnastics, the desires are harmless. However, if a partner consistently prefers fantasy over reality (including pornography, used to fuel fantasies), the relationship is at risk, and professional help should be considered.

Children will help a difficult marriage or relationship.

A pregnancy should never be considered the solution to a problem; in most cases it will only compound the situation. We all know some, some of us have had, and some of us *are* "glue" babies, whose births were intended to patch a crack in the marital foundation. It doesn't work. If something positive happens, it is usually because the marital tension was rooted in the empty nest syndrome, and now that has been averted through a late-life pregnancy. Of course, this solution has a shelf life of only a few years before the marital problems appear again.

A good rule of thumb, for you and for any children you may think about bringing into this world is, if you are experiencing serious relationship problems, do not consider conception or adoption until you have them resolved. (Talk to a professional, even if you are already pregnant. You can certainly achieve improvement in most situations before your child is born. This is your first act as a responsible, loving parent.)

Lydia and Lincoln had been having problems since Lincoln accepted his new job, which required his being gone three evenings a week. This occurred just as Lydia was halfway through her studies at the local junior college. Their combined schedules made it impossible to spend more than a few hours together during the week, and those times seemed to become more and more conflict-ridden. They had talked about how difficult it was going to be while Lincoln established himself in the business community and Lydia prepared herself for a better job than the one she had at a bakery. Now Lydia wondered if it was worth it. She was alone most of the time, and when Lincoln was there, all they did was argue. She began to think a family would be the best way to keep him home, and five months later she announced to him that she was pregnant. They entered therapy two weeks later but dropped out because of complications from the pregnancy and Lincoln's having to take on a second job since Lydia could no longer work at the bakery.

Having children for any reason other than that you are fully prepared to parent is irresponsible. Of course, most of us and *our* children would not be here if we had waited until we matured into mindful adults. And look at all those couples who wait until they're forty and established before they start having babies only to discover that they are so set in their ways that the newcomer feels like a terrible intrusion into their well-organized, highly structured lives.

There probably isn't a "best" time to have children, but there are some reasons that are better than others, and expecting a baby to correct marital malfunction is not one of them.

Marriage is fifty-fifty.

Occasionally it is, but to expect this to be a constant is to be greatly misled. My professional and personal experience tells me that there is more of an ebb and flow to a committed relationship. On a day when I am feeling physically well, emotionally sound, and spiritually intact, I might be up to contributing as much as 90 percent to our marriage. However, later in the week, when I am cranky and need a nap, you couldn't squeeze 10 percent out.

Some of us, by nature, give more than is asked. Others, just as naturally, must be recruited. And still others may require bribes. It is romantic to think we are in fifty-fifty partnerships, but sooner or later reality will come knocking. The important thing to look for is *imbalance*. If one partner is *always* giving more, then serious problems will develop, if they haven't already. The ebb and flow of relationship work depends on trust. The only way I can give 90 percent one day is through knowing that my partner gave more at some point during the previous week and, if necessary, will do so next week. (By the way, "giving more" may mean *not* picking a fight, or taking over one of my chores when I'm too pooped, or just letting me know that even with my bad haircut, he still loves me. Sometimes it's just that simple.)

Leslie and Serena have been seeing me since Serena developed a chronic, progressive disease. They have been lovers for eight years. Serena is considering terminating the relationship because she believes that her increasing disability is a growing burden for Leslie, who has been primarily a self-involved person most of her life. Historically Serena has carried the weight of the relationship. She has had the same job for ten years, while Leslie has changed careers numerous times in a frustrating search for meaning in her life. Serena has also taken on the emotional responsibility for the two of them, attempting to draw out Leslie, who prefers not to confront issues.

Two years ago Leslie went through treatment for chemical dependency. Because they are lesbians, Serena's health insurance would not cover Leslie, even though they had been together six years at the time. Consequently, Serena paid for Leslie's medical costs, and now Leslie wants to show Serena that she can be there for her. She is taking courses to become a nursing assistant, with her goal embracing the fact that she is going to be taking on more and more of Serena's physical care as her disease predictably progresses.

If a couple remains together over the years, there naturally will be shifts in the level of responsibility, degree of emotional involvement, and financial contribution of each. Part of staying committed is the willingness to ride out long periods of imbalance. The key is to step back and look at the larger pattern: Is the burden you carry reasonable and fair? Do you feel resentful or resourceful? Do you believe the imbalance is temporary? Do you have faith that if and when the roles are reversed, your share can be shifted to your partner?

Marriage is forever, no matter what.

This is a very painful expectation for those who find that they must end their relationships in order to maintain their integrity, sanity, health, or all three. In situations of emotional, sexual, and physical abuse, it is necessary to terminate the bond if the abusive behavior continues. Many partners find this contrary to the way they have been raised and their religious education. They remain at risk in life-threatening situations rather than go against their beliefs. They live in pain; some even die. Others, who are not abused but feel "trapped," become depressed, physically ill, or develop out-of-control behavior, such as chemical dependency and eating disorders.

Joy and Walter had been married thirty-three years when they began discussing divorce. She had never imagined a life separate from her husband, and now here she was, *initiating* one.

Joy had "done the traditional thing" even though she always knew that raising five children had barely tapped into her potential. She experienced bouts of depression, as she held back her strong desire for achievement, forced herself to lower her goals, and tried to become satisfied with the activities of everyday family life. When her children were living independent lives, she felt her major responsibility had been accomplished, and she returned to school with—at least initially—Walter's blessings.

Following a spectacular academic performance, Joy was awarded a scholarship to law school. Walter declared that he had no intention of moving and that he wasn't interested in having a "commuter" wife.

Joy's therapy focused on her painful struggle between giving up her thirty-three-year marriage or giving up herself. Because she had entered into a traditional arrangement, she was unable to have *both*, as Walter was. In the end she could no longer ignore her responsibility to herself, and in choosing school, she had to let go of "forever."

In healthy marriages there is room for each partner to become the best he or she can. Sometimes this places a burden on the relationship, when there are long period of absence, chaotic schedules, or shifts in individual domestic responsibilities. But in the end the relationship *benefits* if (1) the partners agree on the decision, (2) the marriage continues to be treated as a priority, and (3) balance is eventually restored.

When partners are unable to express their opinions freely, voice their ideas, exercise their rights, expand their skills, and use their talents, they become stunted. When barriers are erected, growth cannot occur naturally, and in its stymied stage, it goes underground, where the frustration undermines the foundation on which the relationship stands. If a partner reaches this point, a decision about the future of the relationship must be made, and it is often one of the most difficult, most painful decisions of all adult life.

When a marriage remains undeveloped, stuck at a stage where there is possessiveness and insecurity, neither partner can grow, and one partner often becomes overcontrolling in an attempt to protect their relationship. Healthy relationships support individual growth because the partners know that their own satisfaction with life and their satisfaction within their marriage are *interdependent.*

We bring many unrealistic expectations to love relationships. These expectations arise when two people agree to become romantically involved with, and committed to, each other. Most of these expectations we are not even aware of. They are learned so early that they become integrated into our thought patterns and behavior. It is only through purposeful examination of these beliefs, or myths, that we are able to identify them in our lives and appreciate how they cause unnecessary pain and eliminate them.

10

FOREVER:
A LOOK AT COMMITMENT

When (someone) loves you for a long, long time
. . . REALLY loves you, then you become Real.
Generally, by the time you are Real, most of your
hair has been loved off, and your eyes
drop out and you get loose in the joints
and very shabby. But these things don't
matter at all, because once you are
Real, you can't be ugly. . . .

—THE VELVETEEN RABBIT

We human beings seem to possess a universal longing to be attached, to relate to, belong to, need, and be needed. More than four
million Americans will marry over the next year, with the intention
of entering a union that will last until death. Yet more than half of
those couples will not last beyond seven years. Add to this an unknown number of couples who will create nonlegal—but no less
hopeful—relationships that will also fail, and it becomes painfully
evident that although we may want to attach, we certainly have difficulty attaching forever.

Marriage (or its equivalent) offers an oasis in an increasingly
impersonal and competitive world. It serves as a buffer against the
unpredictability of life itself, softening the blows of everyday encounters as men and women go about the business of living.

To be someone's partner means that you have been selected
from almost 249 million people living in the United States today by

someone who wants to share his or her life with you. What a compliment! Creating a shared history, remaining with one partner, and growing together through the years are among the most gratifying aspects of commitment.

So if we all want to belong, and there are advantages to committing ourselves to another person for life, why is it so difficult to achieve? The concept seems simple enough. But human beings are complex, and to appreciate why more than half of those four million couples joined together each year fail to celebrate their seventh anniversaries, it is necessary to go back to the beginning and look more closely at the evolutionary process of long-term intimacy.

THE EVOLVING PARTNERSHIP

A marriage or partnership is not a finished product but rather a work in progress, redefined each morning. Just as each individual goes through stages of development progressing from childhood to adulthood, so a marriage evolves. Relationships of duration can be divided into three separate periods: *courting, adjusting,* and *accepting.* Each phase has its own characteristics, issues, work to be done, and achievements to be celebrated. During each stage, lovers have their own expectations, disappointments, and lessons to be learned. Since partners have individual needs which can lead to conflicting priorities, it follows that developing a committed relationship is one of life's greatest challenges.

The first stage, *courting,* is full of romance, spontaneity, curiosity, and excitement. Two individuals come together and create a separate entity with an existence and future of its own. This newly formed relationship will have its own life cycle. It will be subject to stress and will become "ill" at various times throughout the partnership. If left unattended, it will die of neglect.

Neglect is not an issue in this earliest stage, when the partners first publicly define themselves as a couple. Each is dazzled by the other, and they spend great amounts of time and energy to be together. Companionship is granted priority status, and the lovers vow that it will always be so. Motivation is at its highest peak; there are no limits to what one partner is willing to do for the other. Each idealizes the other, feeling a combination of honor and fascination that he or she has been chosen. The couple possesses a mutual attraction that rivals any competing force; work and other responsibilities are frequently shoved aside in order to satisfy their desires. These are good times.

The primary tasks at this stage are to establish an identity as a "couple," to nurture each other, and to create a mutually satisfying sexual relationship incorporating individual preferences and rhythms. Partners focus on how much they are alike, and emphasis is on merging. The climate is one of passion with high levels of eye contact and physical expression.

But as Frank Pittman reminds us in *Private Lies,* "Those qualities and talents that people develop for success at courtship render them unfit for marriage. [p. 91]" "Romance is wonderful and smells like a new car and fades about as fast and has nothing to do with real life. [p. 93]." For this reason couples have always been cautioned against cohabitation before they know themselves and each other.

Courting (or dating) among adults who seek life partners is intended to be a time during which each lover "assesses" the potential of another as a companion. If it lasts long enough, each can slip out of more formal (and artificial) behavior and ease into being oneself, observing the degree of partner compatibility. When a premature decision is made to cohabit (usually fueled by healthy lust), two "false" selves move in together. The "true" selves are buried beneath the superficial trappings of "romanticism." When they emerge—and they will—this discovery is a rude awakening.

When a couple cohabits prematurely, they are burdened with having to work out the issues of being a family unit while they are continuing to date and learn the very basic things about each other. The desire to create family is so strong that adults tend to commit too early, and single parents continually pull their children into relationships that are too young to bear the weight.

Waiting to move a lover into your space, or joining him or her in his or her place, is especially important when children are involved. It requires discipline on the part of the parent, who may feel that his or her new lover is too wonderful to keep at a distance, to keep from the children. The children, on the other hand, are not romantically involved with this person and are not likely to feel the same way.

Many of today's children of divorce attach themselves to a potential stepparent only to have to unattach a couple of weeks or months later. The most responsible and loving thing you can do, if you are a single parent, is not to bring anyone into your children's home—or worse, move them from their home into someone else's—until the status of the adult relationship has progressed from "potential" life partners to "commitment." Measure your seriousness as a couple by passing time: time to let your "true" selves encounter each other; time to discuss your expectations; time to discover if each is trustworthy and reliable. Don't use your feelings about your lover to determine if you are seriously committed. In the courting stage you aren't even remotely rational.

Dating without cohabitation allows a partner to extricate himself or herself before a relationship is fully established. When children are involved, this means the partners simply cease the forward momentum rather than rip apart another family unit.

If you continue to be involved, over time you will enter the second stage: *adjusting*. This is when the hard work starts, when idealization is replaced by reality. It could happen after the first argument, or it could happen more slowly over the first years. Partners become less mysterious, more familiar and predictable, and this diminishes the excitement from the courting stage. This is the phase in which the partners discover their incompatibilities and conflicting self-interests. This is when they determine their ability to transcend ugly moments.

The major task of this stage is the working through of power struggles as each partner attempts to participate in the relationship without losing a sense of self. Also to be learned during this time are the dance of intimacy and the negotiating and balancing of conflicting needs. Partners relate to each other alternately as ally and foe, helpmate and competitor, asset and liability. The climate is one of primarily ambivalence, peppered with disappointment, celebration, confusion, accommodation, alienation, and confluence.

This is a difficult time for many couples because it brings

the partners face-to-face with their unmet expectations about each other, themselves, and the relationship. Differing assumptions bump up against one another. By now each person realizes the other is not going to change, as each has hoped. The recognition of the mate's essential differentness from the cherished dating fantasy is tough to swallow. Disenchantment sets in as illusion gives way to disillusion and the "perfect" relationship disappears.

Partners who prefer the excitement and magic of the "false" selves during dating to the "true" selves of the adjusting period usually leave at this point. It is precisely this period that is responsible for half the couples' failing to reach their seventh year. *This is the stage that tests commitment.* Anyone can stay committed while having fun. No one gets a medal for hanging in there while dating.

Those who have the most difficulty with the adjusting stage of a relationship are those deeply invested in romanticized love. No other culture expects as much from marriage as we do. We are brought up to believe that love is the sole basis for marriage. We have been socialized to fall in love with a concept. The thriving bridal industry is testimony to this. Hundreds of thousands of families go into debt in order to have the "perfect" wedding. The wedding, not the marriage, becomes the focus. Couples come close to breaking up over such silly things as the color of the icing on the cake. Issues that are completely unrelated to the sacredness of the day begin to take on lives of their own, and the original purpose is lost.

Romanticized love aims at happiness, but as Pittman says, "Marriage is not supposed to produce life's happiness. . . . Happiness, like sweat, is a by-product of hard work [p. 101]."

In the early, romantic phase of a relationship we are tolerant and accepting of a partner's less than perfect qualities. In the adjusting stage those same idiosyncrasies swell to deviant proportions. What was once dismissed as a minor irritation now becomes fuel for many battles as two individuals attempt to blend their lives while protecting their nonnegotiable selves. It is during this stage that couples need a good support system, as Kurt Vonnegut so eloquently states:

. . . couples have to invent for themselves what marriage is
. . . few of us are governed by the customs and attitudes of
a stable extended family in the immediate neighborhood.
Marriage for human beings without extended families is a
two-character play without a backstage crew and, far
worse, without an audience out front that gives a damn . . .
we each expect the other to be as resourceful and sympathetic and various as a large and loving family. Our failure
to communicate is a failure to sound like a multitude.

The couples that successfully navigate the stormy waters of the
adjusting stage are rewarded with the third and final phase of a
long-term partnership: *accepting.* It is in this stage that the couple
finds the payoff for working so hard during their previous time together. It is here that each is cognizant of his or her strengths and
weaknesses not only as an individual but as a life companion as
well. It is here that each appreciates the other's contributions as well
as acknowledges his or her limitations.

The primary task of this phase is that of relaxing into each
other's different ways of being and doing, accepting each other's
limitations and imperfections. In addition, at this time partners
are constructing an even stronger sense of self without losing
touch with their partners. They learn to take responsibility for
satisfying their needs, having set aside their childish desire for
their partners to do so. They stretch to cocreate an even greater
intimacy through a freer flowing of communication. They must
learn to be more actively supportive of each other as aging im-
pacts on both them and the relationship. At this time the partners
develop a more spiritual connection to each other in preparation
for life's inevitable end.

During this third, and final, period the partner is seen as a
teammate, comrade, coworker, and sometimes soul mate. The climate is more relaxed, full of warmth, tenderness, and an interdependence that allows easy negotiating.

By now both partners have relinquished their fantasies about
each other and expectations for the relationship in general. The
thrill may be gone, but it is replaced by security. The partners share
a rich history as well as a powerful and enduring bond.

THREE FACES OF LOVE

In each of the above stages partners state that they "love" each other, yet they may mean very different things. This is explained by the work of Robert Sternberg, a professor of psychology and education at Yale University.

According to Sternberg, there are three components of love: the *emotional,* the *motivational,* and the *cognitive.* The *emotional* aspect is known as intimacy, a deep knowing of each other. Intimacy is expressed through communicating inner thoughts and personal misgivings about who we are and how we look, what we hope for and fear, and, most important, what we truly want and need from our partners. Intimacy also embraces the sharing of one's possessions and one's time as well as offering emotional support. This aspect of love is stronger when a couple first gets together, during the courting stage. Natural curiosity keeps it alive with little or no effort. However, as time passes, the demands of daily life take over, and intimacy is buried under other priorities. This happens in the adjusting stage, after which it takes conscious *effort* to resurrect.

The second aspect of love is *motivational,* or what we call passion. This includes chemistry, that intense desire to be with our partners as frequently as possible. Each person is preoccupied with thoughts of the other until the next encounter. Over time, predictability replaces excitement and passion loses it potency. One's heart still may occasionally race, but the partners no longer go into "withdrawal" in response to each other's absence.

So if both intimacy and passion diminish with time, what keeps couples together? The answer is the third aspect of love: the *cognitive.*

The cognitive is what we call commitment. You express your commitment by regarding your partner as special and separate from all others in your life, by remaining invested in the relationship through difficult times, by following through on your promises, by treating the partnership or marriage as a priority and protecting that relationship from preventable harm (which includes violence toward your partner and self-destructive acts as well as chronic destructive behavior that threatens the partnership, such as alcohol and drug abuse, gambling, etc.), and, finally, by sexual fidelity.

Commitment is formalized through a ceremony. Even the type of ceremony may reflect the degree of commitment. It could be argued that those who elope or rush to a Las Vegas chapel (not to mention the new drive-up window) may be expressing "Let's hurry and do this before either one of us changes our mind" more than trust in their eventual union.

A couple that puts a great deal of thought into the ceremony—even if it is in their backyard—plans it in advance and has family and friends present to witness the vows and celebrate the decision is demonstrating that although they have had plenty of time to change their minds, they have, in fact, chosen not to. They have shown even *before* the ceremony that they have faith in their commitment to each other.

In contrast, the couple who impulsively gets married does not trust that if they took the time to explore their reasons for getting married, they would come to the same conclusion. Quickie wedding ceremonies reflect a lack of respect for the seriousness—not to mention the sacredness—of two people's electing to spend their lives together.

All relationships that end by agreement do so for one reason: The commitment is withdrawn. In relationships that end involuntarily (excluding death), at least one of the partners withdraws his or her commitment. They may talk about issues like sex, money, conflicting parenting, snoring, etc., but in reality the end comes for only this reason: the death of commitment, which is usually preceded by a protracted period of just hanging in there and a sense of helplessness over changing things.

We will see as we explore the work of commitment that it is not about just hanging in there, adding up the years. It is about dedication, not endurance.

CREATING A CLIMATE FOR COMMITMENT

Our first alliance is at birth, when we are thrust into relationship with another. Our vulnerability at that point is so extreme that without a total commitment from the person upon whom we are dependent, we will wither rather than flourish. Without personal experience, without having been able to be fully dependent upon a reliable adult as he or she was growing up, a person lacks an inner core of trust, and trust is essential for commitment because commitment involves faith in another. For this reason some partners find the work of commitment exceptionally difficult, if not impossible. To them commitment is an abstraction, an attractive concept and no more.

These partners are not wrong or evil or dysfunctional, but they *are* disabled in their efforts to connect. At a crucial time in their development, a time when they were supposed to experience the security of reliable, dependable, and dedicating parenting (commitment in action), for various reasons they did not. Now as adults they find it difficult to do the work of the adjusting period, because they have never been the object of another's commitment to them, so they are unable to pass it on. They have not known the rewards; they have not felt the safety and therefore do not appreciate the value in working through the stormy times; the rewards of commitment are unfamiliar. Having been abandoned—if not physically, at least emotionally—when very young, they tend as adults either to avoid opportunities to commit or to jump ship somewhere in the adjusting stage of a relationship.

If you believe you are such a partner or you believe that your lover is (or possibly both), commitment is not impossible, but you will have to work much harder than people who were fortunate enough to have received dedicated parenting. The beauty of human behavior is that it is capable of change. If you want a lifelong partnership badly enough and are willing to do the work, it can be yours, but you should not underestimate the degree of effort and the length of time it will take.

Another reason some people are unable to make full commitments is that they are still attached—even though it might be negatively—to past lovers. When we enter a new relationship prematurely, before old issues have been resolved, we bring emotional baggage to the new partnership. Commitment requires that both partners be actively involved in the present; when one is still living in the past, this creates an extra burden for the couple, as they try to integrate their lives.

A third reason that couples fail to commit is the problem of inertia. Preoccupied with your daily routine, you might find yourself on automatic pilot, not being intentional in your actions or active in your decisions. Everything is done by default. You believe that you do not have enough time to do the necessary work of commitment and hope that just by showing up at home each night, you will have made your contribution.

David Viscott in *I Love You, Let's Work It Out* points out that in the most deeply committed relationships, commitment is never an issue; it is a fact. The commitment is made by the individual, but the work is done as a team. Each partner makes a commitment to the other as well as to the relationship itself.

Lifelong loving at the level of commitment requires a great deal of each spouse. This includes dedication to a common goal, the courage to take risks, maturity and patience, the ability to tolerate ambiguity, the willingness to change, and the daily challenge of keeping intimacy alive while earning a living, raising children, relating to others, adjusting to shifts in social expectations for each gender, and continuing to develop as individuals. You can see why only those who are determined succeed.

Commitment is an ongoing task. Too often couples think that it just happens, that if one day you look at the calendar and see that you have been together for fifty years, then you have been committed to each other. Not true. Hundreds of couples celebrate their fiftieth anniversaries without any sense of wonderment or pride or pleasure. There is no trace of mutual respect or appreciation for the combined effort that forged that particular occasion. Many couples passively arrive at each anniversary, marking an endurance contest more than celebrating teamwork. Paul Pearsall calls this "low" monogamy, as opposed to the "high" monogamy of deeply committed partners. To help keep your relationship highly satisfying, begin using "Love Letters" in the Exercises Section.

Long-term committed relationships are not free of conflict, pain, misunderstandings, etc. It is *how* committed couples approach problems that separates them from other, less dedicated couples. Commitment itself does not resolve problems. Rather it creates a context for the resolution of difficulties. It represents a desire to overcome problems instead of being overcome by them.

Because there is an assumption of permanence, tension and conflicting needs are well tolerated. Each argument is recognized for what it is: a difference of opinion, not a threat to the future of the relationship. Times when the partners do not want to be together are expected, but they are not interpreted as a general uninterest in continuing as a couple. Partners consider separation and divorce avoidance behaviors, escapes from the hard work of resolution.

Committed couples are mutually interested in meeting their difficulties head-on, and they can do so because even in the heat of the moment they know that the argument will pass but that *they* will continue. They believe that they can outlive any disagreement, and even more important, they believe that they can learn and grow from these encounters rather than let an argument destroy what they have built together.

Both David Schnarch and Carl Whitaker, professionals in marriage and family therapy, utilize the metaphor of a crucible when talking about relationships between people who are committed to each other. A crucible is a vessel capable of withstanding severe external stress (very hot temperatures) while internally going about the business of forging a highly valued substance (steel) from lesser substances (crude iron, etc.). It is an extreme test of endurance resulting in transformation. Certainly marital dynamics are another kind of forging, and a satisfying union is the prized product.

CHARACTERISTICS OF COMMITTED COUPLES

In their book *Secrets of Strong Families,* Nick Stinnett and John DeFrain discovered over and over again, as they interviewed couples, that commitment is not about words but about behavior. It is "active and obvious." Think of how many people you know who will tell you that their marriages are their "number one priority," yet they put less time into, and spend less effort on, their marriages than on any other aspect of their lives. After a number of years together, most life mates erroneously believe that the relationship takes care of itself, but in fact, the opposite is true: Its survival is completely dependent upon the joint effort of both partners.

Committed couples never forget that a marriage is its own entity and that all individual decisions must be made on the basis of the impact of those decisions on the relationship. Self-interest must take a back burner on numerous occasions if the relationship is to survive. When each partner is attending only to what he or she personally wants, the relationship is being neglected; if only one partner sacrifices, resentment builds. It takes maturity to keep commitment alive because it frequently requires placing the welfare of the bond before the satisfying of personal desires. Individuals who intend to get their needs met no matter what are poor candidates for committed partnerships.

The most outstanding characteristics of successful committed companions are:

- flexibility and the ability to tolerate change
- a willingness to accept limits
- an assumption of a shared future
- freedom to take risks/trust in each other
- a balance of dependencies
- not only loving but, more important, truly liking each other ("best friends")
- a shared history

These couples stop periodically and examine their relationships for any necessary adjustments; they appreciate that commitment is an ongoing, active process. The partners are capable of working on changes within themselves as well as between them. Their response to external stressors (illness, loss of employment, demands of work, etc.) is one of adaptability. When confronted with a problem, they explore alternatives rather than restrict themselves to a single solution. When one of them grows in a different direction, that growth is celebrated, not regarded as a threat to the bond between them, because their flexibility incorporates an appreciation that they are separate beings as well as united lovers and therefore will have different needs at times. They remember that they form a partnership of *individuals*.

These partners do not expect perfection in their mates and understand when to identify something as an issue to be worked on and when to consider something an irritation to be tolerated, when to focus and when to let go. They recognize the limitations of their ability to change each other and do not consider it their personal responsibility to make each other happy. When necessary, each is able to delay personal gratification for the sake of the relationship without feeling resentment. There is an understanding that this is part of the work of making their marriage mutually satisfying.

There is, for committed companions, an assumption of permanence. This creates the freedom to have disagreements and makes avoidance unnecessary. These couples consider divorce the result of being too passive about marriage and expecting satisfaction without effort. They know that the relationship will survive conflict because they are willing to be unhappy in the moment, knowing that in the long run they will have worked it out. This is one of the greatest rewards of making a commitment.

Both partners feel free to be themselves and express their feelings without fear of judgment or condemnation. They can take risks within the relationship (be more bold sexually or more intimate in their communication) without the danger of ridicule. They remain sexually faithful to each other out of choice, not out of a sense of sacrifice.

By balancing their dependencies, they balance the power in the relationship. They exhibit a high tolerance for exchanging responsibilities when necessary. In those marriages which are more traditional, the roles may be determined by gender, but if one partner is unable to fill his or her responsibilities as the result of illness or absence, the other fills in as best as he or she can. In nontraditional partnerships, in which roles are not rigidly gender-specific, each partner focuses on the task to be done, not on whether it is "woman's work" or "man's work." In both cases the work that must be done by the couple gets done through a cooperative effort. Chores are not a problem because each couple has a means of delegation that works for them.

Partners enjoy each other in spite of their individual flaws. They believe their likable qualities outweigh any deficiencies. Their time together is rich with intimacy, lively conversation, and quite often humor. They possess similar values and often similar personal goals. These couples have developed rituals and frequently refer to each other by pet names. They treasure their "coupleness" as a priority.

Finally they have a common history. This is what gives them a strong sense of connectedness. They live active lives as individuals but are anchored by their commitment to each other. Their shared life through the years has provided multiple experiences from which they have learned many things about each other. Just by being together for so many days and nights, they have grown more sensitive to each other's moods, needs, and preferences. These internalized maps keep them from developing a weekly crisis because as long as they are tuned in to each other (rather than take each other for granted), they can prevent a misunderstanding from becoming a major issue.

In his book *Couple Constancy* Lance Laurence summarizes the struggle that goes on between committed partners as "mastering the task of moving towards someone without losing one's sense of self [p. 109]." His interviews with happily married people echo the facts that none of this can be done without daily dedication and that dedication involves hard work.

THE WORK OF COMMITMENT

Although we might expect it, there does not seem to be a connection between the degree of marital satisfaction and the decision to divorce. People who are miserable stay together for many years, and couples who are only irritated with each other frequently seek divorce. The decision to divorce seems to have more to do with what partners expect from a committed relationship than with what actually happens. Those expectations are based on what the individuals witnessed growing up, what they learned about marriage through their churches, their schools, and their communities at large, as well as what they have assimilated through books, television, and movies.

If a person does not expect very much from marriage, and doesn't get very much, he will report that he is satisfied. However, if an individual expects marriage to make her happy and keep her happy, and she remains unhappy yet married, to her the most obvious conclusion is that there is something wrong with her particular marriage. This is followed by the idea that perhaps finding a new partner is the answer. When this does not work, the pattern is repeated.

Therefore, the first work to be done is that the partners need to be honest about what they expect from the joining of their lives and to discuss this freely. Obviously this should be done in the first weeks of meeting, but lovers are too preoccupied with other thoughts to attend to this task at that time. Discussions about expectations usually occur involuntarily in response to conflict during the adjusting phase when differing or unmet expectations create tension. To assist you in talking about this with your partner now, before a crisis occurs, turn to "Expectations" in the Exercises Section.

Commitment means relinquishing the infantile dream of being unconditionally accepted by a partner who will gratify all your needs and make up for all your childhood disappointments. It means expecting to be disappointed by your partner but not using this as a reason to pull the plug.

When there are problems in a marriage, the first target is our partner, the second target is the relationship itself, and the third, if at all, is our own behavior. Committed companions know, in times of tension and conflict, to look to themselves first in an attempt to understand their contribution to the issue. This is based in the wisdom that we can control only our own behavior and no amount of wishing, hoping, or praying can control our partner's.

Every long-term relationship has to face injustices that one partner has inflicted on the other. If a couple kept score over the years (and committed couples never do), they might see that there is inequity, that one partner may always do more for the other or for the marriage, and that it will never be even. That is not reason enough to terminate the bond. Committed couples understand this imbalance but also believe that both partners make valuable contributions. There is no contest. They are not interested in determining who is the "better," more generous partner, because their effort is focused on the marriage, and for that reason all effort is appreciated.

Commitment also means negotiating, compromising, and sacrificing. It is about joining two individuals who want what they want when they want it. This is why the adjustment phase is the working phase. To remain committed, the partner must want the relationship more than they want anything else. There will be times when that pledge is tested, times when something in the present competes with your future as a couple. It will be up to you to protect your commitment from harm.

Harm comes in many forms. When a partner works long hours, he or she is not available to nurture the relationship. When a husband or wife uses alcohol or drugs to an extent that communication with the spouse is impaired and alienation replaces intimacy, he or she is placing the commitment at risk.

And of most concern is the issue of desire for others. When a commitment is made to one person, everyone else is "out of bounds." When a choice is made, those not chosen are relinquished. If you want variety, if you want to keep your options open, don't enter a committed relationship. It takes maturity to choose one person and let the rest remain fantasy material. Monogamy may not be one's nature, but it can certainly be one's choice.

A committed partner does not feel desire only for his or her partner, but in a relationship in which the partners pledge sexual monogamy, that desire is acted on *only* with one's partner. This seems to be the most crucial factor for most committed relationships.

FAITHFUL ATTRACTION

One thing that professionals agree on is that more couples are sexually faithful than the population would believe. Being unfaithful is certainly a more titillating topic than being monogamous, so it makes sense that talk shows, advertising, soap operas, etc. emphasize the more forbidden. However, interview after interview in my private practice, as well as feedback from colleagues, indicates that monogamy is preferred. Andrew Greeley, in his book *Faithful Attraction,* writes that according to a Gallup poll, 96 percent of married Americans reported that they were faithful in 1990.

Cheating is not always about sex; sex may be where it ends up, but sex is not necessarily the motivating factor. Many partners reach beyond their relationship for solutions that could have been found with their partners if they had only been willing to risk confrontation and resolution. Cheating is investing in another person emotional and/or sexual energy that should have been focused on one's mate, and in doing so, it siphons the primary relationship. Cheating does not have to include sex for it to be harmful to the committed relationship: Anything that creates an inappropriate boundary between a husband and wife diminishes their effectiveness as a team, and when one spouse has secrets and must lie to the other, a boundary is inadvertently constructed. Cheating is a form of indirect communication, a passive way of letting your partner know something that you are not willing to talk about directly.

If most spouses feel desire for or have sexual fantasies about men and women outside their committed relationships, why are some partners able to remain sexually faithful throughout their entire marriage and others not? Harvard psychologist Lawrence Kohlberg's research shines light on this phenomenon by pointing out that infidelity is a choice and that one's ability to make certain choices depends on one's moral development.

Young children tend to be rather hedonistic and self-centered. Their only reason for not doing something they shouldn't is avoidance of pain ("I don't hit my sister, because I might get spanked"). Later the hedonism gives way to the need for approval ("If I don't hit my sister, my mother will like me"). This is followed by a period of conforming to rules and authority. ("I don't hit my sister because we have a no-hitting rule at home"). Finally they come to the stage of decision making in which the higher good is acknowledged and includes the welfare of others ("I don't hit because that is no way to problem solve and only creates more problems").

We don't all achieve the highest stage of moral development by the time we are adults, as witnessed by the reasons given by partners who remain faithful but have reached different levels of development (maturity):

CHILD'S LEVEL: I don't mess around on my wife because I'd get caught and have hell to pay for it.

ADOLESCENT LEVEL: I don't mess around on my husband because people would talk terribly about me.

FULLY DEVELOPED: I don't mess around on my partner because that would be harmful to the trust between us and our commitment to each other.

For committed partners, faithfulness is a choice, not a sacrifice. These couples do not want to risk the loss of a cherished togetherness in order to indulge briefly in the present. They are aware that affairs are preventable. Despite the popular notion that they "just happen," there are very predictable stages to an affair, and stopping at any one of the stages is possible.

The first stage may involve a breakdown in communication between the partners, or loss of couple time as the result of their taking each other for granted, or conflict without resolution, or possibly chronic disappointment of one's expectations. Any of these lead to the necessary step of *rationalization*. If a person is committed to fidelity, then an affair cannot occur until a rationalization is developed. The most common one is believing that one "deserves" better.

Instead of communicating this directly with the partner and bringing in professional help if necessary, the spouse becomes involved outside the couple boundary. If you are truly convinced that you deserve better and that better is not possible within your marriage, then put your energy into exploring the option of divorce rather than have an affair. An affair will certainly not improve the situation at home, and if you no longer care about the situation at home, you are no longer committed to the relationship and should make your partner aware of this.

Another common rationalization is an altered state of mind: "I didn't know what I was doing. One thing led to another." Remember that *you* are in charge of protecting your commitment from harm and that the abuse of alcohol and drugs is one of the most harmful external stressors. If you are so high that you have no control over your behavior, you are already placing your relationship at risk. Stop before you harm it any further. Affairs don't "just happen"; they are choices we make. We deny that we have any active role in them, so that we can continue to feel we are "good" partners, while all the time we are taking chances that can result in irreparable damage.

A third rationalization is "providing support." Being the shoulder for someone to cry on is a powerful feeling and good for the ego. It is an honor to be chosen as the one that someone else opens up to. But empathy can lead to tenderness, and tender feelings easily shift into tender behaviors, which under certain conditions lead to erotic behaviors. Consolation is often combined with isolation, and isolation with an attractive stranger can ignite desire. There is nothing wrong with wanting to "be there" for someone else, but you must first protect your commitment by being very honest with yourself.

Carlfred Broderick, in his book *Couples,* suggests some questions to ask yourself if you find yourself in the position of being supportive to someone to whom you are also very attracted. I have adapted these below. Your answers to these questions can help you determine if you are on the brink of an affair, and allow you time to think it through before taking any action.

1. Does this person make me want to be next to her/him and be caring and nurturing?
2. Do I feel like I want to make up for all the pain and suffering he/she has gone through?
3. Would I still feel this way and be spending this time if this person were seventy-five or had a partner who collected guns?
4. Do I believe that we need to spend long hours alone together so I can help him/her?
5. Do I find myself sharing my own relationship problems as we talk, things I should be talking about with my partner, but don't?
6. Has this person begun to assume a dominant place in my thoughts? More than my partner?
7. Do I long to touch this person? Do I want to do more?
8. Does my partner know where I am and what I am doing?
9. Why are we not helping this person as a couple? [p. 164]

Broderick continues by warning that couples who have affairs have something in common: They all were able to find time alone, apart from others. An affair requires privacy. So if you find that you are identifying with the above questions, you can protect your primary, committed relationship by making sure you are never alone with the person you desire. It sounds too simple, but it actually works.

Remember it is up to *you* to protect what you and your life mate have built. All that can come tumbling down in a careless moment. Deeply committed partners are not that careless.

Frank Pittman helps demolish so many of the myths surrounding sexual infidelity. For starters, he lets us know that "Most affairs consist of a little bad sex and a lot of telephoning [p. 38]." He also believes that most affairs are friendships gone awry because of gender-based expectations and the inability of the sexes to cross gender lines and have relationships without sexualizing them.

Partners who are betrayed almost always come to the immediate conclusion that they are deficient in some way, driving their lover to someone else. Actually most affairs have to do with the ego state of the person having the affair (self-centered, for instance) rather than the person against whom the infidelity is being committed.

Committed couples intend not to have affairs, but committed couples are made up of humans, and human beings are imperfect creatures. Some partners believe that after an affair divorce is inevitable. Others see the possibility of healing. This is different for each couple. A one-time affair may result in the couple's learning more about themselves and each other, but it is not a damage-free event. Once trust has been betrayed, it takes a very long time to reconstruct it. Deeply committed couples usually attempt to do this. On the other hand, chronic infidelity signals a much deeper problem: that the partner is a poor candidate for commitment and should restrict himself or herself to dating.

So how do committed partners keep their desires under control? How do they remain faithful year after year, as their partners become more familiar and less mysterious, as they meet other attractive adults, as they bump up against the constraints of monogamy? The buzzword seems to be "hot" monogamy: eternal faithfulness without boredom or lack of excitement. This requires mental gymnastics.

Good sex is a state of mind. Committed partners know that being turned on is their own responsibility, not something their partners are supposed to do to them. (That's good news, because as you remember, you can't control your partner's behavior, but you can control your own.) This means that you have the capacity to keep yourself interested if you are willing to take the time and energy to do so.

Partners who leave relationships because they are bored with the sex are partners who expect their lovers to make it exciting for them. They are still stuck in the romanticized first stage and doomed to be disappointed. They will fail to take responsibility for their own sexual well-being, blame their partner, blame the relationship, and never get around to looking at their own contribution.

Fidelity requires discipline, and couples determined to remain faithful to each other exercise that discipline on a daily basis. They assume a future together, and they appreciate that each day is a step into that future, which they want to protect from harm.

COMMITMENT: THE LANGUAGE OF "WE"

There is a tremendous security that comes with commitment. Commitment is liberating. Time we might otherwise spend on worrying or trying to control our partner is freed for other activities. Commitment is a leap of faith. There is not now, nor ever will be, a way of proving our partner's fidelity. At some point we must simply let go and trust. We have no guarantee that our partner will be there when we awaken each morning. We can only hope.

It is in this fuzzy area, of faith, trust, and hope, that these lifelong relationships are forged. Perhaps this is why they are so fragile: They rely on human beings to keep them viable . . . and we are imperfect.

Couples who are very similar to begin with may not have as much difficulty arriving at a commitment as do those who are opposite. But those who are opposites may grow more in the process. On their fiftieth wedding anniversary David and Vera Mace, who together have published more than thirty books on sex, marriage, and the family, came to the following conclusion:

> We tried to determine what had been the decisive factors in our years of happiness together. . . . We arrived at an interesting conclusion. In our attempt to assess the favorable and unfavorable factors with which we had started out, and how we had made use of them, we reached the agreement that, on balance, the *differences* [my emphasis] between us and the challenge of working through them . . . had contributed more to our eventual happiness than the similarities that had seemed at first to constitute the promise of success! [p. 261].

As the culture around us becomes more and more comfortable with divorce as an option, couples will have to struggle harder to honor their commitments to one another. They will need larger support systems to help them in troubled times. We will witness fewer marriages of pleasurable longevity, as partners choose not to do the necessary work to keep commitment alive. Those bonds that do succeed will be very special, or as Ken Dychtwald, a specialist on longevity, has said, "Those who celebrate their golden anniversaries will have *mastered* marriage. It will be like mastering the violin or cello." (Wallis, p. 17)

When a couple vows to remain together forever, they are binding themselves to each other not only legally, economically, physically, and emotionally but spiritually as well. In the end partners look back:

> Real-life death scenes aren't like the movies. My husband, too tall for a regulation bed, lay with his feet sticking out of the covers. I stood clinging to his toes as though that would save his life. I clung so that if I failed to save him from falling off the cliff of the present, of the here and now, we'd go together. That's how it was in the netherworld of the intensive care unit. . . .
>
> It seemed that the entire world had turned into night. Cold and black. No place you'd volunteer to enter. Doctors

tried to be kind. Their eyes said, "This is out of our hands. There's nothing more we can do."

A nurse with a soft Jamaican lilt placed a pink blanket over my shoulders. Someone whispered, "It's just a matter of minutes."

Just a matter of minutes to tell each other anything we had ever forgotten to say. Just a few minutes to take an accounting of our days together. Had we loved well enough? [Ascher, p. 30].

Is there anything *you* have forgotten to say or do? Are you "up-to-date" with your companion? It's so easy to slip into the comfort of a long-term relationship and become lazy about attending to it. After you have forged a satisfying union, be careful about thinking your work is done. It's never really done. But it *does* get easier.

11

COUPLES COUNSELING: WHEN TO GO AND WHAT TO EXPECT

One advantage of marriage,
it seems to me, is that when
you fall out of love with him,
or he falls out of love with you,
it keeps you together until you maybe
fall in love again.

—*JUDITH VIORST*

It's harder to get a driver's license than a marriage license. That's certainly part of the problem. Few of the images that bombard us from advertising, television shows, movies, and fiction reveal how much work is actually involved when two individuals create a life partnership. Instead we are saturated with stories of couples who are either blissfully merged or on the verge of murder. There is no hint of what lies ahead for the former or what has propelled the latter into their current state. We are led to believe that committed partnership is something that just happens; we are ignorant of the degree of effort it takes to maintain a mutually satisfying union.

Growing up, utilizing these images as a template, a young man or woman comes to believe that staying together is more a matter of luck than sweat. Relationship failure is blamed on picking the "wrong" person, and as soon as the "right" person comes along, everything will be hunky-dory. Either you pick the right person or you don't. Either you stay together or you don't. It's not necessary to know the messy details.

But marriage* is only an abstraction; people are real. Without knowing the "details," couples are helpless to make right whatever has gone wrong. Our schools endeavor to make sure that all students know algebra when, in fact, only a fraction will ever use it. On the other hand, as a nation we face increasing divorce rates, spousal and child abuse, chemical dependency, spousal depression and suicide, with minimal marriage and family preparation in the curriculum.

Therapists, social workers, and educators will continue to argue for a more balanced approach to educating our youth; one that reflects the skills of not just working but living in our society. Without such an education, couples enter states of commitment poorly informed, unprepared for the work ahead, and deeply invested in romanticism. It is no wonder that they run into problems.

SEEKING PROFESSIONAL HELP

Couples used to seek counseling for two common reasons: Either disenchantment had set in and they felt married to a "stranger," or there was a major crisis that the marriage was too fragile to handle. Today there is a third reason, especially with the increase in remarriages and stepfamilies: a desire to seek help *before* the commitment is made. Men and women who are marrying after living independent lives, or who are remarrying later in life, are taking a more pragmatic approach to marriage. Rather than be swept away by romantic fantasies, these individuals are treating marriage like any other major investment they might make. They are seeking feedback on the potential partnership, and as if it were a business venture, they weigh the pros and cons. While they can't be faulted for their responsible approach, it is easy to imagine them at the altar, sealing the deal with a firm handshake.

---

* Although most of the couples seen in conjoint therapy are married, not all are, and the terms "marriage," "marital," and "spouse" may not reflect you and your mate. The information in this chapter applies to all committed couples seeking counseling.

Most of the couples presenting themselves for counseling today do not fall into this category. They are men and women who have significant doubts not only about whether their marriages have a future but about whether it is even possible to have a committed, mutually satisfying relationship. What they have witnessed growing up, what they observe among their coworkers, and what they hear as they socialize with other couples is discouraging and confirms their suspicions.

By the time they arrive, they either have battle fatigue or are withering from indifference. Like trying to put a jigsaw puzzle together when there are missing pieces, these couples have come up against the impossible, and some are exhausted from their effort. Others try to solve the problems of two by becoming three. If this is done through having an affair or by becoming parents, it never works. The third party they need must be someone outside their everyday lives, someone who is not emotionally invested in either partner, someone who will listen to them objectively.

Hesitation to seek professional help is easily understood. There is usually a reluctance to acknowledge that the relationship is in trouble, fear of being blamed, and shame caused by "failure" at something that was not expected to be difficult. Because of these factors, couples often wait until they are on the verge of separating before they reach outside their families for help. Many have tried to deal with their problems by not talking to each other because there are so many "hot" topics guaranteed to trigger conflict. With no talking, and probably no touching, by the time they make an appointment, intimacy is nonexistent and the partners are alienated, if not completely polarized.

It is too late if one partner has already decided to abandon the commitment. He or she may attend therapy sessions but not with any authenticity. The person's plan is to place the soon-to-be-abandoned lover in the hands of a caring therapist and thereby reduce the guilt of leaving. Entering treatment to please a partner is not a major problem because reluctant mates often change their perspective once they experience the value of an objective, nonjudgmental third party. But *remaining* in treatment to please a partner undermines the team effort and always backfires. If you are aware that you are not invested in your future as a couple, or in counseling, and are only going through the motions, come clean. The therapy can then shift from repairing to disconnecting, and the therapist can focus either on you as a couple needing help with terminating your commitment or on your partner through individual treatment.

With the advent of AIDS, more couples seem to have less of a "disposable" attitude toward their relationship and are willing to work with what they have. For many couples there simply isn't a model for how to do just that. Many try to fit their parents' traditional marriages into a context of dual careers, and that is not workable. Without professional help, these partners feel a personal failure rather than understand that the problem is much bigger than just the two of them. When men's and women's roles change, but expectations about marriage remain the same as the previous generation's, conflict is inevitable.

When a couple begins counseling, there is a vague sense of unmet needs, but frequently no one has clarified whether these are minor irritations or major problems. When a relationship is shaky, so-called trivial issues have the power to destroy. Everything at this point has been thrown together into "We're unhappy" or "We don't seem to communicate anymore." Actually there is no such thing as not communicating. Even the silent treatment is a form of communication. What is missing, however, is effective dialogue in which each partner feels heard and has a sense of impact on the other. "No" communication is really impotent communication.

Counseling is frequently sought after the "true" identity of one or both partners makes itself known. Although therapists anticipate this stage in adjusting to marital life, couples don't understand what is happening, and this triggers a crisis.

In the early stage of a relationship, differences are easily tolerated because attention is focused on how much the lovers have in common (a major component of romanticism). Lovers fall in love with what they want to see and hear. Nearsighted and deaf, they stumble into each other's arms. Nothing is too difficult to undertake. Nothing can separate them. They are intoxicated with each other and with possibility.

Minor irritations, quirks, and habits are "endearing" if noticed at all. His shyness is cute. Her boldness is exciting. As time passes, as the partners become more familiar with each other, they begin to feel safe enough to expose more of their authentic selves. In doing so, they gain a different perspective: His shyness is now understood to be antisocial behavior. Her boldness is nothing but rudeness.

The idealized partners evaporate, leaving real people to struggle with what they have just discovered: Dating is a sham, a shell game. The deception is taken personally rather than appreciated as a predictable step in becoming life partners. Each feels somewhat betrayed (the degree of betrayal depends on the revelation). There is a mutual sense of being paired with a "stranger," which is anxiety-provoking for a partner who feels safest when merged with another.

The realization hits: There are two individuals here, each with his or her own set of expectations and desire for control so that those expectations can be met. All of a sudden it isn't going to be as easy as it seemed. Maybe it was a bad idea to get together. Maybe this isn't the right person. Maybe we should just break up.

If a couple enters counseling at this stage, they discover that what has transpired is not an indicator that they are wrong for each other but rather an indication that their relationship is going through growing pains. Learning this provides tremendous relief if they want to remain together. If they weren't committed in the first place, they will continue to regard the crisis as proof that they weren't meant for each other. It's as good a reason as any if you're determined to bail out.

WHEN TO GO

Long before a couple enters marital therapy, the thought is there: Things are not getting better. For some couples that's enough motivation to schedule an appointment. For others things have to get much worse, especially if seeking help is regarded as a sign of weakness or failure. Our society is based on a fierce independence, which at times is taken to unhealthy extremes. The truth is, it takes courage to make that first phone call because it is frightening to imagine that your relationship may be dying and embarrassing not to be able to save it.

To help you organize your thoughts about the current status of your relationship, complete "Signs of Relationship Dissatisfaction" and "Issues" in the Exercises Section.

You may be wondering if you have good reason to seek professional help, if what is wrong is really all that serious, or if anyone can really help. You may find that you go back and forth between wanting to make an appointment and trying to work on things yourselves. You may even have made an appointment only to cancel it at the last minute. This ambivalence is natural, especially if you don't know what to expect from counseling.

Many problems between partners are resolved through the efforts of the partners alone or just by allowing enough time to pass. In order to help you decide if it is time to reach out, here are some guidelines for couples who are thinking about seeking professional help. It is a good idea to do so when:

- You are unable to communicate undefensively, when there are too many "hot" topics.
- You no longer feel heard; you no longer care about listening to your partner.
- Your perceptions of the problem(s) are so polarized that you can't problem solve.
- Conflict has escalated into name-calling, threats of abandonment, or physical abuse.
- The same themes occur in your arguments; there is never any resolution of disagreement.
- You are feeling out of control or overcontrolled by your partner.
- You have increasing resentments that you are not sharing with your partner.
- You or your partner have been unable to forgive a past hurt.
- You no longer feel psychologically "safe" with your partner, so that true intimacy is impossible.
- Your problems are serious enough so that one or both of you is escaping into alcohol, drugs, food, television, work, etc.
- There is no balance in your effort; one partner is consistently overburdened.

- You know what needs to change, but you are fearful of that change or don't know how to go about it.
- You no longer believe that your partner is concerned about your welfare; you believe your partner has become too self-focused to participate in the relationship.
- You find yourself compromising your values in order to stay together.
- You tend to avoid each other rather than arrange time together.
- You continue to argue, but you fail to make up and learn from the conflict.
- Your motivation is too low to make significant changes on your own.
- You consistently feel unlovable or unloving.
- You consistently feel lonely even when you are together.
- You are more invested in proving you are right than in understanding your partner.
- You hope your partner screws up so you have a good excuse for being mad.
- You are angry at your partner most of the time.
- You can't let go of your unmet expectations, and they are preventing you from enjoying your partner.
- You ignore the effort your partner is making and focus on criticizing instead.
- "Divorce" is a serious topic.

Looking at all the reasons that couples seek counseling, I think David Schnarch summarizes it best:

> Marriage forces us to see (if we have the courage to look) the worst, as well as the best, parts of ourselves: it reveals our capacity for sadism and hatred, our desire to punish and control our spouses, our secret neediness and insecurity, our shame-filled sexual fantasies, and, most of all, our usually unacknowledged terror of being left alone to our own inadequate selves, of being rejected, or losing someone we love.
>
> But these horrors are precisely what people . . . hope to escape when they marry. Each spouse hopes to have fi-

nally found the "other half" that will make him or her a whole self. Marital problems often surface when the thin membrane of this fantasy is stretched to the breaking point, when life and its vicissitudes have shredded the fabric of bogus togetherness . . . [p. 46].

WHEN YOU SHOULDN'T WASTE YOUR MONEY

Any ethical marriage counselor will tell you when you are wasting your time and money. There are certain requirements necessary before therapy can be effective, and if those aren't in place, it is almost always an exercise in frustration. Therapy is not a miracle. It isn't something that is done *to* you. It is a cooperative effort requiring a team, and your participation on that team is vital.

You have probably heard from some of your family or friends or coworkers that they tried counseling, but "it didn't work." Sometimes it doesn't. Following are some of the things that contribute to failure in couples counseling. If you or your partner identifies with any of these, know that you are in treatment with the odds against you and that individual therapy is probably the best choice:

- A partner does not take the work or process seriously enough and simply goes through the motions, without investing in the outcome.
- A partner has already decided to abandon the commitment and is in counseling only so he or she can say "I tried."
- A partner is having an affair that will not be relinquished.
- In spite of warnings about the damage to the marriage, a partner is determined to continue certain behaviors (violence, out-of-control alcohol or drug use, chronic infidelity).
- A partner is too immature to let go of unrealistic expectations left over from childhood and insists on their being met by his or her mate.
- A partner is overly invested in independence and separateness and is not willing to shift to interdependence.
- A partner has no intention of making any recommended changes in behavior or attitude.

- A partner continues to place the relationship low on his or her priority list.
- Partners have come together through an unplanned pregnancy under parental pressure, with little interest in freely forming a bond.
- One partner is invested only in getting his or her needs met and is uninterested in what is best for the relationship.

FINDING A THERAPIST

Your relationship deserves the attention of a qualified, experienced professional who specializes in working with couples. The best way to find that person is to begin asking those close to you if they can recommend a name or two. If you know a couple who has been through counseling and found it to be a positive experience, contacting their therapist is a good beginning but not necessarily foolproof. Sometimes things just don't click.

If you don't know anyone who is seeing a therapist, get in touch with the American Association of Marriage and Family Therapists (AAMFT) at 1-800-374-AMFT. It is in Washington, D.C., and publishes a brochure that can serve as a guide for you. Each state has its own association, and the AAMFT can put you in touch with the one nearest you. By calling the association, you can obtain the names of several qualified professionals in your area.

Look in your local newspaper for announcements of public lectures or programs presented by local colleges and hospitals. See if any of the speakers are addressing relationship issues. Attend several presentations until you discover a speaker who appears knowledgeable, as well as someone you think you might be comfortable working with. These speakers almost always practice therapy in addition to teaching or research. If the speaker is associated with a hospital or university, it usually has a clinic where there are other professionals as well.

When you have decided on a name to call, remember that you are a consumer and are calling about a service. You have the right to ask questions about the service you are considering. You have the right to ask questions about the person who is going to be rendering that service. Find out his or her background, preparation for this field, the length of time he or she has been practicing, and whatever else you need to ask to determine for yourself if this person is indeed qualified.

Once you have determined that the person you are calling is qualified, you must find out if treatment is going to be affordable. What does this person charge per session? How long is a session? Is this negotiable? Does she or he accept insurance? Payment plans?

Therapy is expensive. It has to be considered as an investment in your future and the future of your family. You are not entering treatment simply to put a Band-Aid on the current problem, but rather you are attempting to understand how you got to where you are and how to avoid it in the future. Dollar for dollar, successful therapy yields terrific dividends over the years. If, however, you are unable to pay out of pocket or lack insurance coverage, there are many qualified professionals and clinics that provide services on a sliding scale. These are often the least experienced counselors, but not always. All professional mental health workers have a network of colleagues. If you are not able to afford a particular therapist, ask for the names of two or three others.

Once you have found a person who is qualified and affordable, it is important to inquire about his or her experience with couples. When you are seeking couples counseling, and you have equally qualified and affordable therapists to choose from, the one who specializes in marriage and family therapy is preferable to someone who spends most of his or her time providing individual therapy. There is an entirely different philosophy behind working with individuals from working with couples and families. To help you through the morass of professional help available, here is a brief description of the differences among various mental health professionals:

Psychiatrists are physicians. They have completed medical training like other doctors. They are able to write prescriptions for medication. They use a medical model or disease model and are trained to think in terms of diagnosis and pathology. More are beginning to specialize in working with couples and families and moving away from the traditional disease model.

Psychologists do not dispense medication. They often administer tests to measure (and possibly predict) behavior. They rely on the data from the tests to help them design their treatment plans. Some prefer to remain in research. Others enter clinical practice, working with individuals, families, and groups. Some focus on diagnosis and pathology, while others choose to emphasize health.

Clinical social workers are usually trained in the medical model, focusing on individual diagnosis. Some have extensive experience in medical social work as well and prefer to remain associated with hospitals or clinics. They do not dispense medication or do testing. They see individuals, couples, and families.

Marriage and family therapists are professionals with special training in working with couples and larger family groups. Emphasis is not on disease or individual diagnosis, as the "patient" is the family or the marriage. Focus is on the dynamics between family members rather than individual pathology. They do not dispense medication or do testing.

Other options available for counseling are clergy, psychiatric nurses, and nurse practitioners. Any of the above women and men may hold more than one license or have been trained in more than one profession. For instance, a marriage and family therapist may also be a psychologist; that means that in addition to specializing in treating couples, he or she can administer any necessary psychological tests. Each state regulates what each profession is allowed to do, some more vigorously than others.

Once you have obtained the names of several therapists, before you make your final choice, it might be helpful for you to know what some of the different treatment approaches are. There are hundreds of ways to address the problems you bring to a counselor. The most common practices fall into one of the following categories:

Psychodynamic (Freudian, psychoanalysis, object relations). Emphasis is on the internal world of the individual; marital dissatisfaction is believed to be a result of the failed development of either or both partners, especially failure to separate from parents; inadequate parenting is blamed for current marital problems; little attention is paid to life cycle after adolescence; no mention of external stressors; couples' expectations are both conscious and unconscious; no interest in the dynamics between partners; behavior is motivated by drives (sexual, etc.)

Behavioral (focus on laws of learning that guide human behavior). Not concerned with the unconscious; emphasis on response to environment rather than developmental issues or internal ego states; marital therapy focuses on patterns of behavior exchanged between partners; cost/benefit analysis of these exchanges; reward versus punishment; reciprocity versus coercion; history not important; application of principles in present to alleviate problems; motivation is out of response to stimulus.

Humanistic (emphasis on healthy individual). Client seen in a constant state of growing; creation of a safe environment to be authentic in; risk taking encouraged; focus on individual responsibility; not interested in history; spontaneity encouraged; feelings valued as guide; marriage seen as a place for personal growth to occur through open communication with partner; motivation is out of human desire to be the best one can be.

Cognitive therapy (influence of thoughts on behavior). Focus is on how we distort information as we take it in and the fact that emotions are heavily influenced by these distorted thoughts; little interest in history; couples therapy focuses on self-talk as well as the distortions between partners that lead to misunderstandings.

Feminist therapy (nongendered approach). Involves the resocialization of both men and women based on the belief that much of our behavior is organized by gender and that gender roles limit one's growth, including the development of mutually satisfying relationships; dysfunction traced to rigid role expectations; focus on how damaging sex role socialization can be; goal of equal partnering through shared power; improved intimacy through removal of gender-based expectations.

Family therapy (systems approach). Major impact on field of conjoint therapy; focus is on relational aspects of marital satisfaction instead of isolated individual behavior; concepts of boundaries and triangles (now used in chemical dependency treatment); belief that individuals are part of a larger system; when one family is troubled, all are affected; emphasis is on "between"; issues of under- and overresponsibility of spouses; past explored with regard to issues in each partner's "family of origin."

With regard to being an RB or an LB partner, some types of therapy may appeal to one partner more than the other. For instance, there is often dreamwork involved in psychoanalysis, Gestalt, and Jungian modalities of treatment. Since LBs have difficulty remembering their dreams and do not communicate metaphorically, an LB might feel alienated by this approach. On the other hand, behavioral therapy has great appeal to someone who is solution-oriented. An RB partner is well suited for humanistic therapy with its emphasis on feelings and relationships, whereas he or she might be turned off by what cognitive therapy has to offer. When people talk about therapy's "not working," sometimes it is because there was a poor match in the beginning.

When you contact a therapist and begin asking your questions, pay attention to your first impressions: Do you feel welcome to ask questions, or does the therapist seem defensive? Are you getting answers, or is the conversation being turned back on to you? You are searching for the person you believe will be most helpful. If you don't feel comfortable with the first phone call, try again. It is possible that you reached the therapist at an inconvenient time. If by the second call your questions have not been answered to your satisfaction or you feel as if you are being rushed, then you probably won't be comfortable in session with this person either.

A competent professional will not be offended by your questions. Have your questions organized and written down, however, so you make the call as brief as possible. The object is not to do therapy over the phone but only to establish if this person is a candidate for further consideration. Be a responsible consumer; you need to put at least as much time into this as you would into buying a car.

WHAT TO EXPECT ONCE YOU'RE THERE

Couples initiate counseling with a common thought: "If the therapist would change my partner, things would be just fine." It is a rude awakening to discover that the therapist does not possess this power. Experienced therapists have long given up the romantic notion that they can change another human being's behavior. If you are counting on this particular trick, you will be disappointed.

This first lesson is the hardest: Your partner isn't going to change anything that he or she doesn't want to change. However, a therapist can help your partner (and you) explore how *not* changing will affect your relationship. A therapist can create a safe environment in which experimenting with change is not as frightening as it might be outside the session. It may appear that therapists do in fact change people, but in reality, once a person is determined to change, all the therapist does is facilitate the process.

Couples enter counseling so that their marriage can be "fixed." They often approach the process as if it were a surgical procedure, expecting the counselor to do the operation while they supply a history. They soon discover that more is expected of them than just telling their story. The most common misconception about couples counseling is that the counselor will tell you what to do, that you will only have to follow directions. While some types of therapy are more directive than others (behavioral modification, for instance), in conjoint counseling active participation by the partners is necessary and expected. The therapist serves as an impartial sounding board, commentator, and catalyst to get things moving. The experienced counselor knows that in time the couple's natural wisdom will surface, and the counselor need only assist the partners in finding their own solutions.

Therapists can't make you feel better, correct the past, turn you into different people, motivate you, or be a constant source of strength for you. Just like you, they are people with limits. It's not so much that you have failed to correct things yourselves and now the counselor will step in and be "successful," but rather it is that you are *living in* the marriage, while the counselor is *observing* the marriage. This gives the counselor a tremendous advantage: that of an outsider's unbiased perspective.

It is important that you and your partner believe that the therapist is equally committed to both of you. Each of your viewpoints deserves attention, and although they probably differ, each has merit. There may be times when it seems that one of you is getting special treatment or more attention than the other, and this may be true. It is part of the process, and you have to trust the process if you are going to participate in it. If one partner seems hesitant to become involved in counseling, the therapist may spend a larger portion of a session focused on that reluctance until that partner has a better understanding. At another time a session may be very stressful for one partner, and the therapist may seem to be more occupied with that person.

Don't use an individual session to determine if there is a bias. Instead look back over three or four sessions before you conclude there is an imbalance. If you then continue to feel the same way, discuss it. It is important that you trust the process, whether or not it makes sense at the time. More important, you certainly must trust your therapist.

Trained professional counselors have developed a body of special knowledge to draw upon and have been taught specific skills to facilitate the process of discovery ahead of you. That special knowledge allows the therapist to assist you and your partner in:

- Exploring your strengths as a couple as well as identifying areas that need work
- Helping you increase your awareness of thoughts, feelings, and ideas that may either interfere with or enhance your interdependence
- Identifying your options and probable consequences of each choice
- Changing behaviors in order to achieve desired goals
- Communicating authentically and meaningfully
- Identifying patterns of interaction that are toxic to your partnership
- Learning how to engage in conflict without harming the relationship
- Developing problem-solving skills
- Grieving and healing your past hurts, disappointments, and resentments
- Identifying unrealistic expectations you may have for marriage and for each other

- Constructing a partnership in which each of you feels respected as a separate person
- Creating a mutually satisfying sexual relationship
- Empowering yourselves as a couple
- Developing a plan for confronting issues after graduating from therapy

Couples counseling does not ensure you against separation, but it will, if you hang in there long enough, prevent an impulsive, in-the-heat-of-the-moment decision to abandon your commitment. Once you've gone through the process, if you do decide to divorce, that decision will be a rational one, one that is much easier to live with.

PHASE ONE

Your first appointment is usually an information-gathering session. The amount of information the therapist requires depends on the type of therapy you are entering. (A Gestalt therapist may want nothing more than a few descriptive statements about your relationship. A psychodynamic therapist will ask for both individual and couple histories.) The description of couples counseling presented here is based on my training as a marriage and family therapist and my private practice. Your experience will be similar in some ways and different in others.

During phase one I meet with couples once a week. As they progress through treatment, visits are less frequent. At the initial information-gathering session I am interested in what attracted partners to each other in the first place and what keeps them together. I ask them to describe their parents' marriages and what these marriages taught them about being an individual man or woman, as well as a partner. I want to know the status of their commitment and a brief overview of the time they have spent together. Of great significance to me is their early expectations and what has happened to them.

I ask why they are seeking counseling at this particular time and how they believe I can help them. What do they want to have happened by the time we are through working together? This gives me a sense of how much time our work may take, and people always ask. It took the couple a long time to get to this place, but without exception, they are always surprised at how long it may take them to reach their stated goals. It is my duty to make sure that what they want is feasible. If I pay no attention to their unreasonable time frame, they will feel responsible for the failure ahead. (There *is* a form of brief therapy that focuses only on the "presenting problem." It offers a quick fix but does not focus on the larger picture. A behavior is changed, but underlying attitudes, beliefs, and feelings are not explored, and these may leave the couple open to recurring problems in the future.)

Once we establish what the partners want to have happen and a realistic time frame for the work, I go over the basics. We discuss the seriousness of the work ahead, the importance of keeping appointments, and the cancellation policy. Confidentiality is discussed as well as the fact that sex with a therapist is *never* part of legitimate, professional work. I explain that if either is having an affair, the affair will need to end before serious work can begin because a split commitment is no commitment. If a partner needs help in terminating an affair, we begin our work there.

The partners are told that if either has a private conversation with me, the other will be apprised of it since I cannot be the "keeper of secrets" and remain impartial at the same time. This is an important part of the early phase, when each partner confuses counseling with appearing in court and I am cast as the judge as each pleads his or her case for requesting change in the other.

At this point one or the other often says, "I'm not the one with the problem." Again there is confusion about the process of therapy: the myth that someone must be blamed. This alone keeps the majority of couples out of counseling, especially those who were raised by critical, demanding parents. These partners expect to be blamed and don't see the point in spending money on anything so potentially painful.

My experience confirms the philosophy that problems are between the partners. I assume that both are players, and I am not interested in who started what; my interest is in helping them resolve their issues and resolve them as a team.

Because things can get a bit hairy at times, I mention that one or both of them will feel like dropping out at some point. There will be times when old resentments are exposed, and these can be very painful. Topics that they have been avoiding will need to be discussed, and they can be uncomfortable for everyone. The couple must be helped to believe that they can transcend that pain and discomfort. It is important that they develop not only confidence in themselves to work through whatever comes up but confidence in me to guide them as well as confidence in the process itself. (This may not happen until the first crisis, which usually occurs in the middle phase.)

The early phase, in my practice, is primarily an educational process. One of the most common problems for couples is that they run into difficulty simply because they are ignorant. How can they possibly know about living in a committed partnership when as a society we are not committed to teaching our youth? They learn from their observations, and unfortunately their models are rarely a paragon of marital health. Couples need information in order to act. When they don't have it, they will fill in the gaps with their own assumptions and inherited myths.

I begin with some brief remarks about different types of relationships: dependent, independent, mixed, and interdependent. *Dependent relationships* involve two partners who lean so heavily on each other that neither can develop as an individual. If one lets go, the other falls. There is total merging with the other and a great fear of being alone in the world. *Independent ones* involve two strongly individualistic people who fear needing others. They are self-sufficient to the extreme. Very little relationship actually exists except for pragmatic reasons. *Mixed partnerings* involve one dependent and one independent partner. They have the most difficulty and are the most common type seen in couples counseling; that which is a problem for one is not a problem for the other. Their very needs are polarized, and they cannot manage to meet in the middle.

The fourth kind, *interdependent relationships,* is the model of a healthy couple. It involves a balance of both individual and relationship needs, mutual respect, shared power, reciprocity, individual security as well as teamwork and shared values and goals. Although a marital therapist is supposed to be value-free to a great extent, I admit I use the model of interdependence as a template for couples who seek help.

At this point I usually say something about the difference between immature and mature love. We all would like to meet someone who could meet our every need and let us have our own way all the time; this is a fantasy left over from childhood. *Immature love* is focused on receiving, getting, being filled up, securing reassurance, anxiety about one's lovability and is based on the idea that "I love you because I need you." Immature lovers frequently feel cheated in their relationships. They constantly complain about not getting enough (it doesn't matter what). Their natural state is one of complaining rather than doing. Security is housed in someone else, never in themselves.

Mature love, however, is focused on gratitude for what does happen, a sense of joy about loving the other person and what is possible as a team. The sense is "I love you because you expand my world of possibilities."

About now during the session each partner is likely to decide that he is mature and his partner is immature. We explore this conclusion and eventually revise it to embrace the possibility that both of them have some growing up to do in the relationship department. Spreading the responsibility around is an important task of this first phase. It eliminates blame and increases a sense of possibility. If only one person is the problem, then everything rests on that person's having a personality transplant. If, however, each of the partners is coarchitect of their difficulties, each can decide for herself or himself if she or he wants to make the necessary changes in order to achieve what is desired.

Those changes include a major shift in attitudes toward each other. To do serious work—work that will bring them closer to what they want—each partner must be willing to take some risks. These risks in themselves are a part of the move from immature to mature love. The partners must be willing to:

- Believe each other's reality (if she says something hurts her feelings, don't tell her she's being too sensitive)
- Refocus on their own behavior (if you think your partner is al-

ways after you to do something, look at your own avoidant behavior and how that triggers him)

- Stop blaming the other (begin to acknowledge that you got to this place through your combined actions)
- Give up old ways of being that are harmful to your relationship (these may be things you like to do or have always done out of habit)
- Adjust expectations (about each other as well as the relationship itself)

That last item, "adjust expectations," is one of the simplest ways to feel better about a relationship. During this first phase of counseling I introduce the concept of unrealistic expectations because they pose a serious threat to the work ahead. Too many partners want something that is simply not there. It may have been there during dating, when motivation is at its highest level and when anything can be maintained for a brief period. (Common complaint: "He was so romantic when we were first going out; wrote me little love notes and left them on my pillow. Now the notes are on the kitchen counter and they say 'out of milk.' ")

The mistake is the assumption that any particular behavior is going to continue, that it is a natural act for that person, part of his or her way of being in the world. The expectation is regarded as a given that is then taken away; this is why it feels like betrayal. But in reality it was a role—part of courting—and in time those roles are dropped and the authentic person emerges.

Think about the amount of time you spent together and the hours you kept when you were first lovers. On the basis of those experiences you might expect to feel high levels of chemistry forever, or you might expect that your partner would always want to stay up late with you. But the fact is time has passed and things have changed. Not only has your partner changed, but you're not the same person either. Once you've stepped out of the artificial light of those first months (and even years) together and into the daylight of reality, you may be disappointed, but you can now begin to relate more honestly. You can't even start the process of changing your relationship until you acknowledge your mutual disappointments. As this happens, you move into phase two. If you hang in there during phase two, the most difficult time in counseling, you may be fortunate to discover that happiness is not about having what you want but about wanting what you already have.

PHASE TWO

As couples progress through their counseling, they need to be seen less often. During this phase I tend to see couples once every other week. (On occasion there may be a need to be seen more frequently, and that is arranged.) I shift to every other week so that partners have time to put into action skills they will learn. Changing one's habitual responses to stress, one's partner, even oneself is a slow process. Couples need time to practice new patterns of relating to each other.

Spouses have two movies playing on the same screen, each with its beginning, middle, and end. By playing simultaneously, they create a scrambled, nonsensical world. The individual partner brings a lifetime of experiences to the relationship in the form of her or his own personal film; each partner thinks his film is the only one playing. The marriage counselor is not so much a film critic as an editor. Snipping and splicing here and there, he or she preserves what is vital to work on and relinquishes that which is distracting, extraneous, or irrelevant.

In this phase of counseling there is a lot of communication between partners, usually more talking than listening because they have yet to master that particular skill. It is a time of ventilation. Resentments are aired. Unrealized dreams are revealed. The past still hurts, the present is intolerable, and the future seems very fragile.

This phase can turn ugly very fast in the hands of an inexperienced therapist. The flood of emotions can easily overwhelm anyone who has not rafted these waters before. Even a superior therapist can have a bad day and get swept away, losing sight of the process itself. Some counseling sessions will be better than others. (It's interesting that when couples are asked, following termination of treatment, if any particular session was helpful, it often turns out to be one in which the therapist considered her work to have been mediocre. Proof that when the therapist gets out of their way, couples make the greatest progress!)

All the hurt, resentment, anger, and disappointment are blocking any caring, so as uncomfortable as it is, talking about these things clears the way for healing. There is a danger, however, in doing irreparable harm if you and your partner spend too much time focused on your grievances without committing yourself to the work ahead and moving on. If you should drop out of treatment at this phase, nothing will have been gained, but a great deal will have been lost. The trick is to stay focused on the commitment, the relationship between you, rather than on each other.

Your marriage is a separate entity that is entirely dependent upon the two of you. To be successful in therapy, when you are feeling rage toward your partner, who is being a "jerk," or are unable to summon up compassion for her "stupidity," you must refocus yourself and concentrate on the bond between you. You're not mad at your relationship; you aren't fed up with your commitment. You are mad at *him;* fed up with *her.* These feelings are about a partner who, from your perspective, isn't being much of a partner.

To do the work of this difficult phase, it is important to hold the thought that the two of you have created something and that something has been neglected and now needs your attention. Transfer your attention, your energy to that and away from your frustrating partner. If you are able to do this, you are making yet another shift from immature to mature love. Mature love isn't concerned with who is "right" and who is "wrong." It's about "what can we do to protect our commitment from our own insecurities."

At this point I usually share my observation that some themes seem to be emerging. I might even ask the couple, "If your relationship were a book or a movie, what would be the title?"

A common theme is loneliness. Marriage can be a very lonely place. People expect to have many needs met by marriage. No other society demands as much from marriage as ours. Considering our expectations, it's a miracle that couples are able to maintain something even close to what they desire. We are seeking more from a lifetime companionship than it can provide. There we hope to be loved for who we are, flaws and all. There we seek shelter from an impersonal, sometimes crazy world.

There is a fundamental loneliness in simply existing that can never be erased. Gibson Winter *(Love and Conflict),* notes that we are lonely when "our lives are not knit to others [p. 183]." No matter how close we get to others, the reality of our separate self remains. By trying to merge with others, by joining, by seeking companionship, we hope that the loneliness will disappear. When we find someone special, we are too preoccupied to notice the loneliness, but when the relationship is in trouble or if it ends, that awareness emerges in full force.

Just as no single relationship can handle the weight of all our needs, our partner cannot be expected to carry burdens that are our own responsibility. This becomes apparent during this second phase, as each declares his or her fear of failing the other: "I know you need my support, but I can't seem to give you enough," or "I tell you that you look fine, but you keep asking if you look fat." During this phase partners begin to understand that much of their conflict resolves around individual issues and that the separation of individual issues from couple issues is difficult. When we expect our partner to make up for our lack of esteem, confidence, security, or motivation, we are overburdening the commitment. Conflict is often triggered because we confuse being disappointed with, and angry at, our lover with being disappointed with, and angry at, ourselves.

In this phase I help couples identify "red flags" or things that set them off. Terminal language, like "you always" or "you never," usually triggers an argument. Effective communication skills are learned, and partners begin to shift from "making their case" to "hearing both sides."

We begin to experiment with change, which is frightening for both partners. We all prefer our own way; we prefer to stay the way we are and have our partner do all the changing, especially if our needs are being met. The partner whose needs are met has very little motivation for change. To change under these circumstances is another move from immature love to mature love.

To give up a situation that meets one's needs in order to gratify the unmet needs of a partner or the relationship is an act of personal sacrifice, and immature love does not sacrifice. Immature lovers want it all, and they want it their way. Most partners, by the time they reach therapy, have come to the conclusion that their mates are demanding and that they themselves are sacrificing.

Midway into the second phase partners may begin to think that they do not need to continue. They find that conflict has diminished and that they are now once again thinking about the future. They become carelessly optimistic, forgetting to practice their communication skills and pay attention to their own contribution to the problems. They have a false confidence about being able to tackle whatever arises, leading them to slack off from taking an active role in their relationship and protecting it from individual harm. They have certainly made progress, but how far they have yet to go is reflected in the crisis that almost always occurs at this time.

I ask them to take on a personal challenge. Each partner is asked, "What is one change you could make, which you are willing to make, that would bring about a tremendous positive difference in your relationship?" Once the change is identified, I ask the other partner, "Do you agree? Would that make a significant positive difference?" The change must be small enough to commit to but great enough to have an impact.

Once the change is agreed upon as significant, that partner commits to incorporating it into his or her life for the next thirty days, no matter what. This means that the change is not an exchange; it is not dependent upon what the other partner does or does not do. It is an *individual* commitment, reflecting the fact that individual responsibility is vital to the health of any relationship. The promise is to the relationship, not to the partner. At the end of the thirty days there is no one to answer to but oneself as to whether the commitment was accomplished or abandoned.

Because a relationship is a system, working like a Swiss watch, change in one partner is not isolated but rather triggers change in the other. One partner cannot change without having an impact on the other; the other cannot respond to the impact while remaining the same, so he or she must also change. The couple who was ready to leave counseling, believing that they had learned all they needed to learn, is now thrown into a tailspin because they did not anticipate the power of change.

The crisis may be so severe that one partner may say, "I'm no longer sure I want to keep working on this. I don't even know if I want to stay together." At this point the couple is reminded that they did not commit to staying together when they entered counseling; they committed to doing the work. If at the end of that work they no longer want to be joined, that will be their decision. However, the work is not over, and to make a decision now to abandon not only the counseling but the relationship as well is premature. This is a very difficult time for couples. It is the most challenging time for the therapist. Those couples who keep their commitment to therapy begin to do even deeper and more rewarding work.

It is now that a partner begins to understand that he or she has married "several" people. Each of us is different, given different contexts. I am different with my husband from the way I am with a client, different with a friend from the way I am with my dentist. We humans are complex, multifaceted beings. When we begin to make changes in our lives, different aspects of ourselves emerge. If those changes are significant, anyone close to us must learn to relate to someone "new."

Change means that a partner's behavior is no longer predictable, and that can be threatening when the other partner has relied on their mate to be a particular way: "He was always shy. I could always count on him just standing around at a party. But now he goes right up to anybody and just starts talking. I'm afraid he might find somebody more interesting."

Healthy relationships are relationships that allow for the growth of the individual partners. However, there is very little preparation for the impact of that growth on intimacy. Growth can feel like a betrayal: "He never used to be that way" or "She wasn't into that when I first met her." It is as if we expected our partners to remain frozen in some earlier form so that we ourselves don't have to adjust, change, and grow.

When partners come to therapy, they want their spouses to change, but they have certain changes in mind for them, changes that will ensure that they get *their* needs met. But mates aren't always that cooperative and often change in unexpected ways. Either way, whether a change is expected or not, the couple is totally unprepared for the shift in the system, the relationship itself. Those with a strong foundation can ride it out. Those with shakier footing sometimes don't survive.

Because of the upheaval brought by actual change, partners ask, "What happened? We were doing just fine." Almost always, as they look back, they realize that they have slipped back into old behavior, neglected what they have learned, and once again been taking the relationship for granted, rather than remembering it has a life of its own and is subject to illness and even death if neglected long enough. It takes a crisis to shake things back up again to a level of active commitment. Each may respond to the crisis in a different way.

Therapists and researchers alike agree on one thing: It is not differences between partners that create problems for couples but rather *how they handle their differences.* As each spouse protects his or her separate self, as each lover confesses different needs, as each mate discloses different preferences, the system must adjust if it is to continue.

Following the crisis, the work begins focusing on those differences, for that is what the crisis has revealed. The ongoing struggle between keeping an individual identity and living in a relationship takes on a different light as each partner appreciates that this conflict is a necessary part of true intimacy, that intimacy is impossible without this tug-of-war. Together we look at the function of conflict. It is then no longer personalized but rather understood to be necessary to a working partnership.

With a reduction in personalization, a couple can begin to examine a mate's requests with a more cooperative lens and a partner's motivation with a more forgiving eye. By now the partners have made important discoveries: that each is both alike and different from the other; that neither will probably make any radical changes but that each will become a variation of who he or she was when they first met; that the self is always changing, and sometimes those changes show and sometimes they don't; and that sometimes one partner's changing may be difficult for the other but that together they can work it through.

PHASE THREE

The last phase of counseling is composed of visits every three to four weeks because the couple is now far more independent than when they began treatment. They have more confidence in their ability to intervene themselves before an irritation becomes an issue or communication breaks down. This phase focuses primarily on these tasks:

- Reviewing what has been learned and what has been accomplished in relation to the original goals
- Identifying problem patterns that got the couple into trouble in the first place and how to prevent them from happening again
- Predicting possible future issues and formulating a plan to cope with them in a cooperative way
- Taking full responsibility for one's contribution to the problems within the relationship
- Forgiving one's partner for past transgressions
- Renewing their commitment to the bond between them
- Letting go of the therapy process and the therapist as their guide

The essence of this phase is to reinforce the fact that partner blaming (most of phase one and early phase two) is not as productive as looking at one's own contribution to the problems since that is the only behavior under each person's control. It is about realizing that marital actions are bilateral and therefore any change must be contributed to by both. It is about the lovers' discovering how they have gotten in their own way and that most of what they wanted was there all along, but viewed through the lens of an infant's fears, a child's longing, or an adolescent's stubbornness, all of which make it impossible to participate fully in a satisfying adult partnership in the present.

This stage is about discovering that one's partner is not, nor ever will be, everything one has expected. It is about accepting limitations and letting go of fantasies. It is about confronting reality, embracing differences, and coping with disappointment. It is about celebrating a shared achievement.

Couples who hang in there until the end of treatment know the benefits of doing so. Unfortunately many couples settle for elevating their "unbearable" relationship to "bearable" and stop with phase two. Those who do stay in treatment truly invest in themselves as a couple. They learn that although there may be a problem in the future that they need help with, it does not mean that they have failed. They understand that *knowing when to ask for assistance* is the sign of a healthy partnership. Much of their work has been about shifting attitudes, and by phase three one of the most significant shifts has been the move from rigid thinking to an increased awareness of options. If seeking help is believed to be a sign of weakness, the partners remain helpless to improve their situation. When they discover that it is, in fact, an exercise of choice, they are on the road to empowering themselves.

The final appointment (they know, of course, that they can return for "booster" sessions at any time in the future) is one of mixed emotions. There is a sense of loss in letting go of old arrangements; a sense of rebirth with the adoption of newer, healthier ones; an air of confidence as the couple, wiser than before, returns to their daily lives; and a feeling of jubilation as the couple celebrates a sense of renewal. (Some even choose to renew their vows either in session or in a more formal way with friends and family.)

In that last hour together there is also anxiety mixed with sadness. Therapy is about growing. It is about growing up and letting go. The couple must let go of their dependence on me as their therapist, which they began doing, slowly, as the appointments became less and less frequent.

Termination is about good-byes, and *I* must let go as well. Mine is a letting go filled with joy, pride, satisfaction, and sorrow. After the couple leaves, I look back and remember their first visit, and I smile. What they wanted seemed so impossible to them. It wasn't, and I knew it then. But *they* know it now, and that's the fun. Waiting for that moment is what it's all about for me.

12

OPEN LETTERS

Dear RB Partner:

Many of the ways in which you differ from your LB partner may be seen as strengths. You contribute positively to your relationship through your own way of being and responding, yet problems continue to surface. This is because some of your personal strengths may be *problems* for your partner. That which has served you well—individually—sometimes creates difficulties for your loved one and the bond between you.

Most people are clear about how their less than desirable traits contribute to interpersonal problems, but many of us fail to appreciate how our assets can do the same.

This is an open letter from my heart to yours because I know that you give your best and try your hardest only to wake up to the same unresolved issues. I want you to stop focusing on what is "wrong." The truth is that your problems are rooted in things that are very "right" or "good" about you but still manage to get in the way when you relate to your LB.

We will first explore your strengths as an RB and discover how these play a role in the problems you two may be experiencing. We will then look at what you need to do to prevent these problems from becoming major issues. I will identify as well what you have to gain by making the suggested changes. The idea is first to celebrate your strengths and then to adapt them to the needs of a long-term, committed love relationship with an opposite.

Let's begin with your *spontaneity*. It engages others, enlivens conversation, and energizes interactions. Even though *you* are comfortable with this aspect of your personality, your spontaneous actions may not be fully embraced by your LB partner.

Spontaneous behavior (like all behavior) is on a continuum: At one end is a free, spirited response to life, and at the other is a self-destructive impulsiveness. Even when you express yourself in a healthy, uninhibited—and harmless—way, your partner may have a negative reaction that surprises you. This is due to a number of factors.

An LB is very uncomfortable being the center of attention and will go to great lengths to avoid situations where that is likely to happen, only to be yanked smack into the middle when you do or say something that shifts the focus to you and your partner.

LBs like to be prepared for everything as far in advance as possible. In an LB's mind this reduces the risk of making an error in judgment, making a fool of oneself, or inadvertently offending someone. When you are your spontaneous self, your LB is caught off guard. Without adequate time to prepare a response, he or she will "shut down." Communication comes to an abrupt halt, because you are moving too fast into unknown territory, and you are doing so within the context of a relationship. A spontaneous act is a unilateral decision. Your partner has no time, no opportunity to vote. For this reason some of your actions may be perceived as insensitive. You may discover, to your surprise, that you have wounded or offended your LB, even though that was never your intention.

When you are communicating with your LB, it is important to appreciate the differences in your response times. It is equally important to be aware that just as the LB's lack of spontaneity drains the liveliness out of an exchange, your liveliness at times may overwhelm an LB. This doesn't mean you can't be spontaneous; it means you need to be sensitive to the impact that spontaneity has on your partner.

If you notice that you are being "too much" or that you've overwhelmed your partner, say something like: "I can tell that you weren't expecting me to say that. I caught you completely off guard. When you've had time to think about it, I would be interested in your response," or, "I'm sorry. I think what I just said may have made you uncomfortable. That was not my intention."

Next, we explore your ability to *focus on multiple tasks simultaneously*. This is definitely an asset when you are on a tight schedule. You can be on the phone making travel arrangements, checking a pot roast, and making a decision about what color to paint your office all at the same time. You are not derailed when one task becomes two and two become three. This "chaos" is far less frustrating for you than for an LB, who may become discombobulated and irritable under similar circumstances. Engaging in simultaneous, parallel activities allows you to pack more into your day than your LB partner, who does things in a linear fashion, one after the other, is able to.

However, when you are doing more than one thing at a time, problems develop because you are not able to give your full attention to any single task, and therefore, you are at risk for making errors. This becomes a sore point for your partner because he or she is more likely to be focused on one thing at a time, giving attention to detail and being particularly careful. An LB believes strongly that anything worth doing is worth doing well. You believe that anything worth doing can be done along with something else.

When you and your partner work on a project together, these two styles frequently clash. There will be times when you may need to set aside your natural tendency and instead give each step the singular focus it deserves. If you can do this, the project will go more smoothly.

Another strength of yours as an RB is your *comfort with ambiguity*. Unlike an LB, you don't feel an internal pressure to make choices. You are far less invested in determining that which is absolute. For this reason you don't agonize over decisions. This relieves you of stress because you do not need to be certain before you take action.

This comfort with ambiguity is coupled with a *tolerance for concurrent, diverse emotions*. You do not need to make sense of everything you are feeling. Often you experience completely polarized emotions (such as love and hate) at the same time. Because of this tolerance, there is more of a flow to your inner experience; you are free from the labor of dissecting each feeling and determining its "validity."

Although your comfort with ambiguity and your tolerance for diverse feelings present no problem for you, these two characteristics can drive your LB crazy. An LB relies heavily on rational thought, and when there is so much emotion in the air—especially emotions that don't make sense to him or her—an LB will feel adrift without a compass. An LB feels burdened by having to sort through your contradictory remarks to get to the "bottom line." Of course, there is no such thing in your world because whatever you are experiencing in one moment could take a dramatic shift in the next. However, it is important to remain sensitive to the fact that this creates problems when you communicate with an LB.

Another of your personal strengths is your reliance on *intuition* as your guide in most matters. This internal authority allows you to make decisions without a protracted debate with yourself over the "correct" or "perfect" solution. Because something does not need to make sense to you before you embrace it as real, you are able to be receptive to feelings which defy logic. Intuition, combined with a rich imagination, makes it possible for you to commune and connect through *empathy*.

Needless to say, both intuition and empathy contribute to bonding with others and are vital components of a deep intimacy. However, even though they are prized by those in the business of counseling and therapy, they can—believe it or not—create problems for opposites. The most significant of these is when you assume your intuition is infallible and you develop an arrogance about it:

RB: I can tell that you don't really want to go to the movies.
LB: No, really, it's fine.

RB: You say that, but I know once we get there, you will regret having missed your program on TV tonight.

LB: It's not that important to me. I'd tell you if it were.

RB: I can tell that you're just saying that. . . .

Intuition is truly an asset and often pays off, but it becomes a liability when you use it to "read" your partner's mind and then insist on your perspective, giving your partner no credibility. Not only is this insulting to your partner, but if you don't check it out with him or her, it can be harmful to your relationship. You are creating a problem when you form an opinion or take action merely on the basis of your intuition, *no matter how accurate you have been in the past*. Your responsibility is to communicate what your intuition tells you. Your partner's responsibility is to respond honestly.

Your tendency to *focus on relatedness* allows you to see the big picture. This appreciation of the interdependence of all things fosters a sense of connectedness among issues in your relationship and colors your response to your partner. This ability contributes to your being able to identify problems that might otherwise go unnoticed. It also contributes to your LB's frustration when he or she attempts to communicate with you because you are constantly linking together events that your partner sees as totally unrelated.

This particular difference between RB/LB partners creates a great deal of conflict and misunderstanding. For instance, your partner does or says something that triggers a negative response in you, which he or she assumes is related to what was just said or done. Your partner may spend hours privately trying to figure it out only to discover, once you talk, that it was related to an event two years ago, a connection that you considered obvious.

For you there is a "theme," and you can promote better communication by identifying what it is. Your LB (who thinks in a linear fashion) is protesting, "What does A have to do with B?" You (whose thoughts are more like a pinball machine) explain, "A has to do with E, which has to do with B, which has to do with J, which reminds me of A." Don't expect him or her to follow this, but it will make things easier if you at least make the mysterious connection.

Your *willingness to take risks* brings a playfulness to your interactions with others, frees you to be more adventuresome, and brings you rewards through timely action. It makes it possible for you to be spontaneous and allows you to take advantage of situations which would practically paralyze your partner.

The problem is that sometimes the risk involves him or her, and it is imperative that you be sensitive to the impact this will have. Just because *you* are comfortable with the situation, don't assume it's not a concern for your LB. A good rule of thumb is never to volunteer your partner even if it seems like a very minor thing to you.

My husband and I were at a celebration several years ago. It was an appropriate moment to offer up a toast. I could have done it because I didn't need to plan what I would say ahead of time, but since it involved one of his relatives, I quickly turned to him and said, "Why don't you give a toast?" He looked like a deer in the headlights of an oncoming car. I kept egging him on, thinking, "It's no big deal. Just say something." This was early in our relationship, and I had no idea what that was like for him. Afterward we had a talk, and he explained how terribly uncomfortable the whole situation was for him. Over the years I have grown more sensitive to not putting him on the spot, but I have more growing to do. If I want to take risks, then I can, but I don't have the right to push him into one.

Finally, your ability to *focus on feelings* plays a major role in the health of your relationship. This keeps the relationship from becoming too businesslike. There can be no intimacy without feelings, and because you can access yours more easily than your partner, you will find that you are the one who both initiates and requests intimate communication. This can lead you to believe that you are more emotionally invested in the relationship, but in reality it simply means that you are more comfortable with that particular "language."

So if a focus on feelings is vital to the life of your relationship and you do that naturally, what is the problem? There is no problem for *you,* but your partner sees things quite differently. Your tendency to overemphasize emotion makes certain kinds of communication difficult. For instance, problem-solving discussions can best be undertaken if both the facts and the feelings about those facts are revealed. But you have difficulty separating the two, and this can prevent resolution of the issue under discussion because you tend to personalize everything.

In order to further communication between the two of you, try to appreciate that your desire to express your feelings may at times create a barrier to achieving understanding. That may seem impossible since you believe that understanding depends on expressing how you feel. But remember that your partner relies on a clear presentation of the facts in order to feel understood, and if he or she is not able to do that, frustration will eliminate the desire to continue talking. Only through your mutual effort can communication remain rich, productive, and satisfying.

I hope you see now that many of your problems as a couple are not based on personal faults or weaknesses or "dysfunctional" behavior. They are created when your individual assets come together with those of your partner. This is why it is so difficult to make the changes that are necessary if you and your partner are going to establish a mutually satisfying relationship.

By now you are probably asking yourself, "Why would I want to ignore my intuition or suppress my spontaneity?" These are parts of what makes you the person you are. As an individual, then, it wouldn't make sense. But when the focus is on establishing, developing, and maintaining a relationship, each partner has a responsibility to monitor how his or her individual preference (RB or LB) affects that bond: how it contributes to strengthening it and how it diminishes it.

Now that you have the knowledge you need, you can begin to do your part. Your partner will discover the information he or she needs in the following letter. Even though it is addressed to "Dear LB Partner," I suggest you read it as well.

DEAR LB PARTNER:

By now you have experienced both the ups and downs of being in a relationship of opposites. In the beginning your RB partner fascinated you by being so different. Some of those differences open new worlds for you; others leave you feeling frustrated and misunderstood. When this happens, it is natural to focus on your RB partner and yourself to figure out how each of you has failed. But the truth is that these problems do not stem from personal inadequacy. They are rooted, in fact, in the very opposite. This paradox is intrinsic to RB/LB relationships and marriages: That which is a personal strength of one partner is often a problem for the other.

Most people are clear about how their less than desirable traits contribute to interpersonal difficulties but do not realize that their individual strengths can do the same. This is an open letter to you, inviting you to consider an alternative approach to understanding your relationship. I'm offering you a new tool for problem solving: the realization that what works for you in the rest of the world can be *counterproductive* within an intimate relationship. A strength becomes a liability.

It is important to celebrate your strengths as an individual and then to adapt them to the challenging work of creating and maintaining a mutually satisfying, long-term, committed partnership. Let's look at your assets as an LB and how these can contribute to difficulties with your mate. Then we will explore what kinds of change are most effective in the elimination and prevention of problems similar to yours. Finally we'll relate these changes to your own personal satisfaction, as well as the future of your relationship.

To begin with, your *ability to problem solve* contributes significantly to your relationship. Your natural tendency toward critical thinking enables you to identify the crucial elements of any situation. Once you know what the problem is, your attention shifts to alternative solutions. When your partner brings his or her problems to you for discussion, you are ready with answers. On many occasions this is exactly what your partner is seeking. However, at other times your quickly volunteered advice is not received with the enthusiasm you may believe it deserves.

At those times your RB partner is less interested in answers and more interested in connecting. He or she needs "reflection" more than resolution. This means listening, responding, and sharing—but not sharing your solutions. What he or she wants in these situations is for you to identify with the problem and share any similar experience of confusion, embarrassment, fear, pride, etc. The connection is complete when you communicate that you, too, have known what he or she is feeling. If you haven't had a similar experience, the connection can be made by saying, "I can't imagine what that must feel like. Tell me more."

When you give advice or offer a solution, you end the more intimate level of communication—the level of feeling and experience. When you begin to advise, your RB may lose interest, even though it would be possible to continue discussing how you came to your solution, the many applications, and the pitfalls of each alternative. It becomes a monologue at this point because you now have an audience rather than a partner in discourse.

To prevent this from happening, address the problem immediately when your RB starts talking. If he or she does not ask for help, say, "I have some ideas about what you can do. Do you want to hear them, or do you want me just to listen?"

Because you are solution-oriented, when your partner isn't seeking advice, you may have difficulty figuring out your role. You want to *do* something in order to be helpful, like make suggestions. The truth is that you can be very helpful without taking action; you can demonstrate your support by simply listening and occasionally empathizing when you identify with what your partner is feeling. It will take time before this passive kind of support feels more comfortable to you, but it will certainly be appreciated by your RB.

Your second strength as an LB is your preference for *logical and rational communication.* Your ability to separate facts from feelings enables you to discuss problems without personalizing them. You don't allow your feelings about someone to color a situation. You are able to see the facts on both sides of any argument and bring a balanced perspective to any issue.

The value of logic is obvious, but the problem is that logic is irrelevant when intimacy (feeling language) is the focus. When logic is regarded as the only acceptable path to "reality" and awareness arrived at through emotions is discounted, your partner will have no way of communicating with you. His or her concerns will not be taken seriously.

If your RB's (and your own) feelings must make sense to you before you can accept them, then intimacy will be a struggle and your relationship will wither. By eliminating feelings, by not allowing feelings to influence them, LBs tend to treat everyone the same. That's democratic, but it deprives your partner and your relationship of "special" status. A good rule to remember is that logic and emotion are equally valuable in the maintenance of a satisfying relationship; each—in the absence of the other—can be harmful.

Healthy relationships depend upon a solid foundation. You, as an LB, contribute to this through two more of your strengths: your *stability* and your *preference for order over chaos*. Ask any physicist: Stability is related to predictability. Because you tend to be comfortable with routine, you are less likely to create an unexpected crisis for the relationship. Any changes you make will come only after long periods of thought. This incubation period allows your partner and your relationship to integrate and respond to these changes over time rather than overnight.

This preference for a predictable life is reflected in your effort to bring order to chaos. Emotional upheaval in your partner triggers in you a desire to bring things under control. As long as feelings are ricocheting around the room, you prefer to sit it out. Your unwillingness to join in the emotion fest reduces the likelihood of escalation and increases the opportunity for resolution.

Even though these are strengths which you bring to the relationship, it is important to appreciate how the tendency toward routine and order can become oppressive to your partner. For instance, if your morning ritual is like that of most LBs, it is made up of a series of acts that are always performed in the same sequence. This leaves no room for variation or surprise.

If you always eat two pieces of toast after your shower, then you won't be open to the idea of eating a muffin in bed instead. By not injecting variety into your morning, you close off opportunity. Locked into predictable behavior, you have no mystery about you and risk boring your RB. So for the sake of your relationship, now and then step out of your routine and surprise your partner—and yourself!

Another of your assets is the way you can *channel your attention and energy into a single focus*. This allows you to concentrate for extended, uninterrupted periods of time. Long after your RB has become bored with a project (usually after it has become repetitive), you hang in there and see it through. You are not seduced by either internal or external distractions. There is an end point, and you intend to arrive there. This tenacity enables you to get through the thorns to the roses, producing a sense of accomplishment that is extremely satisfying.

Achievement can be so seductive, however, that its pursuit may take priority over other, more important matters. This single focus, while blocking out extraneous, competing thoughts and allowing you to reach your goal, prevents you from appreciating the big picture.

For instance, let's say you have begun working on your computer when your RB pops in and suggests taking a walk together. You agree, but since it is unrelated to what you are doing, it is difficult to integrate, and soon your commitment is set aside or forgotten. Ten minutes later your partner visits again, this time to let you know he or she is waiting. The walk appears to be inevitable, so you leave your computer and grab your jacket and are out the door.

Your partner does not know that although you have physically changed locations, your focus remains back home on the computer. You are thinking that a walk will give you time to do some mental gymnastics, an opportunity to continue working. Your RB is thinking that a walk will help you two connect since you have been involved in separate projects all afternoon. He or she begins reminiscing out loud about the day you met and looks to you for a response, only to discover that you are preoccupied. Although your need (to remain focused back home) is being met, the relationship is being neglected because you are failing to take this opportunity to reach out to your RB. Because LBs are frequently preoccupied, RBs often complain that their relationships are "lonely"; the LB partner is physically there, but his or her heart just isn't in it.

To prevent problems like this from occurring, don't attempt to fake it. If you are heavily concentrating on something and your partner wants your undivided attention, let your RB know: "That sounds like fun, but I'm really deep into trying to figure something out. I don't think I can let go of it right now. How about if I come find you when I feel free of it and we can walk then? Meanwhile, if you are tired of waiting and want to go on, I'll understand," or, "I could come along, but I'm so caught up in this that I just don't think I'd be very good company—unless you are willing to listen to me ramble on about what I'm doing."

There is great temptation in each of these cases just to let your partner do his or her own thing, so you can continue your focus. Occasionally you will choose your individual need over the needs of the relationship, but be aware of a pattern that you might be doing this excessively. Your relationship needs maintenance, and that requires a certain level of intimacy and a certain frequency of companionship. When you are preoccupied most of the time, the responsibility for initiating intimate communication and companionship falls to your partner or is entirely neglected.

A final strength of yours that contributes significantly to the health of your relationship is your *impulse control*. Because you weigh your thoughts prior to sharing them and monitor your behavior before expressing it, you are far less likely to harm your relationship or hurt your partner through your actions. You have fewer regrets and rarely embarrass your partner or put your foot in your mouth. This is an area where your predictability is definitely an asset. Your RB can always feel safe in public with you, for you are less inclined to focus attention (negative or otherwise) on the two of you.

The downside of all this is that although you are not likely to harm through action, your *inaction* can sometimes cause problems for the relationship. The most common ways you do this are through being reluctant to initiate activity and the lack of spontaneity.

Inaction or overly controlled impulses contribute to your passivity as a partner. The relationship's vitality is diminished and responsibility is lopsided. Your RB is burdened with creating ideas, making things happen, and keeping them lively.

You probably were attracted to your RB because that person helped you connect with a more spirited, but somewhat buried, part of yourself. It is your responsibility to keep that spirit alive, so it can join that of your partner.

While impulse control plays an important role in the stability of your relationship, when it dominates your personality and routine replaces spontaneity, an overall rigidity or intensity can develop. This intensity often suppresses the more playful behavior you engaged in early on, when you were courting and were willing to take any risk that was necessary to win your RB's heart. Now and then take those same old risks, step out of your predicable self, and court your partner all over again.

Why give up a logical orientation to life? What's wrong with impulse control; wouldn't the world be a better place with more, not less? Where would any relationship be without problem-solving skills?

I hope you can see how your personal strengths contribute significantly to the health of your relationship. Now you can also appreciate how those same strengths become problematic at times. Even though each of them has—and will continue to have—great value to you as an individual, each must be evaluated within the context of relationship as well.

You may have noticed, if you read the "Dear RB" letter at the beginning of this chapter, that more strengths are listed for the RB than I have just noted here for the LB. To balance the contribution would be misleading because the RB partner brings a greater variety of strengths to an intimate relationship.

This is not because he or she is a better person but because an RB's strengths are rooted in a tendency to lean toward connection. RBs are more involved in initiating and maintaining intimate relationships, and relationship is the focus of this book. If this were a book focused on the individual, then *your* strengths as an LB would be dominant.

If you have not read the "Dear RB" letter, I invite you to do so. You will recognize some of your frustrations as well as learn what your partner is going to be working on.

Now that you have expanded your own awareness, I hope you feel better equipped to live within a relationship of opposites—one that is certainly a daily challenge!

Dear RB and LB Partners:

We all would prefer to have a partner who could meet our every need and let us have total control of our relationship. This fantasy is left over from childhood, when so much was out of our control we were often frustrated and conflict was scary. When as adults we find ourselves having those same feelings, our tendency is to blame "incompatibility" and abandon the relationship.

My personal and professional experiences have led me to a different conclusion: Immaturity, not incompatibility, is the culprit. Couples need maturity to resolve whatever incompatibility there is. It takes maturity to let go of the hope that our partner can be the fantasy parent who loves us unconditionally, has unlimited faith in us, regards us as the center of his or her own universe, and never frustrates our needs. Incompatibility is what happens when our real live partner appears before us at a time when we are wanting our fantasy parent.

It is easy for opposites to think that adjustment to each other's very different ways of being demands too much work and that it's time to "throw in the towel." This is the thinking that contributes to our current divorce rate, as well as to the ending each year of hundreds of thousands of relationships.

Both of you have developed, over your lifetimes, preferences, prejudices, and personal philosophies that are deeply ingrained. You each have daily habits which are so entrenched that they have become unconscious. A great deal of your sense of security comes from your being able to continue as you have, doing what you have been doing, when you want to do it, without having your needs frustrated or blocked by the needs of someone else.

But as David Luecke reminds us in his "prescription" for marriage, an effortless compatibility is an illusion. He tells us: "Compatibility is not something some couples have while others do not. It is something couples achieve or fail to achieve. Compatibility is something couples build out of their differences."

As opposites you have a great deal of experience in what Luecke is talking about: that partners must learn to be creative about their differences rather than try to force a uniformity on the relationship, that the push to conform not only buries individual gifts but also snuffs the liveliness out of the relationship, that partners need to be stretched rather than defeated by their differences, and that building compatibility is an ongoing task that must be a priority.

EXERCISES

LOVE LETTERS

Partners who are very involved in their busy lives may find it helpful to pick a day of the week and on that day, each week, write and send love letters to each other. Such a letter is not unexpected during courting, but after many years together it is refreshing to have these weekly reminders of what it's all about. Getting a love letter in the mail is always a surprise while you shuffle through the bills. If there have been harsh words earlier in the week, the thoughts in the letter remind the partner that even during ugly times the commitment remains.

The letters should not serve as a forum to stretch out a discussion or an argument. They should not be in the form of a list. They need to focus on disclosure of feelings about each other as well as the relationship in general. If it has been a tough week and it is "letter" day, and a partner can't think of anything nice to say, then something like the following will do. "I'm having trouble thinking of what to say because I am still upset about our fight last night. I know, however, that this will blow over like all the other times. I trust that we will get back to a good place. I have faith that we will be able to work this out together."

(This demonstrates that although there are residual negative feelings, this partner isn't always interested in withholding or punishing the other. Mature love always focuses on getting to a common understanding, not on getting even.)

ACCESSING YOUR RIGHT AND LEFT BRAIN THROUGH DRAWING

(Adapted from *Drawing on the Right Side of the Brain* by Betty Edwards)

It is important to remember that we all are right and left brain dominant along a continuum. This exercise allows you to move along that continuum with a heightened awareness of doing so. The best way to understand the different functions of the right and left brain is to experience those functions. The following exercise will access first one hemisphere and then the other. You will notice the shift, if you pay attention to your focus.

Materials: pencil, one sheet of typing paper

Directions:

1. Right-handed person: Draw a profile of a person's head on the *left* side of the paper, facing toward the center

    Left-handed person: Draw a profile of a person's head on the *right* side of the paper, facing toward the center.

2. Draw horizontal lines at the top and bottom of your profile, forming the top and bottom of a vase.

3. Go back over your profile, naming out loud the features as you trace over them (forehead, nose, etc.). You are using your left brain here as you identify and categorize each feature.

4. Starting at the top, draw the profile *in mirror image* on the other side, with that profile also facing center. (This should complete your vase.)

    As you are drawing the mirror image profile, watch for a sense that you are shifting modes. The second profile will not come as easily, and you will notice that as you were drawing, you were focused on it not as a profile but as a shape you were trying to duplicate. You were scanning to determine when to curve in and when to jut out. You were using your right brain to determine the relationship between different lines.

It was easier to draw if you didn't worry about whether the nose looked like a nose, when you weren't analyzing or playing critic.

In your right brain you are thinking: Where does that curve come close to the next? You are working with spatial, relational comparisons.

If you hear a voice telling you, "That's not a very good face. That doesn't look like a mouth;" that is your left brain asserting itself. It wants to dominate the event and is not used to being shut out.

TALKING

Communication creates many problems for opposites as they attempt to understand each other's language. In addition to speaking from very different perspectives, other aspects of sending a message can obstruct the flow. In this section you and your partner can check any areas of talking and listening that seem to be blocking your effectiveness as a team. Use the list to identify problem areas so that problem solving can begin. If you are unable to discuss the lists without entering into nonproductive conflict, use the list to help organize your thoughts prior to seeking professional help.

First, each partner takes one list and places his or her mate's initials next to the items that reflect the mate's style. Then each partner identifies those items that he or she recognizes as part of his or her own style and places own initials there.

Compare lists. Circle those items that have both partners' initials. These are areas that you both contribute to and a good place to begin. To reduce the chances of conflict, each partner should focus only on his or her contribution.

(For a detailed description of each item, see Chapter 4.)

Partner 1	Partner 2
___ Lack of trust	___ Lack of trust
___ Failure to include partner	___ Failure to include partner
___ One-way communication	___ One-way communication
___ Sending mixed signals	___ Sending mixed signals
___ Lack of self-awareness	___ Lack of self-awareness
___ Aggressive language	___ Aggressive language
___ Abstract language	___ Abstract language
___ Topic avoidance	___ Topic avoidance
___ Withholding	___ Withholding
___ "Mechanical" problems	___ "Mechanical" problems
___ Monopolizing	___ Monopolizing
___ Stress	___ Stress
___ Alcohol and drugs	___ Alcohol and drugs
___ Power struggle	___ Power struggle
___ Doesn't stay in present	___ Doesn't stay in present
___ Personalization	___ Personalization
___ Blaming	___ Blaming

LISTENING

Follow the instructions for the above exercise. Detailed discussion of the following items can be found in Chapter 5.

Partner 1	Partner 2
___ Unsolicited advice	___ Unsolicited advice
___ Polarization	___ Polarization
___ Poorly timed logic	___ Poorly timed logic
___ Passive silence	___ Passive silence
___ Rigidity	___ Rigidity
___ Blind spots	___ Blind spots
___ Loss of attention	___ Loss of attention
___ Triggers	___ Triggers
___ Poor self-esteem	___ Poor-esteem
___ Failure to clarify	___ Failure to clarify
___ Failure to give feedback	___ Failure to give feedback
___ Lack of curiosity	___ Lack of curiosity

___ Self-disclosure: too much   ___ Self-disclosure: too much
___ Self-disclosure: too little   ___ Self-disclosure: too little
___ Failure to allow silence   ___ Failure to allow silence
___ Failure to interrupt   ___ Failure to interrupt
___ Preconceived notions   ___ Preconceived notions
___ Misdirected focus   ___ Misdirected focus
___ Internal distraction   ___ Internal distraction
___ Ill-timed reassurance   ___ Ill-timed reassurance
___ Selective listening   ___ Selective listening
___ Criticizing/judging   ___ Criticizing/judging
___ Name-calling/labeling   ___ Name-calling/labeling
___ Diagnosing   ___ Diagnosing
___ Deflecting   ___ Deflecting

EXPECTATIONS

We all bring expectations with us to any relationship we create. Some expectations are mutual, some are voiced, and some remain unspoken. When we form a love relationship, we often assume that our partner shares similar expectations for us to those we may have for him or her. Those assumptions become problematic when they are not recognized as such and are acted upon without clarification. This exercise will help bring any assumptions out into the open, so that they may be discussed freely.

If you find that you are unable to talk about the results of this exercise without creating unmanageable and unproductive conflict, use the exercise to organize your thoughts on this topic prior to seeking professional help.

NOTE: This exercise is designed to be done with a partner; if you have no partner at the present time, you may complete the questions by focusing on your last relationship. Although you will not be able to get input from the other person, it may help you understand your own expectations.

Materials: pencil/pen, writing surface, comfortable place to sit on floor, copy of exercise for partner

Begin this exercise by sitting on the floor with your backs

touching. Remain in this position for a minute or two with your eyes closed, paying attention to your different breathing rhythms. Try to match your partner's rhythm until you are breathing in unison. When you have done that, slowly turn around and face each other. Take a pencil, and complete the following.

Expectations I have of my partner in this relationship:

    1.

    2.

    3.

    4.

    5.

Expectations I have of myself in this relationship:

    1.

    2.

    3.

    4.

    5.

Expectations I think my partner has of me in this relationship:

    1.

    2.

    3.

    4.

    5.

When you and your mate have done all the sections, begin reading your lists out loud to each other, alternating with each statement. When you both have read all you have written, exchange papers and circle any answers on your partner's sheet that you want to know more about. Did any of them surprise you? Exchange pages again and take turns clarifying your responses.

INFORMATION EXCHANGE

Couples often confuse "intimacy" with "sex." Although intimacy is part of sex, it really refers to our most secret thoughts, dreams, hopes, desires, fears, and humiliations. It is information about the self that comes from deep within and is shared with a trusted other.

Some partners don't know how to find and share that level. Do-

ing so isn't part of their normal communication style. To help partners achieve that deeper level in their exchange of information
about each other, the following exercise was developed.

For best results, don't try to complete the statements and
share answers spontaneously. Copy the list of statements, and give
one to your partner. Ask him or her to take an hour or so to complete it privately; then agree on a time when you can share your
answers.

It is very important to remember that the person reading his or
her answers is in a vulnerable position. It is always a risk to be intimate. Although it is a risk worth taking, it is a very uncomfortable
experience for anyone not used to doing so. The answers must be
respected and never challenged. If the exercise turns into a debate,
it will be a long time before such intimate details are revealed again,
as trust will have been violated.

1. As far back as I remember, I've wanted to be _____.
2. In the area of _____ I feel very competent.
3. On the other hand, I question my ability to _____.
4. I withhold part of myself from you because I fear that you will

   _____.
5. I take great pride in the fact that I _____.
6. It is difficult for me to admit that I _____.
7. I feel shame when I think about _____.
8. If I let you get very close to me, I'm afraid you might _____.
9. I don't understand why it is so difficult for me to _____.
10. I need your help in changing the way that I _____.
11. It is difficult for me to admit that _____.
12. To me this relationship means _____.
13. I am pleased that in this relationship I am able to _____.
14. At this point in my life I worry most about _____.
15. I need you as my partner to understand and believe that I

    _____.
16. Something that you do that drives me nuts is _____.
17. Something I do that I think probably drives you nuts is I

    _____.
18. Something that really turns me on is _____.

19. Something that really turns me off is _____.
20. Something you could do that would make life easier for me is

_____.

21. Something I could do that I think would make life easier for you
is _____.
22. Something that we could do together that I would really enjoy
would be to _____.
23. Something you've taught me about love is _____.
24. The best thing about being your partner is _____.

LOVE MAP

Most partners make the mistake of loving their mates in the way they would like to be loved rather than find out how their mates prefer to have love demonstrated. If you have been trying and don't think your mate appreciates your efforts, you may have been using the wrong "map."

Below are common ways that partners demonstrate their love for each other. You can help your partner by prioritizing these. This will give him or her a "map" to your heart. Place a 1 next to the *most* desirable and a 15 next to the *least* desirable, filling the numbers in between. Then exchange your lists, and compare them. Keep your partner's list, so you have a handy guide to how he or she wants to be loved.

_____Taking a walk together
_____Telling me "I love you"
_____Self-disclosing (telling me your feelings, fears, dreams, etc.)
_____Believing in me/encouraging me
_____Touching me affectionately (nonerotically)
_____Calling me by a pet name
_____Giving me presents
_____Complimenting me on how I look
_____Giving me private time, space alone
_____Tolerating my flaws
_____Making love

_____Showing respect for me
_____Initiating activities together
_____Making time for us
_____Taking over some of my chores

INEVITABLE DIFFERENCES

This is an important exercise for opposites because it focuses on the core of their conflict, differences that sometimes seem insurmountable. Make a copy so that each partner has one. Do not attempt to finish these statements spontaneously. Initially take time privately to complete the sentences and then come together to discuss your comments. Make sure that both partners have enough time to answer without feeling rushed.

These answers come from deep within and create an atmosphere of intimacy when shared. Consequently, it is important simply to listen to your partner's answers rather than challenge them. Take the information from this exercise, and use it to understand each other's perspective better.

1. The ways we are different which I like are:

    1.

    2.

    3.

2. The ways we are different which cause me concern are:

    1.

    2.

    3.

3. I think we have the most difficulty negotiating our differences about:

4. An individual need of mine which conflicts with a need of yours is:

5. When it comes to our differences, I sometimes get frustrated because:

6. I believe that I am flexible about most things, but I know I can be inflexible about:

7. I like the way that we handle our differences about:

FINDING A LIFE PARTNER

Information is power. Information about the self is the most powerful of all if you are trying to make changes in your life. When looking for a life partner, if you don't know yourself, you are at risk for selecting someone who is unhealthy for you. If you have been looking without success, you may want to look at the way you might be getting in your own way. Understanding yourself is the best tool you have.

1. What are five characteristics that your "ideal" partner would possess?
    1.
    2.
    3.
    4.
    5.
2. What are five things about yourself that you have to offer a partner?
    1.
    2.
    3.
    4.
    5.
3. What are five things about someone that would place him or her on your "never" list?
    1.
    2.
    3.
    4.
    5.

4. If you have had several relationships with potential life partners, what similarities do you see in your choices?

5. If you are unable to find the right partner for you, how do you feel about remaining single?

6. Would you rather be similar to, or different from, the person you find? Why?

SIGNS OF RELATIONSHIP DISSATISFACTION

When problems develop, couples often experience a pervasive sense of alienation but are unable to identify specifically what is contributing to it. Use this list to organize your thoughts before you sit down and talk with your partner or before you seek professional help.

Make a copy for your partner, and introduce it by saying, "I'm sure you have noticed that we aren't as close as we used to be. I'd like us to talk about that. Would you please look at this list and check off anything that is a concern of yours? I really want us to work this out."

A good place to begin your talk is with any item that both of you have identified as a concern. To reduce conflict, agree that each of you will speak only to how your *own* behavior has contributed to that problem.

If there have been low levels of communication and high levels of tension, you may find that it is impossible simply to sit and talk about any of these topics. Each may now be so loaded an issue that just a word can trigger an argument. If that is so, don't attempt to talk about these without someone to help you.

_____Lack of communication about expectations of each other
_____Feeling that you are drifting apart
_____Long periods of disappointment
_____Resentment about unilateral decision making
_____Feelings of being used
_____Unexpected explosions

_____Feelings of discouragement

_____Avoiding/escaping through alcohol, drugs, food, TV

_____Criticizing each other in public

_____Chronic criticizing

_____Lack of interest in being alone together

_____Unspoken resentments

_____Chronic nagging

_____Lack of interdependence; seeking outside support too often

_____Losing respect for each other

_____Making jokes at your partner's expense

_____Feelings of pervasive loneliness

_____Feeling trapped

_____Neglected sexual relationship

_____Differing priorities

_____Inability to resolve issues

_____Failure to talk in the future tense as a couple

_____Being mad at your partner most of the time

_____Wanting to hurt your partner

_____Wanting to be with someone else more than wanting to work
       things out with your partner

ISSUES

Sometimes when couples talk, it is difficult to identify exactly
what is bothering one partner or the other. Following are categories
of problems common to all couples, with related concerns. This may
serve to help you organize your thoughts before asking for time to
talk or prior to seeing a counselor.

Again, each of you needs a copy so that you each have an opportunity for input. After completion, sit and compare your lists. Focus on an area that you both consider an issue and then discuss
getting help.

_____MONEY

The role it plays; how it is earned, who earns it; how it is spent;
how it is saved, borrowed, and kept track of; what it means to
each of us

_____HEALTH

The way we eat, exercise; our intake of poor food; our intake of alcohol or drugs

_____TIME

How it is used alone and together; how much time is given away to others, projects, etc.; active versus passive time

_____WORK

The priority it takes in our lives; our feelings about success and failure; whether we like or do not like our choice of work; work-related stress

_____LEISURE

How we play as a couple or family; whether to take vacations together or apart; activities we can share.

_____SEX

The frequency of our lovemaking; the quality of the time we spend in sexual activity; the degree of variation; the degree of privacy we have; the degree of sensitivity we have as lovers; things I feel comfortable with; things I don't

_____COMMUNICATION

The amount of time we spend in actual conversation; the degree of intimacy in our talks; our private language versus our public language; roadblocks we have in our communication

_____CHILDREN

Our responsibilities; coparenting; negotiating our differing ways to parent; our feelings about having children/more children

_____FAMILY OF ORIGIN

Your family and mine and how they interact with us; our responsibilities for family; their expectations for us

_____HOME

The degree of comfort or tension present; chores; where we want to live and why

_____COMMITMENT

Definition; feelings about having/not having; future plans

FEELINGS VOCABULARY

Sometimes when a partner wants to talk about what is of concern to him or her, it helps to have just the right word to express what it feels like. For partners who may have difficulty finding the precise term to describe what is going on internally, the following may be of help. (Feelings that are similar are grouped together.)

glad contented fortunate gratified cheerful joyful
excited pleased jazzed high delighted up elated ecstatic
thrilled fascinated exalted uplifted eager enthusiastic

friendly likable pleasant benevolent connected generous
tender calm loved fond cherished desirous desirable

amazed bewildered mystified baffled shocked dismayed
puzzled

unhappy downcast dejected depressed gloomy devastated
somber distressed weary despondent blue disheartened
scared anxious drained burned out low in the dumps
concerned uncomfortable fearful upset cautious
disenchanted apathetic indifferent

enraged infuriated outraged defiant hostile
spiteful bitter furious disagreeable discouraged
bothered smothered alienated distant

restless pressured impatient nervous disturbed
overwhelmed floundering lost confused frustrated
remorseful

awkward ridiculed disgraced underestimated insulted
belittled deceived dishonest humiliated cheated
betrayed blamed embarrassed accused guilty

absorbed engrossed enraptured focused mindful
interested involved

proud important accomplished talented competent
admiration respected respectful experienced wise
capable secure powerful confident enlightened bold

envious jealous biased resentful rejected ignored

trusting appreciated thankful indebted accepted
safe grateful forgiving embraced hopeful

absurd silly ludicrous irrational childish

sad hurt empty helpless discouraged powerless unsafe

MATE SELF-RATE

At the end of each day, while you're preparing for bed, ask yourself the following questions. They are designed to help you imagine your partner's world.

1. What was it like being married to (or living with) me today? What was good about it? Not so good about it? (Later, for a *real* challenge, ask your partner.)
2. What grade would I give myself today as a mate?
3. What is something simple that I could do tomorrow that would make life easier for my partner? (Challenge: put your answer into action.)
4. What is something simple that I already do that helps us as a couple? Am I willing to do that again tomorrow, even though it might not have been acknowledged that I did it today?

BIBLIOGRAPHY

INTRODUCTION

DILLARD, ANNIE. *Teaching a Stone to Talk.* New York: Harper and Row, 1991.

KEEN, SAM. *Fire in the Belly.* New York: Bantam Books, 1991.

I. LEFT BRAIN, RIGHT BRAIN: WHAT'S THE DIFFERENCE?

ASIMOV, ISAAC. *The Human Brain: Its Capacities and Functions.* Boston: Houghton Mifflin, 1963.

BEATON, ALLAN. *Left Side, Right Side: A Review of Laterality.* London: Batsford Academic and Educational, 1985.

BEPKO, CLAUDIA, AND JO ANN KRESTAN. *Singing at the Top of Our Lungs: Women, Love and Creativity.* New York: HarperCollins, 1993.

BLOOM, FLOYD E., AND ARLYNE LAZERSON. *Brain, Mind and Behavior.* New York: H. H. Freeman & Co., 1988.

BOGEN, JOSEPH. "The Other Side of the Brain: An Appositional Mind." In *The Nature of Human Consciousness,* ed. Robert E. Ornstein. New York: Viking Press, 1973.

BRENTON, MYRON. *Lasting Relationships.* New York: A. & W. Publishers, 1981.

BRYDEN, M. P. *Laterality: Functional Asymmetry in the Intact Brain.* New York: Academic Press, 1982.

CHANGEUX, JEAN-PIERRE. *Neuronal Man: The Biology of Mind.* New York: Pantheon Books, 1985.

COLTHEART, MAX. "The Right Hemisphere and Disorders of Reading." In *Functions of the Right Cerebral Hemisphere,* ed. Andrew Young. New York: Academic Press, 1983.

CORRICK, JAMES A. *The Human Brain: Mind and Matter.* New York: Arco Publishing, Inc., 1983.

COVEY, STEPHEN. *The Seven Habits of Highly Effective People.* New York: Simon & Schuster, 1989.

CSIKSZENTMIHALYI, MIHALY. *Flow: The Psychology of Optimal Experience.* New York: Harper and Row, 1990.

CURTIS, SUSAN. "The Development of Human Cerebral Lateralization." In *The Dual Brain: Hemispheric Specialization in Humans,* ed. D. Frank Benson and Eran Zaidel. New York: Guilford Press, 1985.

DEMBART, LEE. "Bringing Fuzzy Logic into Focus" (review of *Fuzzy Logic: The Discovery of a Revolutionary Computer Technology and How It Is Changing Our World* by Daniel McNeil and Paul Freiberger), Los Angeles *Times,* February 26, 1993.

DONAHUE, PHIL. *The Human Animal.* New York: Simon & Schuster, 1985.

DOHENY, KATHLEEN. "Intuition: Taking a Big Step." Los Angeles *Times,* August 19, 1990.

ECCLES, JOHN C. *The Human Mystery: The Gifford Lectures, 1977–78.* University of Edinburgh. London: Routledge Kegan Paul, 1984.

EDWARDS, BETTY. *Drawing on the Right Side of the Brain.* Los Angeles: Jeremy Tarcher, 1989.

_____. *Drawing on the Artist Within.* New York: Simon & Schuster, 1986.

ELLIS, HADYN. "The Role of the Right Hemisphere in Face Perception." In *Functions of the Right Cerebral Hemisphere,* ed. Andrew Young. New York: Academic Press, 1983.

ETCOFF, N. L. "Recognition of Emotions in Patients with Unilateral Brain Damage." In *Emotions and the Dual Brain,* ed. Guido Gainotti and Carlo Caltagirone. New York: Springer-Verlag, 1989.

FALLIK, BEVERLIE, AND JOHN ELIOT. "An Examination of Possible Age Differences in Inter-Relationships Between Intuition, Cognitive Style and Hemispheric Preference Variable," *Perceptual and Motor Skills,* vol. 63, no. 3 (December 1986).

FEYEREISEN, P. "What Can Be Learned from Lateral Differences in Emotional Processing?" In *Emotions and the Dual Brain,* ed. Guido Gainotti and Carlo Caltagirone. New York: Springer-Verlag, 1989.

GALIN, DAVID. "The Two Modes of Consciousness and the Two Halves of the Brain." In *Symposium on Consciousness: Annual Meeting of the American Association for the Advancement of Science, February 1974.* New York: Viking Press, 1976.

GAZZANIGA, MICHAEL S. *The Social Brain: Discovering the Network of the Mind.* New York: Basic Books, 1985.

____. "The Split Brain in Man." In *The Nature of Human Consciousness,* ed. Robert E. Ornstein. New York: Viking Press, 1973.

GESCHWIND, NORMAN. "Brain Disease and the Mechanisms of Mind." In *Functions of the Brain,* ed. Clive Warwick Coen. Oxford, England: Clarendon Press, 1985.

GORDON, HAROLD W. "Music and the Right Hemisphere." In *Functions of the Right Cerebral Hemisphere,* ed. Andrew W. Young. New York: Academic Press, 1983.

GRINDLE, CARLA. "Intuition: A New Age Advantage in High Tech," *Woman Engineer* (Winter 1989–90).

HARRIS, LAUREN. "Right-Brain Training: Some Reflections on the Application of Research on Cerebral Hemispheric Specialization to Education." In *Brain Lateralization in Children,* ed. Dennis Molfese and Sidney Segalowitz. New York: Guilford Press, 1988.

HOPPE, KLAUS. "Hemispheric Specialization and Creativity." *Psychiatric Clinics of North America,* vol. 11, no. 3 (September 1988).

HORTON, PAUL. "Positive Emotions and the Right Parietal Cortex." *Psychiatric Clinics of North America,* vol. 11, no. 2 (September 1988).

HUTCHINSON, MICHAEL. *Mega Brain.* New York: Beech Tree Books/William Morrow & Co., 1986.

KITTERLE, FREDERICK, ed. *Cerebral Laterality: Theory and Research.* Hillsdale, N.J.: Lawrence Erlbaum Association, 1991.

KRYSTAL, HENRY. "On some Roots of Creativity." *Psychiatric Clinics of North America,* vol. 11, no. 2 (September 1988).

KYLE, NEVILLE. "Emotions and Hemispheric Specialization." *Psychiatric Clinics of North America,* vol. 11, no. 2 (September 1988).

LEDOUX, JOSEPH. "Cerebral Asymmetry and the Integrated Function of the Brain." In *Functions of the Right Cerebral Hemisphere,* ed. Andrew Young. New York: Academic Press, 1983.

"Left-Right Brain Role Is Studied." Chicago *Tribune,* April 22, 1984.

LOVE, DAVID. "Hemisphericity and Creativity." *Psychiatric Clinics of North America,* vol. 11, no. 2 (September 1988).

LURIA, A. R. *The Working Brain.* New York: Basic Books, 1973.

MARSHALL, JOHN. "Is Cerebral Lateralization a Graded or Discrete Characteristic?" *Individual Differences in Hemispheric Specialization,* ed. A. Glass. New York: Plenum Press, 1984.

ORNSTEIN, ROBERT. *The Amazing Brain.* Boston: Houghton Mifflin, 1984.

____. *The Psychology of Consciousness.* New York: Viking Press, 1972.

MARTINEZ, MARTINEZ. *Neuroanatomy.* Philadelphia: W. B. Saunders, 1982.

PECHURA, CONSTANCE, AND JOSEPH MARTIN, eds. *Mapping the Brain and Its Functions.* Wasington, D.C.: Institute of Medicine National Academy Press, 1991.

PINCHOT, ROY B., ed. *The Brain: Mystery of Matter and Mind.* New York: Torstar Books, 1984.

____. *The Brain.* Washington, D.C.: U.S. News Books, 1981.

POOL, J. LAWRENCE, M.D. *Nature's Masterpiede: The Brain and How It Works.* New York: Walker & Co., 1987.

PITTMAN, FRANK. "Gender Myths: When Does Gender Become Pathology?" *Family Therapy Networker,* vol. 9, no. 6 (November–December 1985).

RESTAK, RICHARD, M.D. *The Brain.* New York: Bantam Books, 1984.

RUSSELL, PETER. *The Brain Book.* New York: Hawthorn Press, 1979.

SACKS, OLIVER. *The Man Who Mistook His Wife for a Hat.* New York: Harper & Row, 1985.

SAGAN, CARL. *The Dragons of Eden.* New York: Ballantine Books, 1986.

SCHWEIGER, AVRAHAM. "Harmony of the Spheres and Hemispheres: the Arts and Hemispheric Specialization." In *The Dual Brain: Hemispheric Specialization in Humans,* ed. D. Frank Benson and Eran Zaidel. New York: Guilford Press, 1985.

SEARLEMAN, ALAN. "Language Capabilities of the Right Hemisphere." In *Functions of the Right Cerebral Hemisphere,* ed. Andrew Young. New York: Academic Press, 1983.

SPRINGER, SALLY P., AND GEORG DEUTSCH. *Left Brain, Right Brain.* New York: W. H. Freeman & Co., 1989.

TANGUAY, PETER. "Implications of Hemispheric Specialization for Psychiatry." In *The Dual Brain: Hemispheric Specialization in Humans,* ed. D. Frank Benson and Eran Zaidel. New York: Guilford Press, 1985.

TAYLOR, GORDON RATTRAY. *The Natural History of the Mind.* New York: E. P. Dutton, 1979.

TENHOUTEN, WARREN. "Cerebral-Lateralization Theory and the Sociology of Knowledge." In *The Dual Brain: Hemispheric Specialization in Humans,* ed. D. Frank Benson and Eran Zaidel. New York: Guilford Press, 1985.

WHITAKER, CARL, AND THOMAS MALONE. *The Roots of Psychotherapy.* New York: Brunner-Mazel, 1981.

WILLIAMS, LINDA VERLEE. *Teaching for the Two-Sided Brain.* Englewood Cliffs, N.J.: Prentice-Hall, 1983.

WONDER, JACQUELYN, AND PRISCILLA DONOVAN. *Whole-Brain Thinking.* New York: William Morrow & Co., 1984.

YOUNG, ANDREW. "The Development of Right Hemisphere Abilities." In *Functions of the Right Cerebral Hemisphere,* ed. Andrew Young. New York: Academic Press, 1983.

_____, AND GRAHAM RATCLIFF. "Visuospatial Abilities of the Right Hemisphere." In *Functions of the Right Cerebral Hemisphere,* ed. Andrew Young. New York: Academic Press, 1983.

ZAIDEL, ERAN. "Academic Implications of Dual-Brain Theory." In *The Dual Brain: Hemispheric Specialization in Humans,* ed. D. Frank Benson and Eran Zaidel. New York: Guilford Press, 1985.

ZDENEK, MARILEE. *The Right-Brain Experience.* New York: McGraw-Hill, 1983.

_____. "Right-Brain Techniques: A Catalyst for Creative Thinking and Internal Focus." *Psychiatric Clinics of North America,* vol. 11, no. 2 (September 1988).

2. WHEN OPPOSITES ATTRACT

BERZON, BETTY. *Permanent Partners.* New York: Plume/Penguin, 1988.

COVEY, STEPHEN. *The Seven Habits of Highly Effective People.* New York: Simon & Schuster, 1989.

HOLLANDS, JEAN. *The Silicon Syndrome: A Survival Handbook for Couples.* Palo Alto, Calif.: Coastlight Press, 1983.

SAGER, CLIFFORD, AND BERNICE HUNT. *Intimate Partners.* New York: McGraw-Hill, 1979.

3. FACTS AND FEELINGS: BECOMING A "BILINGUAL" COUPLE

BEAVERS, ROBERT W. *Successful Marriage.* New York: W. W. Norton, 1985.

BECK, AARON. *Love Is Never Enough.* New York: Harper & Row, 1988.

BELENKY, MARY FIELD, et al. *Women's Ways of Knowing.* New York: Basic Books, 1986.

BERZON, BETTY. *Permanent Partners.* New York: E. P. Dutton, 1988.

CAPPON, DANIEL. "The Anatomy of Intuition." *Psychology Today* (May–June 1993).

COVEY, STEPHEN. *The Seven Habits of Highly Effective People.* New York: Simon & Schuster, 1989.

FISHER, ROGER, AND SCOTT BROWN. *Getting Together.* Boston: Houghton Mifflin, 1988.

HOWARD, DORIS. "Couples in Psychotherapy: The Positive Effects of a Feminist Perspective on Interpersonal Satisfactions." In *New Directions in Feminist Psychology,* ed. Joan Chrisler and Doris Howard. New York: Springer Pub., 1992.

KOSKO, BART, AND SATORU ISAKA. "Fuzzy Logic." *Scientific American* (July 1993).

LERNER, HARRIET GOLDHOR. *The Dance of Intimacy.* New York: Harper & Row, 1989.

PEARSALL, PAUL. *Ten Laws of a Lasting Love.* New York: Simon & Schuster, 1993.

PIRSIG, R. M. *Zen and the Art of Motorcycle Maintenance.* New York: William Morrow & Co., 1974.

Running Press, *Quotable Woman.* New York: Worldwide Media, 1991.

SATIR, VIRGINIA. *People Making.* Palo Alto, Calif.: Science and Behavior Books, 1972.

SCHWEIGER, AVRAHAM. "Harmony of the Spheres and Hemispheres: The Arts and Hemispheric Specialization." In *The Dual Brain: Hemispheric Specialization in Humans,* ed. D. Frank Benson and Eran Zaidel. New York: Guilford Press, 1985.

SYNDER, MARYHELEN. "The Co-Construction of New Meanings in Couple Relationships: A Psychoeducational Model That Promotes Mutual Empowerment." In *Equal Partnering,* ed. Barbara Brothers. New York: Harrington Park Press, 1992.

4. TALKING TO YOUR PARTNER

ABLES, BILLIE, AND JEFFREY BRANDISMA. *Therapy for Couples.* San Francisco: Jossey-Bass, 1982.

ACITELLI, LINDA. "When Spouses Talk to Each Other About Their Relationship," *Journal of Social and Personal Relationships,* vol. 5, no. 2 (May 1988).

ANASTASI, THOMAS, JR. *Listen!* Boston: CBI Publishing Co., 1967.

ARGYLE, MICHAEL. "Non-Verbal Communication and Language." In *Communication and Understanding,* ed. Godfrey Vesey. Atlantic Highlands, N.J.: Humanities Press, 1977.

AVERY, CARL. "How Do You Build Intimacy in an Age of Divorce?" *Psychology Today* (May 1989).

BATESON, MARY CATHERINE. *Composing a Life.* New York: Penguin Books, 1989.

BEAVERS, ROBERT W. *Successful Marriage.* New York: W. W. Norton, 1985.

BECK, AARON T. *Love Is Never Enough.* New York: Harper & Row, 1988.

BELENKY, MARY FIELD, et al. *Women's Ways of Knowing.* New York: Basic Books, 1986.

BERZON, BETTY. *Permanent Partners.* New York: E. P. Dutton, 1988.

BOGRAD, MICHELE. "Female Therapist/Male Client: Considerations About Belief Systems." In *Feminist Approaches for Men in Family Therapy,* ed. Michele Bograd. New York: Harrington Park Press, 1991.

BOOK, CASSANDRA, et al., eds. *Human Communication: Principles, Contexts and Skills.* New York: St. Martin's Press, 1980.

BOLTON, ROBERT. *People Skills.* New York: Simon & Schuster, 1979.

BRODERICK, CARLFRED. *Couples.* New York: Simon & Schuster, 1979.

BROWN, JULIE R., AND L. EDNA RODGERS. "Openness, Uncertainty and Intimacy: An Epistomological Reformation." In *Miscommunication and Problematic Thought,* ed. Nikolas Coupland, et al. Newbury Park, Calif.: Sage Publications, 1991.

CHASE, STUART. *Power of Words.* New York: Harcourt, Brace & Co., 1954.

CLARK, DON. *Loving Someone Gay.* Berkeley, Calif.: Celestial Arts, 1987.

DIMBLEBY, RICHARD, AND GRAEME BURTON. *More Than Words.* New York: Methuen & Co., 1985.

EMMERT, PHILIP. *Human Communication: Elements and Contexts.* Menlo Park, Calif.: Addison-Wesley Pub. Co., 1981.

FELBER, STANLEY, AND ARTHUR KOCH. *What Did You Say?* Englewood Cliffs, N.J.: Prentice-Hall, 1973.

FERRIS, TIMOTHY. *The Mind's Sky.* New York: Bantam Books, 1992.

FISHER, ROGER, AND SCOTT BROWN. *Getting Together.* Boston: Houghton Mifflin, 1988.

FISKE, JOHN. *Introduction to Communication Studies.* New York: Methuen & Co., 1982.

GILLIGAN, CAROL. *In a Different Voice.* Cambridge: Harvard University Press, 1982.

GOLDBERG, HERB. *The New Male.* New York: William Morrow & Co., 1979.

HENLEY, NANCY M., AND CHERIS KRAMARAE. "Gender Power and Miscommunication." In *Miscommunication and Problematic Thought,* ed. Nikolas Coupland, et al. Newbury Park, Calif.: Sage Publications, 1991.

HERIOT, JESSICA. "The Double Bind: Healing the Split." *Women & Therapy,* vol. 2, no. 2/3 (1983).

HOPPER, ROBERT. *Human Message Systems.* New York: Harper & Row, 1976.

ISENSEE, RIK. *Love Between Men.* New York: Prentice-Hall, 1990.

KEEN, SAM. *Fire in the Belly: On Being a Man.* New York: Bantam Books, 1991.

KYLE, NEVILLE. "Emotions and Hemispheric Specialization." *Psychiatric Clinics of North America,* vol. 11, no. 3 (September 1988).

LAUER, JEANETTE C. AND ROBERT H. *Til Death Do Us Part.* New York: Harrington Park Press, 1986.

LEEDS-HURWITZ, WENDY. *Communication in Everyday Life.* Northwood, N.J.: Ablex Pub. Corp., 1989.

LERNER, HARRIET GOLDHOR. *The Dance of Anger.* New York: Harper & Row, 1985.

____. *The Dance of Intimacy.* New York: Harper & Row, 1989.

LIEBERMAN, GERALD. *3500 Good Quotes for Speakers.* New York: Doubleday, 1983.

LIBERMAN, ROBERT, ed. *Handbook of Marital Therapy.* New York: Plenum Press, 1980.

LITTLEJOHN, STEPHEN. *Theories of Communication.* Columbus, Ohio: Charles E. Merrill Pub. Co., 1978.

MACE, DAVID. *Close Companions.* New York: Continuum, 1982.

MAMBERT, W. A. *Elements of Effective Communication.* Washington, D.C.: Acropolis Books, 1971.

MONTAGU, ASHLEY, AND FLOYD MATSON. *The Human Connection.* New York: McGraw-Hill, 1979.

PIRSIG, R. M. *Zen and the Art of Motorcycle Maintenance.* New York: William Morrow & Co., 1974.

RICHARDSON, SUSAN. "Right Brain Approaches to Counseling: Tapping Your "Feminine" Side." *Women and Therapy,* vol. 4, no. 4 (Winter 1985–86).

ROGERS, CARL. *On Becoming a Person.* Boston: Houghton Mifflin, 1961.

SARNOFF, IRVING AND SUZANNE. *Love-Centered Marriage in a Self-Centered World.* New York: Hemisphere Pub. Co., 1989.

SATIR, VIRGINIA. *People Making.* Palo Alto, Calif.: Science and Behavior Books, 1972.

SATRAN, PAMELA. "When Not to Talk About It." *Redbood* (March 1992).

SEVERIN, WERNER, AND JAMES TANKARD, JR. *Communication Theories.* New York: Hastings House, 1979.

SHLAIN, LEONARD. *Art and Physics.* New York: William Morrow & Co., 1991.

STEINBERG, MARK, AND GERALD MILLER. "Interpersonal Communication: A Sharing Process." In *Communication and Behavior,* ed. Gerhard Hauneman and William McEwen. Menlo Park, Calif.: Addison-Wesley Pub. Co., 1975.

STUART, RICHARD. *Helping Couples Change.* New York: Guilford Press, 1980.

TANNEN, DEBORAH. *You Just Don't Understand: Men and Women In Conversation.* New York: Ballantine Books, 1990.

TESSINA, TINA. *Gay Relationships.* Los Angeles: Jeremy Tarcher, 1989.

VOLLMER, RYAN. "Silent Partner." *Ladies' Home Journal,* vol. 109, no. 4 (April 1992).

WATZLAWICK, PAUL. *How Real Is Real?* New York: Random House, 1976.

WONDER, JACQUELYN, AND PRISCILLA DONOVAN. *Whole-Brain Thinking.* New York: William Morrow & Co., 1984.

YALOM, IRVIN D. *Existential Psychotherapy.* New York: Basic Books, 1980.

5. THE GIFT OF LISTENING

ABLES, BILLIE, AND JEFFREY BRANDISMA. *Therapy for Couples.* San Francisco: Jossey-Bass, 1982.

ACITELLI, LINDA. "When Spouses Talk to Each Other About Their Relationship." *Journal of Social and Personal Relationships,* vol. 5, no. 2 (May 1988).

ANASTASI, THOMAS, JR. *Listen!* Boston: CBI Pub. Co., 1967.

ARGYLE, MICHAEL. "Non-Verbal Communication and Language." In *Communication and Understanding,* ed. Godfrey Vesey. Atlantic Highlands, N.J.: Humanities Press, 1977.

AVERY, CARL. "How Do You Build Intimacy in an Age of Divorce?" *Psychology Today* (May 1989).

BATESON, MARY CATHERINE. *Composing a Life.* New York: Penguin Books, 1989.

BEAVERS, ROBERT W. *Successful Marriage.* New York: W. W. Norton, 1985.

BECK, AARON T. *Love Is Never Enough.* New York: Harper & Row, 1988.

BELENKY, MARY FIELD, et al. *Women's Ways of Knowing.* New York: Basic Books, 1986.

BERZON, BETTY. *Permanent Partners.* New York: E. P. Dutton, 1988.

BOGRAD, MICHELE. "Female Therapist/Male Client: Considerations About Belief Systems." In *Feminist Approaches for Men in Family Therapy,* ed. Michele Bograd. New York: Harrington Park Press, 1991.

BOLTON, ROBERT. *People Skills.* New York: Simon & Schuster, 1979.

BOOK, CASSANDRA, ET AL., eds. *Human Communication: Principles, Contexts and Skills.* New York: St. Martin's Press, 1980.

BRODERICK, CARLFRED. *Couples.* New York: Simon & Schuster, 1979.

BROWN, JULIE R., AND L. EDNA RODGERS. "Openness, Uncertainty and Intimacy: An Epistomological Reformation." *Miscommunication and Problematic*

Thought, ed. Nikolas Coupland et al. Newbury Park, Calif.: Sage Publications, 1991.

CHASE, STUART. *Power of Words.* New York: Harcourt, Brace, 1954.

CLARK, DON. *Loving Someone Gay.* Berkeley, Calif.: Celestial Arts, 1987.

DIMBLEBY, RICHARD, AND GRAEME BURTON. *More Than Words.* New York: Methuen & Co, 1985.

EMMERT, PHILIP. *Human Communication: Elements and Contexts.* Menlo Park, Calif.: Addison-Wesley Pub. Co., 1981.

FELBER, STANLEY, AND ARTHUR KOCH. *What Did You Say?* Englewood Cliffs, N.J.: Prentice-Hall, 1973.

FERRIS, TIMOTHY. *The Mind's Sky.* New York: Bantam Books, 1992.

FISHER, ROGER, AND SCOTT BROWN. *Getting Together.* Boston: Houghton Mifflin, 1988.

FISKE, JOHN. *Introduction to Communication Studies.* New York: Methuen & Co., 1982.

GILLIGAN, CAROL. *In a Different Voice.* Cambridge: Harvard University Press, 1982.

GOLDBERG, HERB. *The New Male.* New York: William Morrow & Co., 1979.

HENLEY, NANCY M., AND CHERIS KRAMARAE. "Gender Power and Miscommunication." In *Miscommunication and Problematic Thought,* ed. Nikolas Coupland et al. Newbury Park, Calif.: Sage Publications, 1991.

HERIOT, JESSICA. "The Double Bind: Healing the Split." *Women & Therapy,* vol. 2, no. 2/3 (1983).

HOPPER, ROBERT. *Human Message Systems.* New York: Harper & Row, 1976.

ISENSEE, RIK. *Love Between Men.* New York: Prentice-Hall, 1990.

KEEN, SAM. *Fire in the Belly: On Being a Man.* New York: Bantam Books, 1991.

LAUER, JEANETTE C. AND ROBERT H. *Til Death Do Us Part.* New York: Harrington Park Press, 1986.

LEEDS-HURWITZ, WENDY. *Communication in Everyday Life.* Northwood, N.J.: Ablex Pub. Corp., 1989.

LERNER, HARRIET GOLDHOR. *The Dance of Anger.* New York: Harper & Row, 1985.

____. *The Dance of Intimacy.* New York: Harper & Row, 1989.

LIBERMAN, ROBERT, ed. *Handbook of Marital Therapy.* New York, Plenum, 1980.

LITTLEJOHN, STEPHEN. *Theories of Human Communication.* Columbus, Ohio: Charles E. Merrill, 1978.

MACE, DAVID. *Close Companions.* New York: Continuum, 1982.

MAMBERT, W. A. *Elements of Effective Communication.* Washington, D.C.: Acropolis Books, 1971.

MONTAGU, ASHLEY, AND FLOYD MATSON. *The Human Connection.* New York: McGraw-Hill, 1979.

PIRSIG, R. M. *Zen and the Art of Motorcycle Maintenance.* New York: William Morrow & Co., 1974.

RICHARDSON, SUSAN. "Right Brain Approaches to Counseling: Tapping Your "Feminine" Side." *Women & Therapy,* vol. 4, no. 4 (Winter 1985–86).

ROGERS, CARL. *On Becoming a Person.* Boston: Houghton Mifflin, 1961.

SARNOFF, IRVING AND SUZANNE. *Love-Centered Marriage in a Self-Centered World.* New York: Hemisphere Pub. Co., 1989.

SATIR, VIRGINIA. *People Making.* Palo Alto, Calif.: Science and Behavior Books, 1972.

SEVERIN, WERNER, AND JAMES TANKARD, JR. *Communication Theories.* New York: Hastings House, 1979.

SHLAIN, LEONARD. *Art and Physics.* New York: William Morrow & Co., 1991.

STEINBERG, MARK, AND GERALD MILLER. "Interpersonal Communication: A Sharing Process." In *Communication and Behavior,* ed. Gerhard Hauneman and William McEwen. Menlo Park, Calif.: Addison-Wesley Pub. Co., 1975.

STUART, RICHARD. *Helping Couples Change.* New York: Guilford Press, 1980.

TANNEN, DEBORAH. *You Just Don't Understand: Men and Women in Conversation.* New York: Ballantine Books, 1990.

TESSINA, TINA. *Gay Relationships.* Los Angeles: Jeremy Tarcher, 1989.

WATZLAWICK, PAUL. *How Real is Real?* New York: Random House, 1976.

WONDER, JACQUELYN, AND PRISCILLA DONOVAN. *Whole-Brain Thinking.* New York: William Morrow & Co., 1984.

YALOM, IRVIN D. *Existential Psychotherapy.* New York: Basic Books, 1980.

6. CONFLICT: YOU'RE BOTH RIGHT!

BACH, GEORGE. *Creative Aggression.* New York: Avon, 1974.

____, AND PETER WYDEN. *The Intimate Enemy.* New York: Avon, 1968.

BADER, ELLEN, AND PETER T. PEARSON. *In Quest of the Mythical Mate.* New York: Brunner-Mazel, 1988.

BEAVERS, ROBERT. *Successful Marriage.* New York: W. W. Norton, 1985.

BECK, AARON T. *Love Is Never Enough.* New York: Harper & Row, 1988.

BELENKY, MARY FIELD, et al. *Women's Ways of Knowing.* New York: Basic Books, 1986.

BERZON, BETTY. Permanent Partners: *Building Gay and Lesbian Relationships That Last.* New York: E. P. Dutton, 1988.

COVEY, STEPHEN. *The Seven Habits of Highly Effective People.* New York: Simon & Schuster, 1989.

EDWARDS, BETTY. *Drawing on the Artist Within.* New York: Simon & Schuster, 1986.

FISHER, ROGER. *Getting to Yes.* New York: Penguin, 1981.

GERBER, GWENDOLYN. "The Relationship Balance Model and Its Implications for Individuals and Couples Treatment." *Women & Therapy,* vol. 5, no. 2/3 (1986).

GIBBONS, ANN. "The Two-Career Science Marriage." *Science,* vol. 224, no. 5050 (March 13, 1992).

HOWARD, DORIS. "Couples in Psychotherapy." *New Directions in Feminist Psychology,* ed. Joan Chrisler and Doris Howard. New York: Singer Pub., 1992.

JORDAN, JUDITH. "Courage in Connection, Conflict, Compassion, Creativity," work in progress #45, the Stone Center, Wellesley College, Wellesley, Mass., 1990.

LAUER, JEANETTE C. AND ROBERT H. *Til Death Do Us Part.* New York: Harrington Park Press, 1986.

LERNER, HARRIET GOLDHOR. *The Dance of Anger.* New York: Harper & Row, 1985.

MACE, DAVID R. *Close Companions: The Marriage Enrichment Handbook.* New York: Continuum Press, 1984.

MASLIN, BONNIE, AND YEHUDA NIR. *Not Quite Paradise.* New York: Doubleday, 1987.

OWEN-TOWLE, TOM. *Staying Together.* Carmel, Calif.: Sunflower Ink, 1987.

PLATTNER, PAUL. *Conflict and Understanding in Marriage.* Richmond, Va.: John Knox, 1970.

RUBIN, LILLIAN. *Intimate Strangers.* New York: Harper & Row, 1983.

SARNOFF, IRVING AND SUZANNE. *Love-Centered Marriage in a Self-Centered World.* New York: Hemisphere Pub. Co., 1989.

STUART, RICHARD, AND BARBARA JACOBSON. *Second Marriage.* New York: W. W. Norton, 1985.

VIORST, JUDITH. *Necessary Losses.* New York: Simon & Schuster, 1986.

VISCOTT, DAVID. *How to Live with Another Person.* New York: Arbor House, 1987.

____. *I Love You, Let's Work It Out.* New York: Simon & Schuster, 1987.

WEINER-DAVIS, MICHELE. "The Strategy That's Guaranteed to Improve Your Marriage," *McCalls,* vol. 119, no. 4 (January 1992).

WONDER, JACQUELYN, AND PRISCILLA DONOVAN. *Whole-Brain Thinking.* New York: William Morrow & Co., 1984.

ZEROF, HERBERT. *Finding Intimacy.* New York: Random House, 1978.

7. THE ART (RB) AND SCIENCE (LB) OF LOVING

ADELMAN, MARCY, ed. *Long Time Passing: Lives of Older Lesbians.* Boston: Alyson Publications, 1986.

ANDREWS, FRANK. *The Art and Practice of Loving.* Los Angeles: Jeremy Tarcher, 1991.

BACH, GEORGE, AND RONALD DEUTSCH. *Pairing.* New York: Avon, 1970.

BADER, ELLYN, AND PETER T. PEARSON. *In Quest of the Mythical Mate.* New York: Brunner-Mazel, 1988.

BANKS, DENNIS. Letter, Los Angeles *Times,* August 25, 1991.

BARBACH, LONNIE. *For Each Other.* New York: Doubleday, 1982.

BEAVERS, W. ROBERT. *Successful Marriage.* New York: W. W. Menton, 1985.

BECK, AARON. *Love Is Never Enough.* New York: Harper & Row, 1988.

BERZON, BETTY. *Permanent Partners: Building Gay and Lesbian Relationships That Last.* New York: E. P. Dutton, 1988.

BRANDEN, NATHANIEL AND DEVERS. *What Love Asks of Us.* New York: Bantam Books, 1980.

____. *The Psychology of Romantic Love.* New York: Bantam Books, 1980.

BRENTON, MYRON. *Lasting Relationships.* New York: A. and W. Publishers, 1981.

BRODERICK, CARLFRED. *Couples.* New York: Simon & Schuster, 1979.

CLUNIS, D. MERILLE, AND C. DORSEY GREEN. *Lesbian Couples.* Seattle: Seal Press, 1988.

DEVILLE, ROBERTA AND JARD. *Lovers for Life.* New York: William Morrow & Co., 1980.

DOUGLAS, CARL. *Counseling Same Sex Couples.* New York: W. W. Norton, 1990.

EHRENBERG, MIRIAM AND OTTO. *The Intimate Circle: The Sexual Dynamics of Family Life.* New York: Simon & Schuster, 1988.

EVATT, CHRIS, AND BRUCE FELD. *The Givers and the Takers.* New York: Macmillan, 1983.

FISHER, ROGER, AND SCOTT BROWN. *Getting Together.* Boston: Houghton Mifflin, 1988.

FLECK, G. PETER. *The Blessings of Imperfection.* Boston: Beacon Press, 1987.

FORD, EDWARD, AND STEVEN ENGLUND. *Permanent Love.* Minneapolis, Winston Press, 1979.

GAYLIN, WILLARD. *Rediscovering Love.* New York: Viking Press, 1986.

GOLDBERG, HERB. *The New Male-Female Relationship.* New York: Signet Books, 1984.

GOLDSTINE, DANIEL, et al. *The Dance Away Lover.* New York: William Morrow & Co., 1977.

HOLLANDS, JEAN. *The Silicon Syndrome.* Palo Alto, Calif.: Coastlight Press, 1983.

HOWARD, DORIS. "Couples in Psychotherapy: The Positive Effects of a Feminist Perspective on Interpersonal Satisfactions." In *New Directions in Feminist Psychology,* ed. Joan Chrisler and Doris Howard. New York: Springer Pub., 1992.

JAMPOLSKY, GERALD, AND DIANE CIRINCIONE. *Love Is the Answer.* New York: Bantam Books, 1990.

JANDA, LOUIS. *How to Live with an Imperfect Person.* New York: Signet Books, 1985.

KAPLAN, HELEN SINGER. *The New Sex Therapy.* New York: Brunner-Mazel, 1981.

KEEN, SAM. *Fire in the Belly.* New York: Bantam, 1991.

KRYSTAL, HENRY. "On Some Roots of Creativity." *Psychiatric Clinics of North America,* vol. 11, no. 3 (September 1988).

LAUER, JEANETTE AND ROBERT. *Til Death Do Us Part.* New York: Harrington Park Press, 1986.

LEDERER, WILLIAM J. *Marital Choices.* New York: W. W. Norton, 1981.

LERNER, HARRIET GOLDHOR. *The Dance of Intimacy.* New York: Harper & Row, 1989.

LEVINE, LINDA, AND LONNIE BARBACH. *The Intimate Male.* Garden City, N.Y.: Garden City Press, 1983.

LIEBERMAN, GERALD. *3500 Good Quotes for Speakers.* New York: Doubleday, 1983.

MACADAMS, DAN P. *Intimacy: The Need to Be Close.* New York: Doubleday, 1989.

MARCUS, ERIC. *The Male Couple's Guide to Living Together.* New York: Harper & Row, 1988.

MASLIN, BONNIE, AND YEHUDA NIR. *Not Quite Paradise.* New York: Doubleday, 1987.

MCWHIRTER, DAVID P., M.D., AND ANDREW M. MATTISON, PHD. *The Male Couple.* Englewood Cliffs, N.J.: Prentice-Hall, 1984.

MILLER, HOWARD, AND PAUL SIEGEL. *Loving.* New York: John Wiley and Sons, 1972.

NAPIER, AUGUSTUS. *The Fragile Bond.* New York: Harper & Row, 1988.

NOWINSKI, JOSEPH. *Becoming Satisfied.* Englewood Cliffs, N.J.: Prentice-Hall, 1980.

OWEN-TOWLE, TOM. *Staying Together.* Carmel, Calif.: Sunflower Ink, 1987.

PEARSALL, PAUL. *Super Marital Sex.* New York: Doubleday, 1987.

PECK, M. SCOTT. *The Road Less Traveled.* New York: Simon & Schuster, 1978.

PEPLAU, LETITIA ANNE. "What Homosexuals Want." *Psychology Today* (March 1981).

PITTMAN, FRANK. *Private Lies: Infidelity and the Betrayal of Intimacy.* New York: W. W. Norton, 1989.

POLSTER, ERVING. *Every Person's Life Is Worth a Novel.* New York: W. W. Norton, 1987.

PRATHER, HUGH AND GAYLE. *A Book for Couples.* New York: Doubleday, 1988.

ROGERS, CARL R., PHD. *Becoming Partners: Marriage and Its Alternative.* New York: Dell Pub., 1972.

RUBIN, LILLIAN. *Intimate Strangers.* New York: Harper & Row, 1983.

RYGLEWICZ, HILARY, AND PAT KOCH THALER. *Working Couples.* New York: Sovereign Books, 1980.

SARNOFF, IRVING AND SUZANNE. *Love-Centered Marriage in a Self-Centered World.* New York: Hemisphere Pub. Corp., 1989.

SCARF, MAGGIE. *Intimate Partners.* New York: Random House, 1987.

SCHNARCH, DAVID. "Inside the Sexual Crucible." *Family Therapy Networker* (March–April 1993).

SHAEVITZ, MARJORIE AND MORTON. *Making It Together as a Two-Career Couple.* Boston: Houghton Mifflin, 1980.

SINGER, HELEN KAPLAN. *Disorders of Sexual Desire.* New York: Brunner-Mazel, 1979.

TESSINA, TINA. *Gay Relationships.* Los Angeles: Jeremy Tarcher, 1989.

WELLS, CAROL G. *Right-Brain Sex.* New York: Prentice-Hall, 1989.

____. "Sex Blocks: Why Your Mind Says Yes and Your Body Says No." *Redbook* (October 1992).

8. SELECTING A LIFE PARTNER

BADER, ELLYN, AND PETER PEARSON. *In Quest of the Mythical Mate.* New York: Brunner-Mazel, 1988.

BRENTON, MYRON. *Lasting Relationships.* New York: A. & W. Publishers, 1981.

COLEMAN, EMILY, AND BETTY EDWARDS. *Brief Encounters.* Garden City, N.Y.: Anchor Books, 1980.

GOLDBERG, HERB. *The New Male-Female Relationship.* New York: Signet Books, 1979.

PECK, M. SCOTT. *The Road Less Traveled.* New York: Simon & Schuster, 1978.

RUBIN, LILLIAN. *Intimate Strangers.* New York: Random House, 1987.

Running Press. *Quotable Woman.* New York: Worldwide Media, 1991.

SCARF, MAGGIE. *Intimate Partners.* New York: Random House, 1987.

SILLS, JUDITH. *A Fine Romance: The Passage of Courtship from Meeting to Marriage.* New York: Ballantine Books, 1987.

STUART, RICHARD, AND BARBARA JACOBSON. *Second Marriage.* New York: W. W. Norton, 1985.

TESSINA, TINA. *Gay Relationships.* Los Angeles: Jeremy Tarcher, 1989.

9. UNREALISTIC EXPECTATIONS

BRODERICK, CARLFRED. *Couples.* New York: Simon & Schuster, 1979.

LEDERER, WILLIAM J. *Marital Choices.* New York: W. W. Norton, 1981.

LERNER, HARRIET GOLDHOR. *The Dance of Intimacy.* New York: Harper & Row, 1989.

LINDBERGH, ANNE MORROW. *Gift From the Sea.* New York: Random House, 1955.

MASLIN, BONNIE, AND YEHUDA NIR. *Not Quite Paradise.* Garden City, N.J.: Doubleday, 1987.

NAPIER, AUGUSTUS Y. *The Fragile Bond.* New York: Harper & Row, 1988.

Running Press. *Quotable Woman.* New York: Worldwide Media, 1991.

SHAEVITZ, MARJORIE AND MORTON. *Making It Together as a Two-Career Couple.* Boston: Houghton Mifflin, 1980.

VIORST, JUDITH. *Necessary Losses.* New York: Simon & Schuster, 1986.

10. FOREVER: A LOOK AT COMMITMENT

ABLES, BILLIE, AND JEFFREY BRANDSMA. *Therapy for Couples.* San Francisco: Jossey-Bass, 1982.

ASCHER, BARBARA. "Above All, Love." *Redbook* (February 1992).

BADER, ELLYN, AND PETER PEARSON. *In Quest of the Mythical Mate.* New York: Brunner-Mazel, 1988.

BERZON, BETTY. *Permanent Partners: Building Gay and Lesbian Relationships That Last.* New York: E. P. Dutton, 1988.

BLUMSTEIN, PHILIP, AND PEPPER SCHWARTZ. *American Couples.* New York: William Morrow & Co., 1983.

BRODERICK, CARLFRED. *Couples.* New York: Simon & Schuster, 1979.

BRODY, JEAN, AND GAIL OSBORNE. *The Twenty-Year Phenomenon.* New York: Simon & Schuster, 1980.

CAPPON, DANIEL. *Coupling.* New York: St. Martin's Press, 1981.

COVEY, STEPHEN. *The Seven Habits of Highly Effective People.* New York: Simon & Schuster, 1989.

CROSBY, JOHN. *Illusion and Disillusion: The Self in Love and Marriage.* Belmont, Calif.: Wadsworth Pub., 1973.

DAVIS, KINGSLEY. "The Future of Marriage." In *Contemporary Marriage,* ed. Kingsley Davis. New York: Russell Sage Foundation, 1985.

DOMINIAN, JACK. *Marriage, Faith and Love.* London: Darton, Longman and Todd, 1981.

FARRELL, WARREN. "The Evolution of Sex Roles: The Transformation of Masculine and Feminine Values." In *Marriage and the Family in the Year 2020,* ed. Lester Kirkendall and Arthur Gravett. Buffalo, N.Y.: Prometheus Books, 1984.

GRUNEBAUM, HENRY. "Toward a Theory of Marital Bonds, or Why Do People Stay Together?" In *One Couple, Four Realities: Multiple Perspectives on Couple Therapy,* ed. Richard Chassin et al. New York: Guilford Press, 1990.

HENDRIX, HARVILLE. *Keeping the Love You Find.* New York: Pocket Books, 1992.

KARP, DAVID, AND WILLIAM YOELS. "From Strangers to Intimates." In *Marriage and Family in a Changing Society,* ed. James Henslen. New York: Free Press, 1989.

KIM, ANDREW; DON MARTIN; AND MAGGIE MARTIN. "Effects of Personality on Marital Statisfaction: Identification of Source Traits and Their Role in Marital Stability." *Family Therapy,* vol. 16, no. 3 (1989).

KIRCHLER, ERICH. "Marital Happiness and Interaction in Everyday Surroundings." *Journal of Social and Personal Relationships,* vol. 5, no. 3 (August 1988).

KRANTZLER, MEL. *Creative Marriage.* New York: McGraw-Hill, 1981.

LASSWELL, THOMAS AND MARCIA. "The Meanings of Love." In *Marriage and Family in a Changing Society,* ed. James Henslen. New York: Free Press, 1989.

LAUER, JEANETTE C. AND ROBERT H. *Til Death Do Us Part.* New York: Harrington Park Press, 1986.

LAURENCE, LANCE. *Couple Constancy: Conversations with Today's Happily Married People.* Ann Arbor, Mich.: UMI Research Press, 1982.

LEDERER, WILLIAM. *Marital Choices.* New York: W. W. Norton, 1981.

_____, AND DON JACKSON. *Mirages of Marriage.* New York: W. W. Norton, 1968.

LERNER, HARRIET GOLDHOR. *The Dance of Intimacy.* New York: Harper & Row, 1989.

LUECKE, DAVID L. "Prescription for Marriage." Relationship Institute, 1989.

MACE, DAVID AND VERA. "Lifetime Monogamy Is the Preferred Form of Marital Relationship." In *Current Controversies in Marriage and Family,* ed. Harold and Margaret Feldman. Beverly Hills, Calif.: Sage Publications, 1985.

MARANO, HARA. "The Reinvention of Marriage." *Psychology Today* (January–February 1992).

MASLIN, BONNIE, AND YEHUDA NIR. *Not Quite Paradise.* Garden City, N.Y.: Doubleday, 1987.

MCWHIRTER, DAVID, AND ANDREW MATTISON. *The Male Couple.* Englewood Cliffs, N.J.: Prentice-Hall, 1984.

NAPIER, AUGUSTUS. *The Fragile Bond.* New York: Harper & Row, 1988.

PEARSALL, PAUL. *Ten Laws of a Lasting Love.* New York: Simon & Schuster, 1993.

PECK, M. SCOTT. *The Road Less Traveled.* New York: Simon & Schuster, 1978.

PIETROPINTO, ANTHONY, AND JACQUELINE SIMENAUER. *Husbands and Wives.* New York: Times Books, 1979.

PITTMAN, FRANK. *Private Lies: Infidelity and the Betrayal of Intimacy.* New York: W. W. Norton, 1989.

_____. "Beyond Betrayal: Life After Infidelity." *Psychology Today* (May–June 1993).

ROGERS, CARL. *Becoming Partners.* New York: Dell Pub., 1972.

RUBEN, HARVEY. *Supermarriage: Overcoming Predictable Crises of Married Life.* New York: Bantam Books, 1986.

SAGER, CLIFFORD, AND BERNICE HUNT. *Intimate Partners.* New York: McGraw-Hill, 1979.

SCARF, MAGGIE. *Intimate Partners.* New York: Random House, 1987.

SCHNARCH, DAVID. *Constructing the Sexual Crucible.* New York: W. W. Norton, 1991.

_____. "Inside the Sexual Crucible." *Family Therapy Networker* (March–April 1993).

SHAEVITZ, MARJORIE AND MORTON. *Making It Together as a Two-Career Couple.* Boston: Houghton Mifflin, 1974.

SHERMAN, SUZANNE, ed. *Lesbian and Gay Marriage: Private Commitments and Public Ceremonies.* Philadelphia: Temple University Press, 1992.

SIMONS, JOSEPH. *Living Together.* Chicago: Nelson-Hall, 1978.

SMITH, AUDREY, AND WILLIAM REID. *Role-Sharing Marriage.* New York: Columbia University Press, 1986.

STINNETT, NICK, AND JOHN DEFRAIN. *Secrets of Strong Families.* Boston: Little, Brown, 1985.

TAYLOR, ROBERT AND ANITA. *Couples: The Art of Staying Together.* Washington, D.C.: Acropolis, 1978.

TESSINA, TINA. *Gay Relationships.* Los Angeles: Jeremy Tarcher, 1989.

TROTTER, ROBERT. "The Three Faces of Love." *Psychology Today* (September 1986).

VISCOTT, DAVID. *How to Live with Another Person.* New York: Arbor House, 1974.

____. *I Love You, Let's Work it Out.* New York: Simon & Schuster, 1987.

WALLIS, CLAUDIA. "The Not-So-Nuclear Family." *Family Therapy Networker,* (March–April 1993).

WASHBURN, SUSAN. *Partners.* New York: Atheneum, 1981.

ZDENEK, MARILEE. *Inventing the Future.* New York: McGraw-Hill, 1987.

ZIV, AVNER, AND ORIT GADISH. "Humor and Marital Satisfaction." *Journal of Social Psychology,* vol. 129, no. 6 (December 1989).

11. COUPLES COUNSELING: WHEN TO GO AND WHAT TO EXPECT

ARD, BEN. "Assumptions Underlying Marriage Counseling." *Handbook of Marriage Counseling.* Palo Alto, Calif.: Science and Behavior Books, 1969.

BEAVERS, ROBERT. *Successful Marriage.* New York: W. W. Norton, 1985.

____. "Attributes of the Healthy Couple." In *Counseling in Marital and Sexual Problems,* ed. Robert Stahmann and William Hiebert. Lexington, Mass.: Lexington Books, 1984.

BOGRAD, MICHELLE, ed. *Feminist Approaches for Men in Family Therapy.* New York: Harrington Park Press, 1991.

BOWEN, GARY. *Navigating the Marital Journeys.* New York: Praeger, 1991.

CARL, DOUGLAS. *Counseling Same Sex Couples.* New York: W. W. Norton, 1991.

CROSBY, JOHN. *Illusion and Disillusion: The Self in Love and Marriage.* Belmont, Calif.: Wadsworth Pub., 1976.

DE MONTEFLORES, CARMEN. "Notes on the Management of Difference." *Psychotherapy with Lesbians and Gay Men.* New York: Plenum, 1986.

GALLAGHER, FATHER CHUCK. *The Marriage Encounter.* New York: Doubleday, 1975.

GANLEY, ANNE. "Feminist Therapy with Male Clients." In *Feminist Approaches for Men in Family Therapy,* ed. Michelle Bograd. New York: Harrington Park Press, 1991.

GARLAND, DIANA. *Working with Couples for Marriage Enrichment.* San Francisco: Jossey-Bass, 1983.

GERBER, GWENDOLYN. "The Relationship Balance Model and Its Implications for Individual and Couples Therapy." *Women and Therapy,* vol. 5, no. 2/3 (Summer 1986).

GILBERT, LUCIA. *Two Careers, One Family: The Promise of Gender Equality.* Newbury Park, Calif.: Sage Publications, 1993.

HOBAN, PHOEBE. "He Said, She Said." *New York* (June 15, 1992).

HOF, LARRY, AND WILLIAM MILLER. *Marriage Enrichment: Philosophy, Process and Program.* Bowie, Md.: Robert Brady Pub., 1981.

HOWARD, DORIS. "Couples in Psychotherapy: The Positive Effects of a Feminist Perspective on Interpersonal Satisfaction." *New Directions in Feminist Psychology,* ed. Joan Chrisler and Doris Howard. New York: Springer Pub., 1992.

ISENSEE, RIK. *Love Between Men.* New York: Prentice-Hall, 1990.

JACOBS, JUDITH. "Empowerment Themes for Couples Therapy." In *Equal Partnering,* ed. Barbara Brothers. New York: Harrington Park Press, 1992.

JANDA, LOUIS. *How to Live with an Imperfect Person.* New York: New American Library, 1985.

KOCH, LEW AND JOANNE. *The Marriage Savers.* New York: Coward, McCann and Geoghegan, 1976.

LASSWELL, MARCIA, AND NORMAN LOBSENZ. *No-Fault Marriage.* Garden City, N.Y.: Doubleday, 1976.

LAURENCE, LANCE. *Couple Constancy: Conversations with Today's Happily Married People.* Ann Arbor, Mich.: UMI Research Press, 1982.

LEDERER, WILLIAM, AND DON JACKSON. *The Mirages of Marriage.* New York: W. W. Norton, 1968.

MACE, DAVID. *Close Companions.* New York: Continuum, 1982.

_____, and Vera Mace. "Marriage Enrichment: A Preventive Approach for Couples." In *Treating Relationships,* ed. David Olsen. Lake Mills, Iowa: Graphics Pub., 1976.

MANSFIELD, PENNY, AND JEAN COLLARD. *The Beginning of the Rest of Your Life.* New York: Macmillan, 1988.

MARANO, HARA. "The Reinvention of Marriage." *Psychology Today* (January–February 1992).

OKIN, SUSAN MOLLER. *Justice, Gender and the Family.* New York: Basic Books, 1989.

OKUN, BARBARA. "Therapists' Blind Spots Related to Gender Socialization." In *Intimate Environments,* ed. David Kantor and Barbara Okun. New York: Guilford Press, 1989.

PAPP, PEGGY. *The Process of Change.* New York: Guilford Press, 1983.

PLATTNER, PAUL. *Conflict and Understanding in Marriage.* Richmond, Va.: John Knox, 1970.

RUBEN, HARVEY. *Supermarriage: Overcoming the Predictable Crises of Married Life.* New York: Bantam Books, 1986.

RUNNING PRESS. *Quotable Woman.* New York: Worldwide Media, 1991.

SAGER, CLIFFORD, AND BERNICE HUNT. *Intimate Partners.* New York: McGraw-Hill, 1979.

SCHNARCH, DAVID. *Constructing the Sexual Crucible.* New York: W. W. Norton, 1991.

____. "Inside the Sexual Crucible." *Family Therapy Networker* (March–April 1993).

SHELTON, JOHN, AND J. MARK ACKERMAN. *Homework in Counseling and Psychotherapy.* Springfield, Ill.: Charles C. Thomas, 1974.

SILVERSTEIN, CHARLES. *Gays, Lesbians and Their Therapies.* New York: W. W. Norton, 1991.

SMITH, GERALD WALKER, AND ALICE PHILLIPS. *Couple Therapy.* New York: Macmillan, 1973.

SMITH, ROBERT, AND ANN ALEXANDER. *Counseling Couples in Groups.* Springfield, Ill.: Charles C. Thomas, 1974.

SNYDER, MARYHELEN. "The Co-Construction of New Meanings in Couple Relationships: A Psychoeducational Model that Promotes Mutual Empowerment." In *Equal Partnering,* ed. Barbara Brothers. New York: Harrington Park Press, 1992.

SOLOMON, MARION. *Narcissism and Intimacy.* New York: W. W. Norton, 1989.

STUART, RICHARD, et al. *Helping Couples Change.* New York: Guilford Press, 1980.

WEINBERG, GEORGE. *The Heart of Psychotherapy.* New York: St. Martin's Press, 1984.

WEINER-DAVIS, MICHELLE. *Divorce Busting.* New York: Simon & Schuster, 1992.

WINTER, GIBSON. *Love and Conflict.* New York: Doubleday, 1958.

WOODMAN, NATALIE, AND HARRY LENNA. *Counseling with Gay Men and Women.* San Francisco: Jossey-Bass, 1980.

ZINN, MAXINE, AND D. STANLEY EITZEN. *Diversity in Families.* New York: Harper Collins, 1993.

12. OPEN LETTERS

LUECKE, DAVID. "Prescription for Marriage," Relationship Institute, 1989.

EXERCISES

COVEY, STEPHEN. *The Seven Habits of Highly Effective People.* New York: Simon & Schuster, 1989.

EDWARDS, BETTY. *Drawing on the Right Side of the Brain.* Los Angeles: Jeremy Tarcher, 1989.

FISHER, BRUCE. *Rebuilding.* San Luis Obispo, Calif.: Impact Publishers, 1981.

LEDERER, WILLIAM. *Marital Choices*. New York: W. W. Norton, 1981.

"Left-Right Brain Role Is Studied," Chicago *Tribune,* April 22, 1984.

SHELTON, JOHN, AND J. MARK ACKERMAN. *Homework in Counseling and Psychotherapy*. Springfield, Ill.: Charles C. Thomas, 1974.

SMITH, GERALD, AND ALICE PHILLIPS. *Couple Therapy*. New York: Macmillan, 1973.

SMITH, ROBERT, AND ANN ALEXANDER. *Counseling Couples in Groups*. Springfield, Ill.: Charles C. Thomas, 1974.

STUART, RICHARD. *Helping Couples Change*. New York: Guilford Press, 1980.

VISCOTT, DAVID. *I Love You, Let's Work It Out*. New York: Simon & Schuster, 1987.

WONDER, JACQUELYN, AND PRISCILLA DONOVAN. *Whole-Brain Thinking*. New York: William Morrow & Co., 1984.

ZDENEK, MARILEE. *Inventing the Future*. New York: McGraw-Hill, 1987.

INDEX